The Case
AGAINST
Homework

"Provocative. . . . Some of the homework assigned children does not make sense. Bennett and Kalish provide good advice on what parents should do."

— *WASHINGTON POST*

"A wonderful book that is not just about homework but about the sadness and futility of turning children into drudges who learn—if one can call it learning—without passion, without love, and without gaining independence. Every educator, every politician, and every parent should read this book and take it to heart."

— **MARY LEONHARDT**, author of *99 Ways to Help Your Kids Love Reading*

"Very helpful, with practical advice on approaching teachers and working to change district standards. . . . Will appeal to parents who have watched tedious book reports squelch their kids' love of reading."

— *SEATTLE TIMES*

"Most parents have experienced the negative effects of homework on family harmony, family time, and play time, but they accept it as a necessary evil. Bennett and Kalish reveal that the homework emperor has no clothes; there is no good evidence to support piling on homework, especially in the younger grades. They follow through with practical advice for managing homework meltdowns, negotiating with teachers, and advocating for policy changes."

— **LAWRENCE COHEN**, PH.D., author of *Playful Parenting*

"Parents of America, unite! You have nothing to lose but your frustration. *The Case Against Homework* is an important book that takes on the 500-pound gorilla—homework overload—long ignored by educational policy makers. Every parent of a school-age child should buy it and follow the authors' excellent advice in order to protect their children from an educational system gone haywire."

—DAN KINDLON, author of *Raising Cain, Too Much of a Good Thing,* and *Alpha Girls*

"*The Case Against Homework* sends a critical message about how to improve the health and well-being of our children by cutting back on busy work and focusing on meaningful assignments, a good night's sleep, and the value of free, unfettered play time."

—DENISE CLARK POPE, author of *Doing School,* Stanford School of Education lecturer, and founder of SOS: Stressed Out Students

"Bravo to Bennett and Kalish for having the courage to say what many of us know to be true! This book serves as an indispensable tool for parents who want to get serious about changing homework practices in their schools."

—ETTA KRALOVEC, associate professor of teacher education, University of Arizona South, and coauthor of *The End of Homework*

"This very important book makes a powerful case that excessive homework is hurting family life and children's full development. What's more, the book does something that is very rare: It gives parents solid practical advice on how they can deal with teachers and schools to produce significant change."

—WILLIAM CRAIN, PH.D., professor of psychology at the City College of New York and author of *Reclaiming Childhood*

The Case **AGAINST** Homework

HOW HOMEWORK IS HURTING OUR CHILDREN AND WHAT WE CAN DO ABOUT IT

SARA BENNETT AND **NANCY KALISH**

THREE RIVERS PRESS • NEW YORK

Three Rivers Press and the Tugboat design are registered
trademarks of Random House, Inc.

Originally published in hardcover in the United States by
Crown Publishers, an imprint of the Crown Publishing Group,
a division of Random House, Inc., New York, in 2006.

Library of Congress Cataloging-in-Publication Data
Bennett, Sara.
    The case against homework : how homework is hurting
our children and what we can do about it / Sara Bennett and
Nancy Kalish. — 1st ed.
        p.   cm.
    Includes index.
    1. Homework—United States.   2. Education—Parent
participation—United States.   I. Kalish, Nancy.   II. Title.
    LB1048.B46   2006
    371.3'0281—dc22   2006020586

ISBN 978-0-307-34018-4

Printed in the United States of America

DESIGN BY BARBARA STURMAN

10 9 8 7 6 5 4 3 2 1

First Paperback Edition

To Julian and Sophia

SARA BENNETT

To Allison

NANCY KALISH

Contents

Tools for Homework Reform

It is not enough to be busy; so are the ants.

The question is: What are we busy about?

HENRY DAVID THOREAU

The Case
AGAINST
Homework

Introduction

Wherever parents congregate—at work, at pickup time after school, at dinner parties, or at the doctor's office—the conversation often turns to homework. Whether kids go to public, private, or religious schools and no matter what grade they're in, everyone has the same frustrations: How much homework are our children doing? Are they spending much too much time on projects that seem pointless and unrelated to the subject? Do parents drop their own evening activities to supervise and monitor homework? Do kids need a tutor, or even medication to help them deal with it? Do kids—including preteens and teens—have meltdowns over the never-ending grind? Are kids giving up extracurricular activities to hole up alone in their rooms, memorizing fact after fact? Do kids have any time left to play and follow their passions? What is the purpose of it all, anyway? How much is too much—and haven't we reached the point of diminishing returns?

If you're the parent of a school-aged child and have ever wondered whether all the homework is worth what your family is going through, this book will finally provide the answer.

So many parents are confounded and exasperated by how homework affects their children five, six, even seven days a week, during every school vacation and often over the summer. Parents are sick of how every night brings another crushing load and another power struggle. Many "homework experts" claim that one of the benefits of homework is increased parental involvement. But is it really beneficial when we constantly argue about homework or stay up late to do our kids' assignments with them—or *for* them? *The Case Against Homework* will show how homework overload is compromising our parenting choices, jeopardizing our children's health, and robbing us of precious family time.

These days, as many of us know all too well, our kids are burdened with way more homework than we had ourselves. This is especially true for elementary and middle school kids, and this is certainly what we found when we conducted our own national online survey and interviews of more than 1,300 parents, educators, and kids. We were surprised to discover that homework overload is happening everywhere—from Montana to Mississippi to Maine—and parents from across the country shared their stories with us. Of course, even if homework overload affects only a small percentage of children, that still translates into millions of unhappy families. (Please note that some parents, teachers, and children we surveyed or interviewed chose to remain anonymous and some names have been changed.)

Who's to blame for this sorry state of affairs? The finger-pointing goes in every direction: It's the kids' fault, it's the school's fault, it's society's fault. Almost always, it comes back to the parents and the prevailing belief that there's so much homework because competitive moms and dads want their kids to get ahead.

Unfortunately, that's sometimes true. But *The Case Against Homework* will tell the real story. Homework polls and surveys routinely demonstrate that between 20 and 30 percent of parents believe their children get too much homework. More than one-third of the parents we surveyed feel the same way. Ironically, other parents who took our survey insist that the amount is "just right," only to go on to describe all sorts of negative effects their kids suffer—from nightly crying fits to stomachaches to facial tics.

Why is there such a disconnect? One reason is that many parents have faith in the school system and assume that educators have good reasons for subjecting our kids to so much work. But we suspect that these parents—and lots more—will be up in arms when they learn the truth: that the overwhelming majority of teachers have never taken a course in homework, and that, contrary to popular belief, there is little solid research demonstrating benefits from the current homework system—if we can even call it a system.

For example, most parents (as well as many teachers) would be surprised to hear that there's very little proof that homework helps elementary school pupils learn more or have greater academic success. In fact, as this book will explain, when children are asked to do too much nightly work, just the opposite has been found. And study after study shows that homework is not much more beneficial in middle school either. Even in high school, where there can be benefits, they start to decline as soon as kids are overloaded.

That's why educators, child psychologists, and other experts on learning are questioning the value of homework, especially in large amounts. As child psychologist Dan Kindlon, a Harvard professor and author of several books, including *Tough Times, Strong Children,* told us, "The issue of too much homework comes up whenever I talk to parent groups, and the truth is, there's no good research justification for it. The analyses out there just don't make a connection between homework and success."

Throughout homework's up-and-down history, everyone has had an agenda. Ours is simply the well-being of our kids. We have the same goals as most other parents: We want our children to be happy, healthy, and competitive in a highly competitive world, and get an excellent education. We want them to love learning. But the current pile-it-on approach to homework is not the answer. In fact, it's counterproductive.

Many parents know intuitively that something is very wrong with the system, yet might feel unqualified to challenge it. But the truth is, we're more than qualified to advocate for our kids, and there's plenty we can do to bring an end to this mess. In the first part of this book, we'll bring you up to speed on the latest research about homework and all the reasons it's not working for kids, parents, or even teachers. In the second part, we'll deconstruct the most common assignments and show you which ones advance learning and which don't. We'll teach you how to do triage when your elementary or middle school children come home with more work than they can handle, and give you the ammunition to confidently write a note to the teacher about why you've decided your child shouldn't lose sleep in order to create a replica of the Pentagon out of Popsicle sticks. We'll show you how to change things for your family tonight—and every night. If you're interested, we'll also show you how to organize other parents to improve the homework situation at your school or even in the entire district, no matter what grade your child is in.

We know firsthand that this kind of advocacy can change even ingrained school policy. We met as parents in a Brooklyn, New York, school and discovered we shared the same frustration over the homework that was taking over our kids' lives. With four hours of homework each weekday night and many more each weekend, Nancy's then-eighth-grader, Allison, had rarely made it to the family dinner table over the previous few years. Many weekend plans with friends, parents, and grandparents had to be canceled so she could do her assignments. This is time their family will never get back.

Lots of other parents at our school were complaining about the homework load, but no one was doing anything about it until Sara, who had an eighth- and a fifth-grader, organized a parent group to discuss the situation. A former Legal Aid attorney, Sara had been successfully negotiating with teachers for years to reduce her own kids' homework loads, and she decided to push the school to finally change its overall policy. By getting other parents into the act, Sara knew that the school could no longer dismiss each parent's problem as "personal." She was right. As a result, the school appointed a task force, held its first open forum on homework, and instituted major changes. And once the issue was raised, Sara's coauthor, Nancy, who had never seen herself as an activist, had one of those "aha" moments. She finally realized that she wasn't facing this problem alone and could do something about it that wouldn't take all her energy and time.

When you also learn the truth about homework, chances are that you'll want to do something to lighten that heavy backpack your child drags home each night. *The Case Against Homework* will show you how.

PART ONE

Fried Brains

and

Frayed Tempers

1

So Much Work, So Little Time

"We feel like we're rushing our kids from the minute they walk through the door at four until they crawl into bed," says Wendy, a mother of first- and fifth-graders who attend a private school near Highland Park, New Jersey. In the three hours before her six-year-old son's bedtime at seven, they have to fit in twenty to thirty minutes of homework, dinner, a bath, and some reading time. "That leaves a whopping fifteen minutes to play. My son will often take out a game and ask one of us to play before he even starts his homework. We grit our teeth as we gently break the news that he has to get his homework done first. It hurts to have to do this—we want him to play! He's six! He's worked hard all day." Wendy's daughter, a fifth-grader, goes to bed at eight after slogging through an average of 90 to 120 minutes of assignments. "My daughter has no time to herself between Monday and Friday—no exaggeration," says Wendy. "And this schedule does not include time for spontaneous events,

such as phone calls from grandparents (especially precious from those that live a plane ride away). My daughter goes to ballet one day a week, and that is a challenge. We don't do other activities because the stress level is just not worth it. We truly feel that homework is taking away from the quality of our lives."

"During our daughter's third-grade year at our parish Catholic school, the volume of homework coming home increased on a daily basis and led to much frustration," says Beverly of Beaufort, South Carolina. "The only way the children could keep up was because very involved parents 'homeschooled' each evening."

"My son hasn't been able to attend his last five Boy Scout meetings and has had to skip weekend camping trips because of his heavy homework load," says Linda, whose ninth-grader attends public school in Woodbury, Minnesota, and tackles three to three-and-a-half hours of homework each night. "He holds his head in his hands and cries. He also gets very angry and vents his anger by yelling. It's not good for any of us!"

"I sit on Amy's bed until 11 P.M. quizzing her, knowing she's never going to use this later, and it feels like abuse," says Nina of Menlo Park, California, whose eleven-year-old goes to a Blue Ribbon public school and does at least three-and-a-half hours of homework each night. Nina also questions the amount of time spent on "creative" projects. "Amy had to visit the Mission in San Francisco and then make a model of it out of cardboard, penne pasta, and paint. But what was she supposed to be learning from this? All my daughter will remember is how tense we were in the garage making this thing. Then when she handed it in, the teacher dropped it and all the penne pasta flew off." These days, says Nina, "Amy's attitude

about school has really soured." Nina's has, too. "Everything is an
emergency and you feel like you're always at battle stations."

These aren't just the gripes of a few chronically disgruntled parents,
though many school principals and teachers would like to think so.
In fact, more than one-third of the families we surveyed and interviewed
admit to feeling crushed by the workload. This is true no matter where
they live (urban, suburban, or rural areas) or what kind of school their
kids attend (public, private, or parochial). So if you feel overwhelmed,
too, you're not alone.

Some people insist that kids aren't working any harder than they did
in the past. But a 2004 national survey of more than 2,900 children done
by the University of Michigan found that the time kids spend doing
homework has skyrocketed by 51 percent since 1981. For some kids, that
adds up to just a few minutes more. But for many kids, the amounts have
become staggering.

In fact, the hours of homework many of our kids are doing far exceed
guidelines from the National Education Association, an organization of
more than 2.7 million teachers and other educators founded in 1857, and
the National Parent Teacher Association. Those guidelines specify that
kids should be assigned no more than ten to twenty minutes per night in
kindergarten through grade 2 and thirty to sixty minutes per night in
grades 3 through 6. And some experts recommend even less—or none.

According to Duke University professor Harris Cooper, a top researcher on the subject and the author of *The Battle Over Homework:*
Common Ground for Administrators, Teachers, and Parents, schools should
follow a "ten minutes per grade per school night" rule—in other words,
ten minutes per night in first grade, twenty minutes per night in second
grade, thirty minutes in third grade, and so on, up to a maximum of two
hours per night in high school.

You might be surprised at these low totals—especially if your child does several times more than that. According to a 2006 Associated Press–America Online poll of 1,085 parents, elementary school students are averaging seventy-eight minutes per night while middle school students put in an average of ninety-nine minutes. Another 2006 poll from NEA/Leapfrog indicates that eight- to thirteen-year-olds average even more— 90 to 105 minutes a night. And at just one public high school in Needham, Massachusetts, a 2006 survey of 1,300 students uncovered that more than 28 percent were doing at least four hours of homework each night. In fact, according to the hundreds of families we surveyed and interviewed, the majority of their kids in all grades were doing amounts that far exceeded the recommended guidelines each night.

And you might be even more surprised to find out that, according to Professor Cooper's 2001 review of more than 120 studies of homework and its effects, and his updated 2006 research reviewing an additional sixty studies, there is very little correlation between the amount of homework and achievement in elementary school and only a moderate correlation in middle school. Even in high school, "too much homework may diminish its effectiveness or even become counterproductive," writes Cooper in his latest research review. And as he told us, "It is not going to improve a ninth-grader's achievement to do 2.5 hours of homework per night versus 1.5 hours."

Moreover, as Cooper writes in his latest research review, "it is not possible to make claims about homework's causal effects on longer-term measures of achievement, such as class grades and standardized tests, or other achievement-related outcomes." Indeed, "because the influences on homework are complex, [there is] no simple, general finding applicable to all students."

In other nations, high amounts of homework also fail to produce high-achieving students. Many of the countries with the highest scoring students on achievement tests, such as Japan, Denmark, and the Czech Republic, have teachers who assign little homework. On the other hand, countries such as Greece, Thailand, and Iran, where students have some of the worst average scores, have teachers who assign high quantities of homework, according to David Baker and Gerald LeTendre, education professors and authors of *National Differences, Global Similarities: World Culture and the Future of Schooling.* Meanwhile, American students do more homework than many of their peers in other countries, but still only manage to score around the international average. "It seems like the more homework a nation's teachers assign, the worse that nation's students do on achievement tests," says Professor Baker.

Even though there are some studies that attempt to show a relationship between homework and higher grades and test scores, "It's impossible to determine whether more homework causes better achievement, whether teachers assign more homework to students achieving better, or whether better students spend more time on home study," writes Professor Cooper in *The Battle Over Homework.* "Any or all of these causal relationships are possible."

Some vital aspects of homework have never been studied at all. Many educators tout homework as a great way to teach children responsibility. Yet according to Etta Kralovec, associate professor of teacher education at University of Arizona South and coauthor of *The End of Homework: How Homework Disrupts Families, Overburdens Children, and Limits Learning,* "There's been no research done on whether homework teaches responsibility, self-discipline, or motivation. That's just a value judgment. The counterargument can just as easily be made that homework teaches kids to cheat, to do the least amount of work, or to get by." With parents increasingly involved in assignments every step of the way, we think homework *undermines* the teaching of responsibility.

More to the point, no one has ever studied whether something other than homework—independent reading, for example—might improve test scores. Is a rich home life a better way to improve achievement than even the best-designed homework assignments? "That's an important question," says Frances L. Van Voorhis, a consultant to the Center on School, Family and Community Partnerships at Johns Hopkins University, "but I don't foresee getting an answer to that any time soon."

This is why some experts recommend no homework at all. "There's no evidence that homework is good for reinforcement," says Professor Kralovec. "If parents are going to give up their home life for homework, there should be evidence that it will produce something."

Is Anyone Listening?

Whether the research is positive or negative, the schools keep piling on homework, and elementary and middle school kids have been hit with the biggest increase in their overall load. Many parents told us that their middle schoolers never had *any* homework in kindergarten, yet now homework for kindergarteners is the national norm. This is true, even though, as Professor Cooper writes, "The effect of homework on the achievement of young children appears to be small, even bordering on trivial." He explains that, as any parent knows, young children have very short attention spans and trouble tuning out distractions at home to concentrate on the work at hand. They can't tell when they make mistakes or prioritize what they need to study. In short, they're just too young to get much out of it on their own. That's why Professor Cooper's examination of the research found that, for elementary school students, in-class study with a teacher proved superior to homework in terms of learning.

On top of that, our kids are currently spending an average of two more hours in school each day than we did. As a result, they're getting home a lot later and a lot more tired. The younger the child, the earlier the bedtime, and the less time there is to squeeze in everything. "When do I fit in the homework?" asks a single mom of a first-grader and a younger sibling in childcare, whose kids arrive home at 4:30 and go to bed three hours later. "Am I supposed to keep them up later to do the homework? I'm a teacher and know what kids act like the next day at school when they are overly tired!"

WHAT THE JAPANESE KNOW

Starting in the late 1990s, many Japanese elementary schools began instituting no-homework policies so that children had more time for family and to pursue outside interests. They're not handing out hours of homework to their middle schoolers, either, according to researchers Baker and LeTendre. For example, contrary to what you might think, Japanese teachers assign less than an hour of math homework *per week* to seventh- and eighth-graders.

The time crunch gets even worse in middle school, when our children start to get homework from many different teachers who don't coordinate assignments. Taking into account the average seven-hour school day, a middle schooler who does just one hour of homework each night is putting in a forty-hour work week. If she has ninety-nine minutes of nightly assignments, as students in the Associated Press–AOL Online poll report, her work week jumps to 43.25 hours. That means that many sixth-graders are working longer hours than the average adult.

Plenty of kids exceed even those amounts. "Counting bus rides, classroom time, and homework, my son is putting fourteen hours a day into school," laments a dad from Raleigh, North Carolina, whose public school eighth-grader does two-and-a-half hours of homework each night. Hundreds of miles north, Svetlana, a New York City college professor, has the same complaint: "I've figured out that, between school and homework, my seventh-grader does ten to twenty hours more schoolwork a week than my college students do in total."

And it's worse still in high school. "In order to handle huge homework loads, even good students are popping NoDoze and Ritalin to stay awake," says Denise Clark Pope, a professor at Stanford University School of Education, who spent a year at a California high school to research her book *Doing School: How We Are Creating a Generation of Stressed-Out, Materialistic, and Miseducated Students.* "They get to the point where they're only sleeping three or four hours a night."

All around the country, high schoolers find they need to push themselves harder and harder. Says Eden, a tenth-grader at a public school in Shaker Heights, Ohio, who does about four hours of homework each night and more on the weekend, "Often my homework is pointless and simply takes time. Teachers are supposed to have a test day on which they can give tests and a flex night when they are not allowed to assign homework, but no one follows the rules. Sometimes, I'll have five tests on one day. There is very little time to be a kid with the amount of homework I get." Adds Jon, a senior at a public school in Cambria, California, who does three to four hours of work every night, including weekends, "Homework is my life. It is all I do. Every day, I cannot bear to wake up. I hate homework. I cannot believe how much of my childhood has been wasted on homework! I will never have that time again. All I can think of is school! HELP!"

And parents are along for the exhausting ride. When Phoebe, a mother from Pelham, New York, arrives home at 6:30, she often finds her limited time with her kindergartener and second-grader filled with busy-work assignments. "My kindergartener was supposed to find letters in magazines and cut them out. But it was really frustrating. His motor skills weren't really good enough to handle the cutting, so we'd just end up doing it for him." Often, he didn't want to do it at all. He'd say, 'Mommy, I'm really tired. I just have to go to bed.'"

"If my kids aren't done with homework and showers until ten, that's a six-hour work day for me that starts at four in the afternoon," says Gail, an Upper Montclair, New Jersey, mom of a fourth- and an eighth-grader, who works at home. When you add it up, it makes you wonder, Are there enough hours for everything?

ADDING IT ALL UP IN REAL LIFE

Here's how the clock runs out each day for four public school kids across America:

KINDERGARTEN GIRL FROM FAIRBANKS, ALASKA

5:30 . . . . home from afterschool program
5:30–6:00 . . . . needs cajoling from parent to do homework, while parent tries to cook dinner
6:00–7:00 . . . . dinner, cleanup, and "a little time to play and interact"
7:00 . . . . bath
7:30 . . . . reading time
8:00 . . . . bed
Total downtime: 30 minutes at most

FOURTH-GRADE GIRL FROM NORTH CANTON, OHIO

5:30 . . . . home from afterschool program
5:30–6:00 . . . . work on spelling while Mom cooks dinner
6:00–6:30 . . . . dinner
6:30–7:15 . . . . homework
8:30 . . . . get ready for bed
Total downtime: 1 hour 15 minutes

EIGHTH-GRADE BOY FROM HAYWARD, CALIFORNIA

3:30 . . . . home from school
3:30–4:00 . . . . snack

4:00–6:30 . . . . homework
6:30–7:00 . . . . dinner
7:00–9:00 . . . . homework
9:00–9:30 . . . . favorite TV show
9:30 . . . . get ready for bed
Total downtime: 1 hour

TWELFTH-GRADE BOY FROM FAIRFAX STATION, VIRGINIA

3:00 . . . . home from school (unless there's an afterschool
            activity or club)
4:00–6:30 . . . . homework
6:30–7:00 . . . . dinner
7:00–10:00 . . . . . . homework (with a little IM'ing)
10:30 . . . . bedtime
Total downtime: 1½ hours

And this is how this senior's mother describes his life: "We live in a highly competitive school district, and in order to be considered for the state colleges, you must obtain at least a 3.8 GPA and graduate with an Advanced Placement diploma, do sports, clubs, volunteer, and have a part-time job. Occasionally, my son goes out on a Saturday night with a few friends. But generally, he spends much of his time at home studying, especially on the weekends. Often he doesn't join the family in an activity because he just doesn't have the time. If he does go, he always brings along homework."

No Holiday from Homework

These days, homework is not just a weekday phenomenon. It spills over into weekends, school breaks, and summer vacations—sweeping aside trips to the zoo, the beach, the park, and the movies and eliminating time for everyone to recharge.

"I resent all weekend homework," says Nora, a Brooklyn mom of a second- and a seventh-grader in public school. "As a working parent, the weekend is the prime time I get to spend with my kids. But instead of doing fun, enriching things, we end up fighting about when their homework will be completed so that we can do the fun stuff. One of the reasons I chose to raise my kids in New York City is because of all the culture, art, and diversity available here. But with four to six hours of weekend homework, we do not get to take advantage of the events around us."

Cultural enrichment and recreation aren't the only things families sacrifice: Religious education can suffer, too. "Our church youth director would like my kids to come to church on Wednesday nights for Bible study, but my kids have never been able to go because of homework," reports Teresa, the mother of a public school ninth- and a twelfth-grader in Mesquite, Texas. Even basic childhood pleasures fall by the wayside. "My daughter has had to decline invitations to birthday parties to finish projects over a weekend," reports Pam, the mother of a first-grader from Pittsburgh.

School breaks are no longer breaks, either. They're often filled with "vacation homework," an oxymoron that sends many of our children back to school burned out afterward. Think twice before giving your child a book as a holiday present. There's no time to read it—at least if you live in Grand Island, New York, where one ninth-grader had to read four assigned novels and write essays on each of them over the break. "It was a large assignment for eight days, one of which was Christmas," says his mom. And if you live in Lancaster, Texas, you ignore holiday homework at your peril. In January 2006, nearly one thousand students were suspended for not completing their Christmas assignments and some were even visited by police. If you live in Raleigh, North Carolina, homework doesn't leave much time for celebrating, either. "At Advent last year," says one dad, "we had to cut short our family rituals—sharing readings, talking about ideas, singing Christmas carols—from forty-five minutes a day to fifteen." And prepare to multitask if you live in New York City. "Before Christmas break, the school sent a note home to all the parents about getting our third-graders ready for the standardized tests," says Jennifer. "We were assigned to teach our kids the multiplication tables over the break. The teacher said it'd be fun to practice them while we're ice-skating."

Not even summer vacation is sacred. "Last summer, I had to read twelve books and write two pages on each of them, and I had one hundred math exercises to complete," reports John, a seventh-grader in Boston. And one New York City family's experience took a toll on all of them. The summer after first grade at a charter school, Rhonda's son had to do ten book reports, math assignments, a report on China—including a written essay and a handmade doll dressed in costume—as well as keep a daily log of his activities and the weather. "After going to summer camp during the day, he was exhausted from all the running around and playing and he didn't want to do it," Rhonda recalls. "He'd say, 'I'm tired, I'm sorry, I'm just a kid.' My husband would go, 'Let him rest,' and I'd have to force him to do it. I shouldn't have to be like that."

Some summer camps have also gotten into the act, making sure children do their assignments by providing quiet reading areas and enforcing attendance. A few even offer SAT-prep courses. Our kids can forget about lazing on their bunks or under a tree with the book of their choice. As Molly, a ninth-grader, puts it, "There's only one way to describe summer homework: painful."

There's a very sound academic reason why children shouldn't do homework on vacation. "Learning is maximized and made most efficient and effective when you allow a period for consolidation," says Kate McReynolds, a clinical child psychologist and director of the City College of New York's Gateway Academy. "Consolidation can only happen in times of rest. When we are wrestling with a problem—personal or financial or intellectual—we'll say, let's sleep on it. Then when we wake up in the morning or come back to it a few days later, we suddenly see the solution. When we take a vacation, we come back to our work with a new vigor; taking a break allows for that consolidation." But by assigning vacation homework, children today are denied that consolidation time. And when parents are told that their children's skills will slip during the break, we have to wonder: If those skills are so fragile, what kind of education are they really getting?

"Do we, as teachers, regularly expect more out of our students than we are able to give?" asks Todd Seal, an award-winning high school English teacher from San Jose, California, in his blog. "Because of the fact that I didn't do a shred of work during the Christmas break, I returned feeling like I actually had time off from work and I have been more excited about things, ready to take on the rest of the year. I wish my students felt the way I do and maybe having a two-week break without work would help make that happen."

Why Ten Minutes Is Never Just Ten Minutes

Ten minutes per grade level might not seem like much. But it always stretches out to more. Even under ideal circumstances, children work at different rates—and circumstances are seldom ideal. As a mom from Shawano, Wisconsin, reports, "I spend thirty minutes fighting my first-grader to do homework she doesn't want to do each night, which doesn't allow time to do other things like swimming, soccer, playing."

The result is not what anyone would call a positive educational experience. "My daughter is exhausted at the end of the school day and the additional work just makes her hate school," says a parent in Jamesville,

Maryland, whose first-grader gets twenty to thirty minutes of homework daily. "She sees the entirety of her homework as overwhelming. She cries . . . and cries . . . and cries." And these are just first-graders.

Of course, kids fight homework and procrastinate. Plenty of books insist that if parents just established a good homework routine (a quiet spot to work, neatly organized school supplies, a tasty but healthful snack, and an adult available to answer questions), kids would happily buckle down and do it. But it's not that simple. For many kids, homework is like having to do their taxes *every night*. How would we feel if we came home to hours of work from five different bosses? At least some of us would quit or enter therapy—which is where some of our children now find themselves.

"I'm seeing a lot of kids come in with homework anxiety," explains Dee Shepherd-Look, a therapist and professor of psychology at California State University at Northridge. "Kids tell me, 'I've been at school all day. I've had to be good all day. I just want to do nothing for a little bit.' They've used a lot of energy competing academically and socially, and to get right into hours and hours of homework is mind-boggling. They can do it, but it takes them twice as long sometimes because they need some space."

Students who are labeled "gifted and talented" can struggle, too, especially if they have a perfectionist streak. Says Stanford University's Denise Clark Pope, "Ironically, they could do that poster charting the course of the moon in a few minutes. But they take it to the extreme, so it can take hours."

If a child has a learning disability, it can be even worse. These kids may have already been struggling and compensating all day long. "On a good night, when my son is not too tired, his three assignments will take about an hour," says one mom of a fourth-grader with learning issues. "On a bad night, when he's exhausted, it will drag out to two hours."

No Time to Be a Family

Even if every assignment our children received had great educational value, homework shouldn't be allowed to crowd out the other aspects of childhood. "Human development comprises a great deal more than working on specific academic skills," says Steve Nelson, the head of the Calhoun School in New York City. "Kids should be smelling stuff, they should be having time to aimlessly relax. In terms of their development, throwing three or four hours of homework at middle school kids is crazy. Something else has to suffer."

The first thing to go is often the family dinner hour. That's a real shame because the table is often the only place where everyone comes together once a day, sharing not just stories of school and jobs, but morals and values, too. "You have to have a time every day when you can sit down as a family and just talk about what you want to talk about without having to figure out a math problem or read a book," says Geri, a former teacher and Raleigh, North Carolina, mother of two kids, ages seven and ten, who eat together no matter what. But fewer and fewer families can afford this "luxury." As one mother from Montana says, "The reality is that our family time has become a thing of the past, and with it the spontaneous and relaxed learning that comes from family dinner-time conversations and games."

THE HIDDEN BENEFIT OF EATING TOGETHER

While the number of families who eat dinner together has risen slightly since 1998, a 2006 national survey done by the University of Minnesota shows that 42 percent of families still don't get the chance on most weekdays. We suspect this is often because of homework. This is particularly ironic, given that, according to a

University of Michigan study, family meals are the *single strongest predictor* of better achievement scores and fewer behavioral problems for children ages three to twelve. That's right—*a better predictor* than the amount of time spent studying.

Children who don't spend much time at the dinner table also miss out on the opportunity to learn the arts of conversation and manners. Perhaps not surprisingly, colleges now offer remedial etiquette courses to help prepare their graduates for the job market. "Many of the college students I work with can't make conversation," says clinical child psychologist McReynolds. "Socializing is practiced at the dinner table."

Dinner conversation can benefit students' vocabulary, as well as their knowledge of current events and the world around them. Says Lawrence Cohen, a Brookline, Massachusetts, psychologist and author of *Playful Parenting: A Bold New Way to Nurture Close Connections, Solve Behavior Problems, and Encourage Children's Confidence,* "When kids have a long leisurely conversation over dinner that's full of lots of different topics, that's going to be much better for their education than doing homework and memorizing vocabulary words."

If families do manage to squeeze in dinner together, parents often end up doing chores that once would have been shouldered by their children. After all, it seems unfair to ask our children to load the dishwasher or take out the garbage when we know they have three hours of studying ahead of them. Yet chores offer a valuable opportunity for parents to teach basic life skills and values and for a child to feel like an integral part of the family. Could we be raising a generation that feels entitled or compelled to always put work before sharing household duties? Will future spouses have even more arguments over who should do the chores?

There's no time for fun and games, either. "My first-grader would love to participate in our family's 'Game Night' with her grandparents, but often can't because of homework," says Robin of Richlands, North Carolina, whose six-year-old has sixty to seventy minutes of work each night." Says Dr. Shepherd-Look, "The way things are now, we're giving kids the wrong message: that work is more important than family."

NO TIME TO SOCIALIZE

Children fourteen and under spend an average of only twenty-five minutes each weekday socializing with family and friends outside of school, according to a 2004 study conducted by the University of Michigan's Institute for Social Research.

One unrecognized side effect of homework is that it isolates siblings from one another. A sixth-grader who is stuck at her desk doesn't have time to play with a younger sibling. This means that their play relationship is severed earlier than it might have been. And because the parent needs to help each sibling with homework, reading a nightly story to them together becomes difficult. Gwen, a mother of a third-grader in Oakland, California, spends large amounts of time helping her older son with homework. "My younger son has nothing to do during this time and uses negative behaviors to get my attention. My third-grader feels put out when I can't focus on his work with him and I end up ping-ponging back and forth between them."

Another mom, with three kids in New Jersey, has a similar problem. "Regular homework does not really foster much in the way of closeness. It actually tends to create competition. If I spend a lot of time with one child, the others can't help but be a bit resentful of that time—even if it is doing homework. It's hard to balance when one needs my help more than the other two." So the school is, in effect, deciding which of

our children will get that all-important, undivided parental attention—
and it might not be the one who needs it most.

Sometimes trying to keep siblings involved with one another requires too much fancy footwork. "My fourth-grader was on the baseball
team this past spring. When his seventh-grade brother wanted to watch
him play, he had to bring his homework with him," reports Deanne, a
mother of four from Houston. "A baseball field is not the best place to do
homework. But it was either that or miss the game. So we struck an unhappy bargain: Our older child could only halfheartedly support his
younger brother—one eye on the game and the other on the homework."

A lot of people think that family time is cut short not because of too
much homework, but because of too many extracurricular activities.
And it's true that some children are overscheduled. But, according to the
hundreds of kids who took our survey, many are dropping out of activities they love in order to have time for their ever-increasing homework
assignments. "I had to quit ballet and I don't get enough sleep and I don't
have time to read," says Caroline, a fifth-grader in a Memphis public
school who does seventy to eighty minutes of homework each night.

In fact, for many of our children, reading for pleasure is a thing of
the past. And even those who do manage to read still only get to do it for
an average of eleven minutes each day, according to a University of
Michigan study. It's not just that kids don't have time to read a magazine
or learn how to execute a perfect pas de deux. How will our children
know what they want to do, or even what they like, if they don't have the
chance to find out? Exploring these aspects of life outside of school is
more important than ever since many school districts have scaled back
art, music, and physical education programs.

When our kids give up such extracurriculars, they also give up the
chance to learn teamwork, socialize with other kids, relieve the stress of
their lives with something that they really enjoy, and build self-esteem
by being good at something other than school. Many of us have fond

memories of forming a special bond with teammates, a coach, or a music, art, or drama teacher. Sadly, many of our kids are missing these opportunities.

Kids often pay dearly if they try to pursue what they love on top of homework. "My daughter was in a play at school with rehearsals until 9 P.M. every night and she still had all her homework," says psychologist Lawrence Cohen. "She was exhausted and it was really upsetting to her to fall behind. What could have been a playful experience became a burden."

Taking the Play out of Play Dates

Many adults blame cell phones and instant messaging for replacing face-to-face contact and harming kids' social skills. But we think one of the biggest—and unrecognized—culprits is homework. These days, nightly and weekend assignments eat up much of the time kids used to spend playing with peers and honing their abilities to share and cooperate. "It's upsetting when my child wants to stay in the schoolyard and play with his friends, but he can't because everyone is rushing home to do homework," says Lisa, the mother of a second-grader at a public school in Forest Hills, New York.

Even when kids do have play dates, they often don't include much actual playing. Forget about baking cookies, playing tag or dolls, or just hanging out together. For some children, getting together with a classmate or friend means doing their assignments side by side during "homework play dates."

"There's no playtime after school," explains Maria, a mother with three kids in the Pelham, New York, public school system, including a first-grader who gets eighty to ninety minutes of homework each night. "We must hit the books because of the workload in their planners. The kids don't like it. But if that's the only way they're going to get a play date, they'll take it."

So maybe the homework play date is better than nothing—but that's not saying much. The "play" part is still missing, and that's a big problem. Many of our kids come home stressed from dealing with school all day long. As Dr. Cohen writes in *Independent School Magazine*, "In order to recover from these worries and pressures—small or large—children need to play after school. Young children might play school, or they might make up dramatic games where they slay dragons. They might play at sports or seek out one-on-one time with a parent to soak up some of that individual attention every child needs. . . . Developmentally, young children need lots of time to run around, to act goofy, to not have to be anywhere at any given time, to play endless games of Barbie, or fantasy dress-up games, or what I call disorganized sports, where children get to argue about the rules and work out conflicts and figure out fairness and decide for themselves whether to keep score or not."

It's not just little kids who need playtime. "Older children and teen-agers, developmentally speaking, need hanging-out time," explains Dr. Cohen. "Their developmental task is to figure out who they are, and all the pressures to be involved in—and excel at—seventeen different things can interfere with that."

ABANDONED DOLLS AND TRUCKS

Six- to eight-year-olds spend 33 percent less time playing today than in 1981, according to the University of Michigan. The American Academy of Pediatrics is so concerned that it issued a 2006 report lamenting this lack of unstructured playtime and urging its quick return.

It probably comes as no surprise that when kids don't have the chance to work out their stress through play, they can develop behavioral problems. There can be academic consequences as well. As we'll discuss in Chapter 5, there have been many studies confirming the importance of play in children's cognitive development and its role in increasing attention, planning skills, creativity, and sophisticated thinking. That's why, as Dr. Cohen says, "Play is what will get your children into Ivy League schools."

"I'm being deliberately provocative," he admits. "But I really do believe it. To succeed, you need not to just simply memorize, but to be creative and imaginative." And it's not just creativity that suffers. When playtime is cut, kids' decision-making power is also being compromised. As kindergarten programs around the country have become increasingly academic and the sand play and dress-up areas have disappeared, so have "children's ability to make up their own games or think of what to do when they aren't being told what to do," says Olga Jarrett, associate professor of early childhood education at Georgia State University. "Kindergarten teachers report that there is some evidence that children are less self-directed because they are constantly being structured." Adds Chris Eliot, head of Tenacre Country Day School in Wellesley, Massachusetts, "Our second-grade teachers had to teach the kids how to pick teams. Our society is so adult-driven that kids don't even know how to pick teams."

This might not seem like a big deal, but it could have long-lasting effects. "We never let kids have any decision-making power anymore," says Harvard University child psychologist Dan Kindlon. "Homework is about following orders all the time. It's hard to feel that you have any power when you're always the 'employee.' Research shows that the adults who end up being successful in business, the entrepreneurs, are the ones who formed the garage bands as kids, who did self-directed stuff that let them follow their passions. But few kids are passionate about homework."

No Time for Doing Nothing

And what about the balance that adults are always seeking in their own lives? In an age when every magazine exhorts us to meditate, practice yoga, and carve out more time to relax, schools often seem oblivious to the stress they're putting on our kids, who are way less equipped to handle it. "It's go, go, go, go . . . go to bed. It's not like there's even a wind-down period," says Gail, the Upper Montclair, New Jersey, mom of a fourth- and an eighth-grader. "If you're only relaxed when you're sleeping, I just don't think that's healthy. What are we teaching our kids for the future? That they all have to be type A workaholics, and if you find yourself with downtime during the day, it's a sin? Where do they learn that it's an important life skill to say, enough, I need a break?"

Children are even expected to complete homework when they're sick. "My seventh-grade twins hated to get sick because if they had to stay home, then they had triple homework—the homework they couldn't do because they were sick the night before, the homework from the day they missed, and the homework from the day they got back," relates Maureen, a pediatric nurse in Florence, Kentucky. "Kids need to be kids. Being an adult is hard enough. And we've taken so much away from them by not letting them enjoy life."

FORGET FREE TIME

Kids today have twelve hours less free time each week than they did in 1981, according to the University of Michigan.

Some educators are wary of allowing children too much free time. They imagine that homework helps kids stay out of trouble—and away from the TV. But some parents say they don't appreciate that kind of help. "If I could make one request to teachers, it would be: Please value my children's time," says Pamela, the mother of sixth- and ninth-graders in Brooklyn, New York. "Please do not give out thoughtless, repetitive homework with the misguided sense that you are saving them from too much television. As a parent, I will take care of what happens with their free time, so don't think you are helping by simply *filling* it."

Without homework to occupy them, "some teachers say kids will just sit around and watch TV and IM their friends. But is that so bad?" asks child psychologist Dan Kindlon. "Kids do need downtime. Fred Rogers used to say that one of the reasons kids took drugs is that they didn't know how to *not* be stimulated."

And sometimes all we want is to cuddle on the couch and enjoy some TV together. One college history professor told us, "It's very pleasant to relax with your kid watching something stupid like 'Wheel of Fortune.' But I feel like the school is prepared to scold me for that." Dr. Kindlon agrees: "Schools shouldn't make the assumption that they are the only ones who can make a decent person and decent society, that parents are clueless. When you watch TV with your kids, you form a bond over that. You can talk about the characters on 'Lost.' It gives you a common language that can bring you closer, make the kids feel like you really understand and connect with them. I do that all the time with my kids. And teachers don't know what's going to fill up the downtime. One Thursday night when we had nothing scheduled, I said to my daughters 'What do you want to do?' And they said, 'How about we build a fire, and we do needlepoint while you read out loud to us?' So that's what we did and it was wonderful."

Paradise Lost

The truth is, homework overload has changed childhood significantly—and not for the better. Gone is that wonderful feeling of having all the time in the world to explore, think, dream, what many would say is the essence of childhood. "Sometimes I feel like the world is about to drop from right beneath me like a ride in an amusement park. I cannot for my life balance anything—like time, homework, or just getting a snack," says Sophia, a ten-year-old from Brooklyn, New York. "I have to rush, rush, rush, rush, rush, rush, rush through my day, actually through my seven days, and that's seven days wasted in my life." Another ten-year-old who does 90 to 120 minutes of homework each night puts it more simply: "It's not fair. I don't have enough time to be a kid."

The consequences? Many of the parents who responded to our survey reported that their children showed physical signs of stress from overwork. "For the first time in her life, my daughter is having stomachaches," says Jenny, a single mother of a twelve-year-old in rural Virginia. "She'll show up in my room, complaining 'I can't sleep, I'm worried.' She needs to spend time playing piano, she needs to have sleepovers, she needs to have Saturdays to walk in the woods with friends and not do things that are school related."

MORE THAN A LITTLE STRESSED

According to a 2000 report by the American Psychological Association, typical schoolchildren today report more anxiety than did child psychiatric patients in the 1950s. And a 2006 survey of 1,300 students at a public high school in Needham, Massachusetts, found that more than 42 percent reported that homework caused them "a lot of stress"; nearly 16 percent said it caused "extreme stress." Georgia Witkin, Ph.D., director of the Mount Sinai School of Medicine Stress Research Program and the author of *Kidstress: What It Is, How It Feels, How to Help,* has found that kids' anxiety levels have only gotten worse since her book was published in 2000. As she says,

"There's been no let up in the symptoms that define stress in children, such as the earlier onset of migraines, gastrointestinal problems, and sleep problems. And it's not because they're worried about Iraq or terrorism or global warming. Homework and school are a major part of it."

Still, many of us are willing to put our kids through the nightly hell of homework overload because we believe that our schools know what they're doing or we feel we don't have a choice.

Even if we feel something is deeply wrong, most of the time we don't know what to do about it. (We'll give you some ideas in Part Two.) If we do voice concerns, we're sometimes told that it's *our* kid with the problem—that every other kid breezes through the assignments without complaint or help, that every piece of homework is well thought out and valuable. So we keep quiet. After all, we're not educators. We have to have faith in our school system. Don't we?

"A lot of people think that so much homework is unfair, but I do believe that my kids are getting a better education than I did, that they're learning more," says Robyn, a single mom of three in Houston whose entire evening revolves around homework each night. "They *have* to be learning more."

But what if they're not? What if the educational system to which we've entrusted our kids isn't much of a system at all?

2

The Myth of the Homework System

Like miniskirts and peasant blouses, homework has gone in and out of fashion. Right now, of course, it's in. And economic concerns—not educational ones—are behind the current thinking that more is better.

In fact, homework was once decried as child labor. In the early 1900s, doctors led a movement to abolish it, insisting that children needed at least five hours of fresh air and sunshine each day. At that time, those kids who today would be diagnosed with attention-deficit/hyperactivity disorder (ADHD) were told to go outside and play more—not take medication so that they could sit still. For the first half of the last century, homework was minimal. Just as workers were winning rights to a forty-hour work week, children were winning the right to a childhood, secured in part through stricter child labor laws and a school day that ended at the schoolhouse door.

But in the late fifties, the space race spawned a new hyper-competitiveness that translated into more work for kids. As Brian Gill, a social scientist and homework historian, writes in the journal *Theory Into Practice,* "After the Soviets launched Sputnik in 1957, the homework problem was reconceived as part of a national crisis; the U.S. was losing the Cold War because Russian children were smarter; that is, they were working harder and achieving more in school. Progressive education was blamed for causing America's failures in space and for undermining its economic and military supremacy."

By the late 1960s and 1970s, parents were again arguing that, like adults, children were entitled to an evening without work, and again homework eased. But by the early eighties, the economy was weak and everyone was looking for someone or something to blame. In 1983, the U.S. Department of Education published *A Nation at Risk,* a report that pointed the finger at our schools, saying that poor education was the root of our economic troubles. The report explicitly called for "far more homework." Americans were fed the line that our kids' nightly assignments were the key to regaining our country's competitive edge in the world economy.

By the 1990s, the homework machine was in full gear—and it's been building steam ever since. In 2002, the No Child Left Behind (NCLB) Act called for raising educational standards. It's a goal that no one can disagree with. But the efforts to reach it have been plagued by poor planning and execution. Driven by fear that we're falling behind in the global marketplace, policy makers have turned to the schools to save us once again. They seem to believe that everything will be fine if we can just get America's students to pass their standardized tests. And the only way to make sure they cover all the material: homework. So we're now at a new high point in the history of homework—a point where many kids, from kindergarten through high school, are working for hours each night to help the U.S. economy succeed.

The trouble is, all this is based on one huge—incorrect—assumption: that more homework boosts test scores, which in turn boosts business. In fact, there is *no* correlation between increased homework loads and any nation's economic success, according to analyses of the most recent data from fifty nations performed by Dr. David Baker, a professor of education and sociology, and Dr. Gerald LeTendre, associate professor of education theory and policy, both from Penn State University, for their book, *National Differences, Global Similarities: World Culture and the Future of Schooling.* "The economic health of a nation is not just driven by the academic success of its workers," explains Professor Baker. "More homework does not equal a better economy."

Most of us simply aren't aware that the homework system rests on such a shaky foundation. After all, homework is such an enormous part of our children's education, we assume that teachers have studied how best to design worthwhile assignments that will truly promote learning. We assume that they wouldn't waste our family's limited time with anything less.

That's certainly what Nancy, one of the authors of this book, used to think. True, she'd feel helpless as she watched her daughter plow miserably through hours of homework every night during middle school. "But I was resigned, too," she admits. "I just thought that the teachers must know what they're doing, that there had to be a system behind it all."

But today's homework system isn't any more "systematic" than it has been in the past—perhaps even less so. As Tanis Bryan, a research professor at Arizona State University, writes "[H]omework practices tend to be based on individual teachers' beliefs rather than on consensually agreed upon or research-based practices." That's why the type and amount of homework our children get, and how much it counts, seems to depend mostly on which teacher is handing it out. The quantity and quality of assignments often vary tremendously from teacher to teacher within the same grade, from grade to grade (sometimes going up, sometimes down), and from school to school within the same district. In addition, many teachers fail to coordinate assignments, leading to light loads some nights and crushing ones the next. No wonder we never know what to expect.

If your child is in one of the heavy-homework classes, it seems unfair and illogical. As a Bradford, Pennsylvania, mother of a second-grader receiving an hour's worth of homework a night explains, "Other second-grade classes at the same school get no homework, and those students seem to perform as well academically as those in my daughter's class who often bring home seven to eight tasks that need to be completed." And it's not just quantity. Another mother of two kids in a New York City public school noticed huge discrepancies when she hosted homework play dates, "I was shocked at the differences in the quality of the homework assignments from one teacher to another, even in the same grade."

So what's going on here? Haven't teachers been trained to make homework an effective learning tool that's worth all the time and trouble? Isn't there a well-thought-out, well-established homework system in place at our nation's schools?

Not quite. "There is no homework system or explicit rules for homework," says Duke University professor Harris Cooper. "If your book is an investigative report to uncover the homework system, you certainly won't find it in the schools of education and you definitely won't find it in the [public] schools when only one in three districts even has a homework policy. Most teachers are winging it."

Professor Cooper's observation sounds harsh. Of course, he's not blaming teachers, and neither are we. After all, we know that the majority of teachers are dedicated and want to do their best for their students. Many of them spend hours preparing for their classes and give up personal time to correct the homework they assign. But they're being short-changed during their training.

There are several different ways to become a teacher—from majoring or minoring in education at college to jumping feet first into teaching and acquiring a credential later. Still, you would assume that, no matter what the method, future teachers would be required to study homework in great detail, from how much to give, to what makes an assignment worth doing, to how to evaluate the finished product properly.

But they're not. Some educators have been worried about this for years. In 1994, the University of Minnesota's Center for Applied Research and Educational Improvement issued a report that said, "It is surprising how little attention is paid to the topic of homework in teacher education. Most teachers in the United States report that in education courses they discussed homework in relation to specific subjects, but received little training in how to devise good assignments, how to decide how much homework to give, and how to involve parents."

Not much has changed. "In my experience working with teachers, they get little or no instruction in homework. It's not something that's highlighted," asserts Frances Van Voorhis, the consultant to the Center on School, Family and Community Partnerships at Johns Hopkins. LeTendre, of Penn State University, agrees. "There's no adequate training of new teachers in homework at all. It's considered an afterthought. We allow the homework policy in the U.S. to be teacher-centric and yet we don't guide the teachers."

NO HOMEWORK 101

Out of the more than three hundred teachers from around the country whom we surveyed or interviewed, only one claimed to have ever taken a course specifically on homework during training. Why? Because no such course is offered at most teachers' colleges. And according to a large 2003 survey of working teachers by California State University at Fullerton associate professor Stephen Aloia, only 18 percent had ever attended a professional workshop on homework.

What did your child's teacher actually learn about homework during teacher training? Here's what some told us.

I never had a class on homework. I felt like my professors had never thought much about homework—and a lot of them had never taught—so they didn't know or really weren't sure what to tell us, beyond saying to make sure that all of your grade isn't based on homework, or to make sure it's meaningful, whatever that means. You could tell they didn't even know.

Lily, who became a teacher in New York City after receiving a bachelor's degree in history with a concentration in education from Northeastern University

Homework was not discussed in school. When we did our student teaching, I saw teachers give out homework and was told that I had to grade papers, but that was it.

Lori, a kindergarten teacher in Sorrento, Florida, who became a teacher after receiving a bachelor's degree in elementary education, with a certificate in early childhood education and reading

I never learned anything about homework before going out to teach. We covered content and how to teach, not what kind of homework you were supposed to give.

Sara, who became a second grade teacher in Waterbury, Connecticut, after receiving a bachelor's degree in sociology from a state university in Connecticut and a teacher's certification at the same time by taking education classes and student teaching

Homework is talked about in most student-teacher method courses. But the professors do not elaborate on the need to assign home-work or how much is necessary. I have no knowledge of any work-

shop or training program that focuses on homework in the classroom. Do beginning teachers need such a workshop? I think so!

Peggy, a recently retired sixth-grade teacher from Sierra Vista, Arizona

What *do* teachers-in-training learn about giving assignments? They might go over the theoretical purposes of homework: practice, preparation for the next class, the development of good study habits and responsibility, and the assessment of a student's skills. But they don't learn much about how to put those theories into practice. While teachers-in-training generally have to make up homework as part of sample lesson plans that they present to their professors, and assign it when they do student teaching, there's little instruction on the nuts and bolts of how to create assignments that actually fulfill the goals mentioned above.

"We talk about homework in terms of how it has to be worthwhile and useful, and that it has to further the student's ability to achieve specific learning goals," says Vicki Jacobs, associate director of Teacher Education at the Harvard Graduate School of Education. "Are my folks equipped to devise meaningful homework? Absolutely. Was it addressed? Yes, but in the context of overall lesson planning. Do we have a separate course on homework? No."

Another thing that's seldom covered in teacher preparation courses is how homework affects family life. "I often hear from starting teachers that they never realized what a big issue homework would be—until they have their first parent-teacher conference," says Professor Cooper of Duke University. "The huge role homework plays in the interface between schools and families goes largely unaddressed in their education."

Most surprisingly, many teachers never learn about the myriad studies showing that homework has little correlation with academic success in elementary school and only a moderate correlation in middle school.

Says Cooper, whose extensive reviews of previous homework research came to that conclusion, "When I speak to teachers, it's always remarkable to me how unaware they are of the research literature—especially young teachers or student teachers."

Yet when it comes to homework, most teachers are true believers. In a 2003 California State University study of teachers of all grade levels, every single one believed in giving homework—despite the fact that not one of their schools or school districts had ever studied whether their system was really working. "These teachers have no data to support their assumptions that homework is beneficial, they simply think it is beneficial," writes Professor Stephen Aloia, who conducted the survey.

If you're puzzled at this point, we don't blame you. The solution to this problem seems pretty obvious: Why not just give teachers-in-training the detailed homework instruction they desperately need?

"I wish I knew the answer to that question," said Professor Cooper. In fact, most of the professors of education we interviewed couldn't explain why their institutions didn't offer courses on homework; it seemed as though no one had ever asked any of them before. Finally, one offered this explanation with a rueful chuckle: "Teaching students how to give homework properly is boring. Faculty want to concentrate on more abstract things about education. There are currently some commissions looking at teacher training. But, unfortunately, I don't think there will ever be a course on homework. It would take a major revolution in education schools."

Fail to Plan, Plan to Fail?

According to a 1998 U.S. Department of Education survey of more than four thousands teachers, more than 60 percent of new teachers reported that they did not feel "very well prepared" to assess student performance, implement curriculum standards, or implement new methods of teaching, such as cooperative learning. And the situation might get worse. As teacher prep programs are discovering for the first time, many elementary, middle, and high schools are now reluctant to help train student teachers. For example, 80 percent of schools that previously hosted student teachers from Antioch College's program will no longer accept them. The reason: Schools are afraid that having inexperienced student teachers in the classroom will bring down scores on the all-important No Child Left Behind tests. This means that many teachers will miss out on a key component of their training.

Yet once teachers graduate and are given their own classrooms, many are under considerable pressure from principals, school districts, policy makers, and, yes, parents to get children to perform well on standardized tests. Many teachers told us that the stress was overwhelming. In some cases, teachers' bonuses depend on their pupils' test scores.

Teachers have been told that kids need lots of homework to test well. So, many assign a lot—even those who would rather not. Even if they attended a program that exposed them to the research behind homework, "they're not allowed to teach the way they've learned," says William Crain, a psychologist who often teaches child development to teachers at the City College of New York's School of Education and author of *Reclaiming Childhood: Letting Children Be Children in Our Achievement-Oriented Society.* Many teachers blame the focus on testing, which forces them to seek ways to squeeze in material and test-taking practice they aren't able to fit into the school day.

"I think there is an increasing push for our students to do more, instead of focusing on doing better," says Michelle, a middle school teacher in Mountain View, California. "Teachers feel pressured to assign homework to get more content in." As one elementary school teacher confided to us, "You have to teach to the test. It's unfortunate, but that's what the schools are reduced to."

Besides requiring teachers to assign homework, however, few schools give much specific direction. As Sara, the second-grade teacher from Waterbury, Connecticut, puts it, "I was told to give homework in one subject a night in first and second grade, and that it probably shouldn't take any longer than twenty minutes. But I wasn't given any guidance on what the homework should be."

WHAT POLICY?

Only 35 percent of school districts in the U.S. have written homework policies, according to Duke University professor Harris Cooper.

Even when schools do have homework policies, they tend to refer to quantity and quality in vague terms that remain undefined. (In contrast, a New York City principal attempting to fire a teacher will find detailed, step-by-step procedures that must be followed to the letter in the more than two hundred–page contract with the teachers' union.)

"So homework is often an afterthought, a ready-made sheet that isn't even linked to the curriculum or what the kids have learned," says Frances Van Voorhis of Johns Hopkins. As one third-grade teacher in Brooklyn, New York, says, "I inherited the assignments from the teacher before me, and she may have inherited them from a teacher before her." The school administration told her to give sixty minutes of homework each night, so that's what she did. She didn't even realize that it was twice the recommended amount for that age group. "I never really stopped to think about the assignments—about how long they take, or whether they're really even necessary," she admits. Adds Sara, the second-grade teacher from Connecticut, "Teachers fall into a rut where they have to give work. I think my homework is busywork, basically fluff. It's just to show that I'm giving it."

Many teachers would like to give more thought to their assignments, but can't because they're buried in work, too. The average U.S. teacher is in class for 18.5 periods per week. Some have to teach even more hours, sometimes outside their subject. As a frustrated fifth-grade teacher in Minnesota puts it, "They give us more and more to do. But they never take anything away." She's not trained to teach the kids science, for example. The result: "Science is most difficult for me as a teacher, so I cheat them on that."

In addition, short-staffed schools have cut teachers' planning time. Instead of being able to thoughtfully prep lessons and assignments, teachers are stuck doing cafeteria or bus duty, coaching, or supervising afterschool programs. In fact, American teachers spend an average of six hours per week—almost an entire school day—doing activities that have nothing to do with teaching or planning.

ON THEIR OWN

According to Penn State University researchers, only 37 percent of American teachers get to meet at least once a week to discuss curriculum and teaching issues with colleagues.

Ironically, new teachers, who could use the most planning time, often have the greatest number of outside duties because of their lack of seniority. "Some teachers probably have their whole week planned out, including their homework," says one new elementary school teacher. "But personally, I scramble each day."

Even Teachers Can't Agree

One teacher's opinion about homework often directly contradicts another's. Reading the comments from the hundreds of teachers who took our homework survey was a dizzying experience. Everyone seems to be doing something different, and most believe they know what's effective. Here's a sampling:

SHOULD KINDERGARTENERS EVER BE ASSIGNED NEW MATERIAL FOR HOMEWORK?

I give review and introductory homework. It helps my students ease into a new concept in class if they have already begun it as an assignment at home.

Melissa, a kindergarten teacher in Broadview Heights, Ohio, with less than three years' experience

No new material should ever be assigned—only brief practice in what a child has already learned in school.

Danielle, a kindergarten teacher in Lake Peekskill, New York, with less than three years' experience

ARE SPELLING AND MATH DRILLS EFFECTIVE HOMEWORK FOR SECOND GRADERS?

I think spelling homework is effective, because it helps to reinforce the spelling of words they will use every day of their lives. We don't have enough time in our already curriculum-packed day to drill

and practice these rules with them. I think math homework is effective, because they need to try the formulas/math problems they learned in class by themselves at home to see what they get stuck on before they get tested on it.

Karen, a second-grade teacher in Monroe, Connecticut, with more than ten years' experience

Computational problems and spelling are not effective types of homework because they are just learning by rote.

Rosemarie, a second-grade teacher and learning specialist in New York City with more than fifteen years' experience

SHOULD PARENTS HELP WITH HOMEWORK IN THIRD GRADE?

If any homework is assigned, it should be something the child can do alone.

Wendy, a third-grade teacher in Tucson, Arizona, with more than fifteen years' experience

Probably the most effective type of homework is that which involves the parents.

Nadia, a third-grade teacher in Brooklyn, New York, with more than ten years' experience

SHOULD MIDDLE SCHOOLERS DO
HOMEWORK PROJECTS?

Projects are not effective. I've found that parents frequently do projects for, not with, their children.
    Mark, an eighth-grade history teacher from Washington,
    Pennsylvania, with more than fifteen years' experience

Creative work that requires family support in construction is effective homework.
    Anonymous eighth-grade math teacher

Even when schools or districts have homework policies, teachers don't seem to pay much attention. Some teachers we surveyed or interviewed weren't even sure whether their school had a policy or not. Most seem to be "doing their own thing." As Barb, who's been teaching first grade for fifteen years in Tucson, Arizona, puts it, "District homework policies are kind of guidelines. No one mentions homework much, so we do what we think best."

For an experienced teacher, winging it might not be a big problem. But for those who haven't been in the classroom as long, following their gut instead of the research can create some unforeseen problems for their students—and for themselves.

Figuring Out How Long It Takes

Even if teachers want to follow the standard recommendations of ten minutes of homework per night per grade level, it isn't easy. During training, teachers aren't taught how to determine how long their assignments actually take. So here are a few of the inventive methods they've come up with:

> *I see how much time it takes the slowest and the quickest workers, divide that in half, and then assign work that should take from one to two hours.*
>
> Fifth-grade public school classroom teacher, New York City

> *I often check textbook recommendations, do the work myself (students often take two to three times as long as a teacher). Sometimes my assignment is too lengthy and I need to make adjustments the following day (which I note for the future).*
>
> Ninth-grade public school math teacher, Livermore, California

> *I base it on how long it takes my own daughter (who is in the same grade as I teach) to complete her assignments in a focused and uninterrupted manner.*
>
> Third-grade public school teacher, Fairlawn, New Jersey

> *I time the assignments as I write them, then add twenty minutes.*
>
> Ninth-grade language teacher

> *I just plain guess.*
>
> Teacher who desired to remain anonymous

It's not surprising that studies have shown teachers are often way off in their estimates. As Lisa, the mother of a fifth- and a seventh-grader from Croton Falls, New York, complained, "Teachers tend to dramatically underestimate the time that homework takes. One teacher actually wrote out a time schedule that was *totally* unrealistic. She felt my child should do math from 3:50 to 4:00, spelling, 4:00 to 4:10, etc. It was obvious this teacher has not given birth yet. May she have twin boys!"

Interestingly, parents aren't the only ones with this perspective. Other teachers made similar comments. "Homework is designed to reinforce the concepts taught in school, not manipulate people's schedules," says Maura, a math teacher and mother of five from Grand Island, New York. "It seems as though the teachers who do not have children of their own send home the most ridiculous assignments." Adds Carmen, a high school teacher from Henderson, Nevada, "I don't think that I realized what a burden homework was for my students until I had my own child in school. After working all day on academic work, the *last* thing that I want to do is to spend my evening with my first-grader doing the same thing."

Not surprisingly, the more experience teachers have, the less homework they tend to assign. "I do not believe that the structure of our families (two parents working outside the home, kids not getting home until dinnertime) fits with the old model of homework," says Barb, the Tucson first-grade teacher with more than fifteen years of experience, who doesn't give any homework except optional reading. "I think it's harmful to take away the only interaction and touch time children have with their parents on weeknights in favor of mandatory homework, which is most often busywork. Six hours of school work a day is plenty for young children, and, in fact, for *all* ages of students!"

Mark, the eighth-grade history teacher and learning specialist in Washington, Pennsylvania, also tries to keep homework to a minimum. "I give maybe twenty minutes of homework, about twice per week," he explains. "It doesn't squash outside activities, yet it encourages the students to think beyond what we have time to consider in the classroom. I check with my students about how their week is looking and try to schedule my homework around their busiest times. It doesn't always work, as they all have difficult schedules, but we try. After all, I genuinely want them to consider the ideas I ask them to consider, and they can't do this well if they have three hours of other assignments. I used to assign a lot more work, thinking it was just part of the learning process. I think (I hope?) that I use my class time a lot more effectively now."

In fact, giving lots of assignments might be one sign of a weak teacher—and school. "It may be the poorest teachers who assign the most homework," explain Baker and LeTendre. "Effective teachers may cover all the material in class without the need to assign a large amount of homework, especially drill and memorization assignments." As LeTendre wrote in his 2007 report, *A Nation Spins Its Wheels: The Role of Homework and National Homework Policies in National Student Achievement Levels in Math and Science,* "[w]hen schools are effective, students gain little from doing more homework."

Making the Grade?

Another assumption many teachers make about homework is that it must be graded to be worthwhile. Many experts, however, think that homework doesn't have to be graded to be useful. In fact, it's better if it's not.

Still, American teachers have the dubious honor of leading the world in grading homework, with 82 percent giving it marks, according to professors Baker and LeTendre. Only 22 percent of teachers in Hong Kong grade homework, and that figure drops to 14 percent in Japan.

If you want to build student responsibility and love of independent learning, Professor Harris Cooper says, assignments should be designed so that almost all students can complete them successfully and get a good grade. Fear of a bad homework grade, he explains, "turns a situation ideal for building intrinsic motivation ('I must enjoy this; I'm doing it and the teacher isn't standing over me') into one that implies that the teacher believes students need rewards or punishment in order to complete assignments."

And of course, says Cooper, homework should never be given as a punishment for bad behavior. "If kids think teachers give homework to punish, the lesson that they learn is that even the teacher thinks that homework is boring and tedious."

In addition, just because a teacher has graded homework doesn't guarantee that he or she has looked at it carefully. After all, the huge assignments many teachers give make that nearly impossible. For example, if a third-grade teacher assigns her thirty students a sheet of 25 long-division problems, it means she has a whopping 750 problems to grade. If she assigns 30 problems, the total climbs to 900!

When teachers take on even more students in middle and high school, the workload becomes impossible. "If you have 150 to 185 kids, do the math—nobody has the time to grade all that homework on a daily basis, much less offer meaningful feedback," explains one former assistant principal of a New York City public high school. "Assigning homework is a game, it's to show that they're doing it. The teachers just spot-check it. My son used to bury things inside his homework to see if his teachers were reading it."

This is counterproductive for everyone. "I used to assign work almost every night," says Owen, a seventh-grade teacher from Auburn, Maine. "But I wouldn't be able to read the assignments carefully—I could just spot-check them. This was not helpful, especially for kids who were not thinking carefully while doing it. Also, students can cheat easily this way. Now I assign less and check more carefully."

In addition, when a grade is assigned to homework, there's a tendency for parents to fix their kids' mistakes and "edit" their work. And if a student takes a little longer to catch on to a concept, she might be punished with a succession of poor grades, even if she eventually masters it.

Evaluating homework—not grading it—is key. "It may be that teachers who use homework to identify skill deficits—and then provide feedback to students about how to build up their skills—are using homework in the most effective way," say Baker and LeTendre. According to their research, however, only about half of our teachers give such feedback.

This is unfortunate because "if a child is not getting feedback on his homework and he's making mistakes and not getting caught, then he'll continue to practice the skills incorrectly until he takes a test and gets a bad grade," says Olga Jarrett, the associate professor in early childhood education at Georgia State University. That's also what happens when teachers use the common practice of "trade and grade," in which students exchange and mark each other's homework in order to curtail cheating. As Jarrett concludes, "Teachers simply don't have the time to evaluate all that homework properly. And it seems to me that's another good reason not to assign so much."

Not Much of a System, After All

No wonder we parents find the whole homework "system" so unsystematic. Upon examination, there really isn't one at all.

Why aren't our teachers getting the training they need before they set foot into a classroom? And why don't our schools have a consistent and straightforward approach to homework that's based on solid pedagogical research instead of half-baked, unproven beliefs?

Unfortunately, we don't have the answers. But as parents, we are outraged. As California State University education professor and father of five Stephen Aloia puts it, "In light of the fact that teachers and districts are eminently aware of the importance of accountability and evaluation, it is a sad tribute to education and especially to children that the efficacy of homework is not being addressed on a systematic and continuous basis."

This much is clear: "Homework is making learning a miserable experience," says professor of psychology William Crain. "I wish schools would place a moratorium on it until they can figure out how to make it a positive and creative experience from the viewpoints of both students and their families."

3

The Family Fallout

FROM PARENT TO TASKMASTER

Each evening, we start off promising ourselves that tonight will be different—no struggling, no yelling, no tears. But then there's that homework again—too much, too boring, too confusing, and sometimes too difficult for even parents to comprehend. So as the hours pass and our children procrastinate or whine, the recriminations start ("Why did you leave it all for after supper?" "If you can't manage your work, you'll have to give up soccer!") and the punishments soon follow ("No TV for the rest of the week if you don't finish that history essay tonight!").

Say hello to Homework Cop (aka Mom or Dad).

With three hours of homework a night, my partner and I end up being the teacher's enforcers.
    Mother of a seventh-grader

I have to be a taskmaster, forcing my kids to do busywork that I know has no value, or fill out worksheets that were out of date decades ago.

Father of an eighth-grader and an eleventh-grader

I often feel like the big bad wolf when I have to tell my daughter, "No you can't play. You have to do your homework." I even have to keep her awake or wake her early in the morning to finish on nights when she's especially tired. I often get angry at the situation and sometimes find myself taking it out on my child.

Mother of a first-grader

Is there any way to avoid this role? It's tough because in the United States today, homework has become a family affair, with parents managing every aspect from start to finish. According to our informal survey, a majority of parents:

- proofread
- edit
- help prepare for tests
- brainstorm on projects or papers
- explain math concepts

More than a third of parents:

- help decide what order to do homework in
- type or handwrite assignments
- read aloud required reading
- help design projects
- help complete projects

- help create sentences for spelling words
- go over work and correct errors

And some admitted to staying up late after their child has gone to bed to put finishing touches on homework.

Who has time to cuddle on the couch and discuss the day when there's so much work to be done?

It wasn't always this way. "The level of involvement today has increased one thousand percent and it's every single night," says Carolyn of Atlantic Beach, Florida. She didn't have to help much with assignments when her three grown daughters were young. But now that she's raising her granddaughter, she spends at least an hour getting the first-grader through her homework each night.

Most of our own lucky parents spent their evenings blissfully homework-free. It wasn't that we didn't have assignments. But much of the time, our moms and dads didn't feel the need to get involved. Few people over forty can even remember their parents asking them if they *had* homework, let alone supervising their assignments. And doing work for your child—a common practice today—was unheard of. Partly, this was because homework was seen as the child's job and the amounts were so manageable that it could stay that way.

And our relationships with our parents were the better for it. After one New York City grandfather witnessed his daughter's struggles over assignments with her own child, he told her, "I'm glad we didn't have to do that with you. It would have ruined our relationship."

In fact, countless authorities are still counseling us that the best way to end the "homework wars" is to let our kids handle their assignments on their own. The problem: Homework has changed drastically, and the way it's structured today makes the hands-off approach nearly impossible. Many teachers expect high levels of parent participation and assign homework that kids can't complete on their own. As Lois, a mother of a sixth-grader in Port Washington, New York, says, "There are so many mixed messages: Help with the homework; don't help with the homework. You should be involved; you shouldn't be overinvolved. It's really confusing!"

Since the 1990s, *parental involvement* and *parent-teacher partnerships* have been big buzzwords. Parental involvement sounds wonderful on the face of it. Who doesn't want to share in the excitement and joy of learning and have a great relationship with your child's teacher?

But there's little excitement or joy when most parental involvement consists of haranguing, cajoling, bribing, or begging kids to do their assignments, as well as teaching them the concepts and study skills they need to complete them. Schools say that parent participation is vital to show us what our kids are doing in school and to give us an opportunity to show them how much we value education. Yet couldn't we find out what they're doing in school simply by asking them or from brief weekly updates the teacher could send home? Couldn't we demonstrate that we're pro-education by doing things *we* choose, such as reading together, discussing world events, and taking our children to museums or concerts?

Moreover, few parents would call what we have with our kids' schools a "partnership" when we rarely have a say about our "part" or whether we want to turn our homes into second classrooms at night. Yet many of us feel we don't have a choice.

"I feel like I am constantly 'on' in terms of making sure the homework is getting done, that it's complete, that long-term assignments are being managed appropriately, et cetera," says Leslie, a mother in Brooklyn, New York. "With three kids, it's a full-time job once they're home from school. I cannot commit to any activities that might involve going out on weeknights. Also, it sets up a very negative parent-child dynamic.

The kids often complain, 'Can't we ever talk about something other than schoolwork?'"

But unfortunately, most parents can't resist asking about the nightly homework forecast the moment they see their kids after school. "As soon as my sixth-grader gets into the van, I ask: How much homework do you have? When is it due? Do you have any tests?" says Marcia from San Francisco. "Tonight at my daughter's school, they have an orchestra performance. And I'm already thinking, Well, how much homework will she have and how will we carve out the time?"

The answers to those questions dictate not just how our kids are going to spend their evening, but how the whole family will. Parenting magazines and books urge us to slow down and reconnect with our children and partners when we get home. But if our child's response is a heart-sinking "I have a lot of homework," we can say good-bye to any hope of meaningful together time.

Family Therapy, Here We Come

Some parents do report that doing homework with their children brings them closer together. Chances are, their kids have a lighter-than-average workload and can breeze through it without being strong-armed. Or the homework is of such high quality and the child is so engaged that he enjoys sitting down to do it.

But those are rare circumstances indeed. Much of the time, the quantity is high and the quality is low, and we feel we've got to force our kids to do it anyway. "This creates a very bizarre dynamic," says Svetlana, the New York City mother who is also a college professor. "Your child comes home with this homework that's intrinsically boring and doesn't want to do it because she knows it's boring. You are then put in the position of having to encourage your child to have to do something that you don't think she should be doing in the first place." That doesn't feel right—*and it isn't.* In fact, homework overload is turning many of us into the types of parents we never wanted to be: nags, bribers, and taskmasters.

BATTLE STATIONS, EVERYONE

Half of the 1,200 parents surveyed by Public Agenda, a nonprofit, nonpartisan research group, said they've had a serious argument with their children over homework, and 34 percent said it's become a source of struggle and stress for them and their child.

For many kids, simply getting started is daunting. A number of parents in our survey, as well as those at homework workshops we attended, reported nightly hysterics when it came time to sit down to loads of work. "In third and fourth grades, my daughter had so much homework that she started developing personality problems—big ol' tears and crying and frustration," says Christine of Houston, who often felt like crying herself. She felt obligated to keep her daughter inside while friends with less homework played. "She would see them outside and couldn't join them. She started to act out in certain ways. She would take her hand and scratch her own face. There was another little girl in her class who was literally pulling her hair out in big clumps. It was horrible."

Did her daughter have learning issues that made the work take longer? No, it was just facing the relentless grind, day after day, without hope of relief. And like many parents, Christine had to hold her daughter's hand (sometimes literally) to get her through it. "It wasn't enough to help her get started, she just felt better if I was right there," adds Christine. "Meanwhile, I didn't get to spend any time with my younger son, who didn't need homework help."

The homework situation got so bad that Christine finally decided to move both her daughter and her son to another school in the Houston area where the homework load is much lighter, and her daughter soon stopped scratching her face and needing the security of having her mother beside her every single evening as she worked. But similar scenes play out in homes all across America every night, and not every parent has the option of switching schools. "I have to continually chivvy my daughter along to keep doing the work," says Pam, a mother from Pittsburgh. "My daughter was sent home (in kindergarten, mind you) with a sheet of fifty-five math problems to solve and return the very next day. This took her well over an hour as they had just started to do math and she still had to work hard at it. She and I both were in tears by the time the assignment was finished."

Dealing with never-ending homework overload can make even the best parents lose their patience, tempers, and good judgment. Prodding her three kids under ten through several hours of homework drains the joy out of every evening for Maria, a mother from Pelham, New York. After several hours of nothing but work, her oldest child, a daughter in fifth grade, almost always starts to cry, and Maria has no emotional resources left. "That's when you snap," she says sadly. She finds herself screaming that she doesn't care if it all gets done, then that her daughter can't stop until she *does* get it all done. "So we go to bed angry at each other, and you just feel so lousy about the world. You've hurt your child's feelings and you don't know what to do."

In fact, for many of us, homework is such an emotional tinderbox that sometimes we find that none of our usual strategies works. "The only conflicts I have with my oldest child are about homework. I have basically run out of ideas to motivate her," says a New Jersey mom whose public school eighth-grader has two hours of work each night. "We've tried weekly motivation charts complete with stickers. She helped set the 'prizes' (books, movie of her choice, homemade cookies). It worked for about three weeks. We've tried taking things away. But what do you take away from a kid who only wants to sit and read all day? We tried reasoning. When she was in elementary school, I would sit next to her for hours prodding her to do the next question. I'm ashamed to admit we tried yelling in moments of frustration." No wonder this mom is at her wit's end. She feels forced to stop her child from reading—which educators endorse as the most important learning activity—and make her knuckle down to work that's less worthwhile.

She's not alone. More than half of the parents we surveyed or interviewed report using negative measures, such as threatening, bribing, and cajoling, to get kids to do homework at least sometimes. Using such methods might get the job done in the short run. But if a child's motivation is external rather than internal, homework isn't even fostering personal responsibility, which educators cite as one of its virtues. "The whole point of homework is for a child to become an independent learner," explains Mary Leonhardt, a teacher for more than thirty years in Concord, Massachusetts, and author of several books on education. "If he's got to have his mother or father sitting beside him, it defeats the whole purpose."

Taking an active role might sound sensible if your child is lagging behind in school. But being too controlling with homework can really backfire if kids aren't doing well. A 2004 study sponsored by the National Institute of Mental Health and published in the journal *Child Development* found that when parents issued commands about assignments or took over part or all of a task for struggling kids, the kids disengaged from their work, became more reliant on their parents to feel competent, and did even *less* well in school. Yet when parents stepped back, and were available for discussion but allowed their children to take the lead (what researchers call an autonomy-support approach), school performance improved.

Whether your child has learning issues or not, continuous power struggles over homework can have an enormous impact. "The constant trauma can really take the warmth out of the parent-child relationship, and you can't underestimate the damage done if that warmth and closeness are lost," says child psychologist Lawrence Cohen. "Kids' relationships with their parents are more important than anything. As these same kids get older, we're going to want them to open up to us about the important emotional and life struggles they're having. But they are not going to open up to us if all we do every day is yell at them to do their homework."

Homework overload isn't just harming parent-child relationships. It takes a toll on parent-parent relationships as well. Many parents reported to us that they frequently disagreed with their spouses or partners about how to handle homework.

> *My husband and I disagree about how to handle homework. Some days, he'll just say, let 'em do it—or not do it. Usually, it's because it's 9:45 and it's past bedtime and we're all going to have a meltdown. He wants to make his life easier. But that's not good enough for me. I won't do it just because it makes my life easier. We can't even always agree on the right answers to some of the problems.*
>
> Jackie, mother of a fourth- and a fifth-grader in a Catholic school in Buffalo, New York

> *My wife tends to think my way is too regimented and I feel her style is too laid back. I use the Socratic method, which puts the responsibility for an answer squarely on my son's shoulders, and my wife tends to think this unfair since he is only seven.*
>
> Joel, father of a second-grader in public school in Haughton, Louisiana

> *My wife believes that the family must take responsibility for all assignments. It is very hard for her to be less involved with my younger son's homework, and she speaks very harshly to my older son in a way that I feel is stressful and demeaning. I have intervened*

with teachers on occasion to get out of certain assignments or to
have them modified to better suit my sons. But this made her very
nervous or even angry at me because she thought we would get
branded by the school as uncooperative. My wife felt that to ask for
a change would just add to the perception that our son was a prob-
lem. This caused great turmoil in my whole family and was one fac-
tor that nearly led to the breakup of my marriage.

William, father of an eighth- and a third-grader in Brooklyn,
New York

Obviously, it's not any easier if there's just one of you. Single parents
have no one with whom to share the burden, and divorced parents who
share custody may resent devoting precious time to assignments instead
of simply enjoying their limited time with their children. One divorced
dad from Houston told us that he'd love to kick back at Cub Scouts with
his son each Thursday, but can't because they're often stuck studying for
the weekly spelling test the next day. He can't play catch with his daughter, either. "I hate being a homework taskmaster when I have so little time
with my kids. There are a lot of other things I would rather be doing with
my children," he says. "I think that schools are depending upon parents
for a lot of the teaching."

What if your ex is not so conscientious? "When my children visit
their father, he does not make them do their homework," says a mother
from Santa Clara, California. "I'm left holding the bag and enforcing that
it gets done. It makes for a stressful week after they return."

Fear for Our Kids' Futures

Nobody wants their kids to remember their childhoods as one long
battle over homework. But many of us are scared about their futures. We

hear all the news reports about how badly the schools are failing and, since we can't do much about what's happening in the classroom, we tend to focus on the one area of school to which we do have access: homework. We feel like we're letting our kids down if we don't do everything we can to help them—but often, our "help" is actually harmful.

"Parents today are in a constant panic about their kids' success," explains William Crain, the professor of psychology at City College of New York. "They're scared to ease up and let their children enjoy life because they're afraid they won't get into Harvard. One woman told me that she had a nightmare that her kid will be a fruit delivery man, and she'll be exposed to the world as a failure as a parent. Her son has various interests, but she can't let him explore them. She has to corral him into doing more homework because she feels that's the only way to achieve success." Adds Helen Leatherwood, an educational therapist and tutor in Hollywood, "I think parents really lose sight that there are a lot of different paths to the same place. Parents end up putting enormous pressure on their kids to excel, and push the hell out of them to get to places that they might not even be well suited for."

Even mental health professionals are not immune to these anxieties. One child therapist in Bethesda, Maryland, admits haranguing her own high schooler to do more work—even when he insists he's finished his assignments and although he receives good grades. "I feel like I'm failing if I'm not pushing him hard enough or micromanaging him. If homework didn't exist, then that dynamic wouldn't be there."

Some of us also worry that other parents are doing more to give their kids an edge educationally. "Let's be real, many parents push for more homework," says Gail, the mother of a fourth-grader and an eighth-grader in Upper Montclair, New Jersey. "At Back to School Night in second grade, they told us to read for twenty minutes to our child. And one woman raised her hand and said, 'We already read one hour a night. Should we start reading for an hour and twenty minutes?' It's like her kid read *Pippi Longstocking* in the womb and now she's on to *Anna Karenina*. There's a kind of peer pressure, and you get whipped up into a frenzy together."

Anything for an A

If you walk by your local playground and your local tutoring center, it's not surprising to see where more kids are congregated after school. (Hint: It's not the playground.) Tutors used to be reserved for kids who were truly struggling. Now there are tutors for kids who are performing at grade level, as well as for high-achieving kids seeking an extra edge. There are tutors for every subject and every kind of test—from those mandated by No Child Left Behind to the ERBs and SATs. There are tutors to preteach tots the skills they will learn in pre-K and kindergarten. And there are even tutors who will do your children's homework for them—although every reputable company denies going that far. Still, it's easy to see why tutoring has grown into a $6-billion-a-year business.

"Everyone is trying to give their kid a leg up. If your neighbors are tutoring their kids, then you have to as well or you feel like you're being left behind," says Chris Eliot, the head of the Tenacre Country Day School in Wellesley, Massachusetts. Adds Hollywood tutor Helen Leatherwood, "We have to acknowledge that most children are either getting outside help from their parents or outside tutors if they want to compete."

Lisa Jacobson, founder of Inspirica, a tutoring and college counseling company with offices in New York and Boston, reports that she knows families who employ up to five weekly tutors for their kids. "People think that parents have become crazy," she says, "but it's really that the whole society has changed under our feet." With the huge bulge of baby boomers' kids now applying to college, the competition for top schools is fierce, and parents are reacting with desperation.

But while tutoring can be a blessing for struggling students or those with documented learning issues, it can backfire in unexpected ways. For one thing, the tutoring center might not be aligned with your child's curriculum. "It can be counterproductive if the program is teaching Kumon math and we're teaching math a different way," says Tenacre's Chris Eliot.

Giving little kids a "head start" can also cause problems. "I think it's inappropriate to hire tutors to teach preschoolers how to read," says Jacobson, who routinely turns down scores of parents seeking tutoring for kids under the age of six. "Parents will say that the kids want to learn. But it's hard for me to believe that kids that age are begging for a tutor." Instead, she says that parents want to ensure that their kids will be seated at the top reading table in class. "I don't think little kids need tutoring and I don't want to be a part of it," says Jacobson. "They're little kids. They just need to go out and play."

Tutoring can also make your child feel *less* confident and competent. "You're unwittingly sending your children a message that you don't believe in them, that they can't do it on their own even with the regular teacher's help," says Jacobson. "From a very young age, kids get the feeling from all the adults around them that they need to be the best at everything. That's a recipe for disaster. By the time I get them in high school, they're crying every day. It's just too much pressure." Kids can also suffer what Chris Eliot calls an anxiety backlash. As he explains, "Kids think: I'm being tutored for this test—I better do well. Then at the test, the kid freezes."

In addition, tutors report that their pupils sometimes become overdependent on them. "An academic tutor's job should be to go in when a student is having trouble, help him get out of trouble and get caught up, and then get out," says Jacobson. "A tutor shouldn't become a crutch." But often, that's exactly what happens. Some students no longer bother to pay attention in class because they know the tutor will cover the material with them later. A class of tutored kids (and Jacobson reports there are indeed classes where most or all of the students are being tutored) might also make the teacher think he's doing a better job than he actually is.

Some parents take things one step further in the effort to give their kids an edge: They try to get them diagnosed with a learning disability, even if they don't have one, says one family therapist from Northern California. "Most of the kids I see are pretty normal, average kids. They don't have learning disabilities. But the parents want to do all this testing and get all these special arrangements," she says. Such arrangements include extra time on tests and tutoring.

Of course, while learning disabilities are a serious problem, this kind of overdiagnosing doesn't always benefit kids. Some parents who complain to teachers about the homework load are told that they should consider having their children take Ritalin or other medications to keep up. "I can't tell you how many conversations I had with teachers that ended with them basically saying 'medicate your kid,' " says one frustrated New Jersey mom of an eighth-grader. "Not one of them would consider that the problem might be the delivery system—even after the school tested her for a learning disability and (surprise!) found that she scored in the ninety-ninth percentile for intelligence."

While some kids clearly benefit from prescription drugs, there is a valid fear that "the diagnosis of attention-deficit/hyperactivity disorder and the medication of children has turned into a classroom management style as opposed to a medical treatment," says David Goodman, a psychiatrist and assistant professor at Johns Hopkins University School of Medicine. "There's a reason why we don't let teachers make diagnoses and medicate kids. A teacher or school system that insists on medication puts themselves in legal jeopardy."

Why Parents Don't Speak Up

Families suffering from homework overload often don't realize how many other families are in the same situation. That's partly because we tend to clam up when our kids are having trouble. No one wants to admit, "We're having a hard time. Are you?" No one wants to reveal that they're arguing with their children every night. As a result, we might feel as though we're alone. "I just assume that everyone else has kids who can sit down and do five hours of homework and excel at it," says one New Jersey mom. "You start to think there's something wrong with my child— and ergo, with me—if he can't handle it."

Such anxiety and parent-to-parent peer pressure makes us compete in ways that aren't helping anyone. Jackie, the mother of the boys in fourth and fifth grades in Buffalo, New York, spends a minimum of three hours each night (yes, that's three *hours*!) checking her sons' homework and making them correct mistakes. "The teacher has asked us not to do it so that she can see what the kids are getting wrong and adjust her teaching," confesses Jackie. "But if I don't do it, every other parent is going to do it, and it's going to impact my kids' grades. What if my kid is the only one getting it wrong?"

Jackie's afraid that as her boys get older, the time she needs to spend reviewing their work is only going to increase. "I work full-time, and I'm close to maxing out now. I don't know what I'm going to do." She admits that her own parents barely glanced at her assignments, and she got great grades all the way through college. "But if everyone's parents are helping them now, what's going to happen to the kids with parents who don't? I don't know if I can bear to find out."

We've come to see our kids' homework as our homework. "What many parents don't realize is that they are contributing to the frenzy this way and they are hurting their kids," explains Denise Clark Pope, the professor at Stanford University School of Education and author of

Doing School: How We Are Creating a Generation of Stressed-Out, Materialistic, and Miseducated Students. Moms and dads like these have been dubbed "helicopter parents," because they hover over their kids, swooping in before they can make a mistake. But without ever experiencing failure as children, they may be unable to cope with it as adults.

Where does this leave us? We might rage against homework to our spouses. But for all our anxiety and frustration, many of us are reluctant to question our school's approach to homework. After all, we want to believe that all the work will be worth it. And if we admit that something is wrong with the situation, our kids might begin to think so, too. Then how will we force them to tackle the grind each and every night? (We'll tell you how to handle this in Chapter 7.) "Parents feel so helpless about homework because they don't want to undermine the teacher's authority," explains associate professor in early childhood education Olga Jarrett. "As a parent, one wants to be supportive."

Even if we know that the problem doesn't stem from us, and that the school's homework practices need reform, we still might not say anything. After all, we don't want ourselves or our children to be seen as a problem, or for them to face negative consequences. As one Brooklyn mom put it, "We made our daughter do the homework even though we didn't believe in it because we were obedient parents, which I really regret, and because I was worried about what would happen to her." However, as we'll demonstrate in later chapters, parents who do learn how to speak up in an effective way often find that teachers will cut down or change assignments.

Surprise, You're a Teacher!

Did you know that you can become instantly qualified to teach math, science, history, writing, and a slew of other subjects? You don't even need any special qualifications or training. All you have to do is give birth to a child who gets homework assignments.

In kindergarten last year, Winter's daughter had one teacher during the day and another one at night, her mom. "She was bringing home assignments she couldn't possibly do by herself," explains the Canyon Lake, Texas, mother. "She didn't understand them, so I had to take on the teaching. I wanted to ask the school, Why is she doing this? You have her for all these hours each day. Why aren't you teaching her what she needs to know?"

As schools try to cram more and more into the day to prepare kids for No Child Left Behind testing or simply to stay competitive, there's no way teachers can get through all the material, especially with ever-growing class sizes. The result: assignments that cover concepts and techniques that haven't been taught thoroughly in class or that are brand new—even though this is ineffective, according to educators. "Homework seems to have supplanted teaching," says Marcia, the mother from San Francisco. "Whatever the teacher hasn't finished becomes homework." Increasingly, parents are expected to take up the slack.

That's what happened to Janet, the mother of a second-grader in San Jose, California, who was told that all the prep for standardized tests left no time for extra math practice at school. "Once the school has taught you that two plus two is four, they don't do anything more than test you on it," she says. The teacher explained that if Janet wanted her son to master the math concepts, she would have to work with him herself. "She told me to get flash cards."

Even Lisa Jacobson, the head of her own tutoring company, balked last year when her son's fourth-grade teacher at their public school in Chappaqua, New York, insisted that she help him through his three hours of homework each night. "I said, I don't want to tutor him," Lisa recalls. "But the teacher said, 'You have to be the tutor. In a town like this, where real estate values depend on how good the schools are and test scores, I'm expected to teach kids at a certain level so that when they go to middle school next year, they are completely prepared. I can't do that by myself all day. So I need the parent to continue at home.' "

In some cases it's the school that is on a mission to make sure parents participate in homework. "The principal told me that it is really the parents' job to educate their children and that his teachers are only facilitators," says Melinda, the mother of two kids in public school in New Orleans, Louisiana. "He said that they purposely send home a lot of work that is over the kids' heads so that the parents will get involved with the kids and teach them at home. He said, 'Melinda, you don't have time because you have a career. But the majority of kids who go to this school, they have stay-at-home moms, and their moms want this.' So my kids are being punished because I'm a career woman."

While few principals would come out and say what this one did, many schools seem to operate under the assumption that we won't bother to do educational activities with our kids unless we are forced. Schools also seem to assume that there's a stereotypical mom at home at 3:00, ready to pitch in with assignments and run out to the crafts store for project supplies. But what if your job doesn't allow you to be there during the critical homework hours? Will your child be penalized?

Even if we are stay-at-home parents or can arrange flexible hours, we don't necessarily want to be drafted by the schools. As Peg, a New Jersey mom of a first- and a fourth-grader, explains, "This is a major issue at our school. I feel that I should be reviewing what the kids have learned during the day, not teaching them what the teacher couldn't get to." Indeed, even parents who are willing partners may quickly discover that helping their children with homework requires a whole new skill set—one they don't have time to acquire. After all, most of us are not trained teachers. "If I wanted to be a teacher, I would have gone and gotten a teaching degree," explains one mom. "I'm not particularly gifted at it anyway."

Some educators argue that parent involvement in homework can enhance and accelerate a child's learning. But it can easily have negative effects, says researcher Harris Cooper, author of *The Battle Over Homework.* "Involvement might also interfere with learning," he writes. "This could happen if parents are uncomfortable or unable to take on the role of teacher or if parents use instructional techniques different from those being used at school."

So why is the school system relying on us? If we wouldn't want an unqualified person teaching our kids during the day, why would we want one doing it at night—especially when that person is also tired and distracted? After all, it's not easy to explain how to do fractions while you're trying to get dinner on the table and perhaps take care of an infant at the same time.

Even those parents who are professional teachers don't want to continue teaching at night. "The worst assignment is the one where the teacher is trying to improve parent-child time," says Maura, the mother of five from Grand Island, New York, and a math teacher herself. "I think I am a good parent. We read with our kids and play games and talk. My kids have had assignments (particularly our oldest) where we had to spend forty-five minutes one-on-one with him. Other children were not supposed to be around. He was six, and I had three other children younger than him. How do you have forty-five minutes for one child in that situation? I think homework assignments should be for the child. If a child cannot do the assignment alone, then it is parent homework."

But when assignments begin in preschool, before kids can even understand the instructions, we have to pick up the chalk—and fast. "Last year, my daughter was assigned book reports in kindergarten," reports Sarah from New York City. "She couldn't read, so one of us had to be involved, or it couldn't get done. It frequently turned into a nag-fest." Adds Gwen, from Oakland, California, "Since my son's a third-grader, almost everything involves our input. The math games require another player, the 'research' projects require someone to search the Web, take him to the library, read and explain the research, teach him about organizing thoughts, help him write it and design the presentation board, and practice it until he feels comfortable. The homework is as much *my* homework as *his*."

Sometimes we'll find ourselves teaching key skills from scratch. As the mother of one second-grader relates, "I was in the middle of a parent-teacher conference when, out of the blue, the teacher says, 'Listen, if you don't work with your daughter's penmanship, I'm going to have to send her to occupational therapy.' This was the first time I'd heard that my daughter was not forming certain letters properly, so I asked: 'Well, at what point did she fail to keep up with penmanship in class?' And out came the answer: 'We don't teach them penmanship.' So there I was with *my* extra homework assignment, which of course meant extra homework for my second-grader because after all her other assignments, she was supposed to practice her letter formation with me. This creates an ugly battle in an area that you would think school would tackle on its own, but for some reason isn't."

Power struggles are another reason why parents make poor teachers, says tutor Helen Leatherwood. "When I tutor other people's children, they treat me as a teacher. They don't whine, there are boundaries, they don't say, 'You don't know what you're talking about.' But when I try helping my own child with homework, it's a different story."

Some schools actually hold special workshops for parents to help them deal with their new job. "Our school has actively instructed parents how to be homework helpers," says Deborah, a California mom of a second-grader and a fourth-grader in a charter school. "They have told us how to guide a child's thinking through thoughtful questioning, rather than just giving an answer. This works nicely when the child is willing to go through the steps. But when they are just tired and don't want to do it, then nothing works."

Around the country, parents are even taking classes to brush up on middle and high school math, specifically so they can help their kids with assignments. A math teacher in Virginia hosts a weekly show on local television called *Algebra for Parents.* Mindy, a sixth-grade math teacher in San Diego who gives homework every single night including weekends, holds a one-hour class for parents each Monday night. "I teach the parents what the kids are going to learn on Tuesday through the following Monday," she explains. "That way it is fresh in their minds and they know how the concepts are being explained to their children. I started it three years ago and I had such a good response that I continued it. Most parents want to help their children, but aren't really sure how and are embarrassed that their eleven-year-old knows more than they do. But as I explain to the parents, 'You were in the sixth grade a long time ago, and the material that your sixth-grader is being asked to learn is material that you probably learned in eighth or ninth grade.' "

Where does this leave those of us who don't take a review course—or just don't want to? At a loss, trying to remember how to solve for X or Y. And chances are, our attempts at teaching math concepts we learned twenty years ago aren't making things any clearer for anyone. When Maria's third-grader came home with her first algebra assignment, Maria studied the problems carefully. "But I learned algebra way back in seventh grade, and the teacher didn't send home any explanation of how to help with the homework," says the Pelham, New York, mother. It wasn't long before her daughter became hysterical because Maria wasn't teaching algebra the way the teacher did it. Maria wants to know, "Why are they even learning algebra in third grade?"

"A Little Help"

After hours of being a taskmaster and a teacher, something's got to give, and often it's our best instincts as parents. An astonishing number of us have at one time or another jumped in to do our children's homework—

yet another way that too much homework is turning us into the types of parents we never wanted to be.

More than a quarter of the parents we surveyed admit to having done all or part of a homework assignment for their children. Parents justify their actions in different ways:

> It's ten o'clock at night, your kid's been doing homework since 6:30, and she looks at you and says, I've got one more page of math, and you say, Give it to me. You don't think that happens? It happens. I'm still able to do the math. But you've got to learn how to write like your child.
>
> A mother of three from Texas

> In Georgia, they really pile it on during elementary school. It can be an awful time for kids and parents. Some of the social studies work at this age involves so much reading that it's nearly impossible for the kids to grasp concepts such as how a bill becomes a law, and they're whining before it's all done. I must admit, there are times when I just do it for them to get them to bed.
>
> A mother of four from St. Mary's, Georgia

> I look up vocab definitions for my son. They are all words he knows, but he is required to write out the dictionary definitions. It seems like busywork, and so not worth his time. I can do it very fast and it feels like something I can do to help. Then we laugh about how much better it is to read to increase vocab, not study words out of context.
>
> A mother of an eighth-grader from Jamaica Plains, Massachusetts

> I wouldn't do anything I'd consider cheating. But when my kids miss a day of school, my goodness, the amount of work that comes

home for them is an easy four hours. Even if they're deathly ill, you have to put them in the car, take them back to school, pick up the assignments, and then begin the drastic ordeal of teaching the material to them. So I'll do whatever needs to be done to get it done. I don't think there's anything wrong with that.

A mother of a third- and a fifth-grader and a former teacher from Baton Rouge, Louisiana

My daughter takes a half hour for dinner and during this time she often brings a book to read as part of her assignment or asks me to drill her in French or in science for an upcoming quiz. Sometimes she works until she falls asleep at her desk. I will then look over her work to see what needs to be completed and I will complete it for her. There are times when the assignment is so inane or so "busy-work" that in order to relieve the stress that this may cause, it has been necessary to do the work for her just to get it out of our faces. I believe that this is the biggest "dirty secret" about homework! Although most parents will never admit it, they are very involved in the work. There is no way that many of these assignments could be completed by a child in the amount of time given.

A mother of an eighth-grader from Brooklyn, New York

If my kid couldn't do the homework, for whatever reason, I'd just do it for her. As an educator, I know it sends a terrible message. The kids see through it. Children are not fools.

A mother of two and an elementary school principal from suburban New York

When it's 11 P.M. and your child is upset about an uncompleted worksheet, taking over can seem like the simplest solution. But while it might save strife, stress, tears, and a confrontation with the teacher in the short run, it also sends a clear message that you'll do your kid's work if he can't, teaching him to rely on the work of others when he's in a jam.

We shouldn't be surprised, then, that cheating on homework and tests has become epidemic. According to a 2005 Rutgers University survey of eighteen thousand students at sixty-one high schools, 60 percent have copied work from a classmate or the Internet. Of course, the Internet has made it easier for unscrupulous kids to plagiarize. But have we unwittingly given them permission to do so with our own actions? Only 27 percent of students who took an earlier Rutgers' survey even believed that such cheating was a serious offense. As one respondent wrote, "You do what it takes to succeed in life."

Creating Dependent Children

The truth is, many of the ways we try so hard to "help" our kids might not really be helping them in the long run. In fact, it could have the opposite effect. When Amy's second-grader was assigned a research paper that was too difficult for him to do on his own, the San Leandro, California, mother spent one whole weekend reading the material and helping him organize paragraphs. But in the end, she says, all her efforts "made him feel stupid because he didn't understand how to do the assignment himself."

In fact, we could be creating a bunch of kids who are so dependent on Mom and Dad or their tutors that they can't do their work by themselves. "Think about it," says Gail, the Upper Montclair, New Jersey mom. "When you start homework in kindergarten, there's no kid on the face of the earth who can do it on his own. Things have to be read to kids, explained to them, so of course you have to sit there with them. That means they come to view us as homework helpers from the get-go. The expectation is there with the teachers and it gets to be there with the kids, too."

We don't like what homework has done to our kids or ourselves. But once we've become enforcers or enablers, it can be difficult to turn back. "I have been an overseer, forcing my son to do everything," says Lori, the mother of a tenth-grader from Raleigh, North Carolina. It's put a lot of strain on their relationship, and she knows her sixteen-year-old finally needs to learn to be responsible for his own work. Still, she says that it's hard to retreat because she's so used to being involved.

Jackie, the mom from Buffalo, New York, who spends three hours each night checking her fourth- and fifth-graders' homework, agrees. "In my mind, I was going to start doing this and then little by little, I'd be backing off and they'd be more independent," she says. "But the reality is that the work will get harder and they'll need more help, so they'll remain dependent."

The way homework is forcing us to interact with our kids could have even more serious consequences. "There's a weakness in kids now. They can't do anything without their parents and don't want to, unless they develop a real rebellious streak," explains Peter Loffredo, a psychotherapist who has worked with children and families for almost thirty years. "It's a lose-lose situation. We're going to end up with a lot of kids who are developing a weak sense of self and a false sense of entitlement, expecting that everyone is going to take care of them."

Jackie, who teaches at a college, has seen this firsthand. "Parents of twenty-year-olds often call me to give homework excuses for their kids." In fact, some parents even buy extra copies of their kids' college textbooks so that they can help with homework, and Lisa Jacobson of Inspirica says that some actually hire tutors to edit their kids' college papers. College administrators shake their heads and beg parents to cut the umbilical cord. But we've been involved in our children's work for so long, it seems natural for us to continue ad infinitum.

4

The Creation of the Homework Potato

T elevision is evil. Homework is good.

It's a prevailing belief in America. But the two have one essential thing in common: Both involve long periods of sitting still, and so both can contribute to childhood obesity and other serious health problems. We're quick to blame television, along with computer and video games, for turning our kids into couch potatoes. But what about all the "homework potatoes" out there, parked in one place while they hit the books for hour after hour, evening after evening? Could homework overload be helping to create a nation of fatter kids? Parents should consider these statistics we mentioned in Chapter 1:

- Since 1980, the time children spend on homework has ballooned by 51 percent, according to a large survey by the University of Michigan. For some, the increase is minimal. But for many, it's significant.

- Since 1981, the amount of time kids spend playing sports has decreased by 58 percent for six- to eight-year-olds, 19 percent for nine- to eleven-year-olds, 43 percent for twelve- to fourteen-year-olds, and 28 percent for fifteen- to seventeen-year-olds, according to another large survey by the University of Michigan.

At the same time:

- Since 1980, the number of overweight children in the U.S. has tripled, according to the Centers for Disease Control (CDC). Even since 2000, there's been a significant increase. More than 17 percent of American kids between the ages of two and nineteen are now considered overweight.
- Since the 1980s, the number of children with diabetes has increased dramatically, according to the American Diabetes Association. In addition, during 2002–2005 alone, the number of ten- to fourteen-year-olds taking medications to prevent or treat type 2 diabetes jumped 106 percent. The CDC predicts that one in three children born in 2000 will become diabetic.

Just coincidence? We don't think so.

Certainly, many things contribute to childhood obesity, from too much screen time to too much junk food. But we believe that homework overload is a big factor that's been overlooked and ignored. Remember: Homework is an extremely sedentary activity, just like watching television. In fact, "there is absolutely no physiological difference between watching TV and doing homework," says Melinda Sothern, an exercise physiologist who runs the pediatric obesity laboratory at Louisiana State University Health Sciences Center in New Orleans and coauthor of *Trim Kids,* a guide for parents of overweight children. Sitting burns only 33 to 50 calories an hour, and it makes no difference whether kids are watching TV or doing homework. Too much of either one can lead to weight gain.

In fact, homework is a major obstacle to kids who need to lose weight. "Homework is the number one reason parents of overweight kids say they don't have time to exercise. It's very discouraging," says Dr. Sothern. Kris von Almen, who runs Committed to Kids, a pediatric weight-loss clinic in San Jose, California, and who coauthored *Trim Kids,* adds "We're up against homework all the time. The kids are highly motivated to lose weight. But if we ask them to do a few minutes of exercise three times a week, they'll say, 'I can't. I have too much homework.' "

Sure, most kids, overweight or not, also consume a lot of junk food. But the time they devote to homework might be hurting them even more. "All the evidence seems to suggest that the increase in childhood obesity is related largely to reductions in physical activity, more so than major changes in diet," says Robert Malina, a professor of physical education at Tarleton State University in Texas and a top researcher who co-authored a 2005 review of 850 studies on exercise and children for the CDC. "Diet plays a part. But the lack of physical activity has a bigger impact."

SEDENTARY SCHOOL KIDS

The CDC recommends that kids get at least sixty minutes of moderate to vigorous exercise daily. Many of us assume our children are getting more than enough physical activity at school and tell ourselves that it doesn't matter if they're sedentary afterward.

Unfortunately, that's probably not the case. Recess and physical education have been slashed at schools across the country to save money and increase the time for academic instruction. According to 2006 figures, more than 4,600 U.S. elementary schools have no recess at all. And most physical education classes simply aren't that physical anymore. A study conducted by the National Institute of Child Health and Human Development found that third-graders spend an average of just twenty-five minutes *per week* engaged in moderate to vigorous activity. Even when kids do have P.E., that same study found that after teachers managed kids' behavior and taught them rules, there was an average of just 4.8 minutes left per class for vigorous exercise. What's more, research shows that kids who are inactive at school are also more likely to be inactive *after* school.

Lots of kids do play organized sports at school or elsewhere. But as these teams have become more competitive, those children who aren't highly skilled are often made to stay on the bench, says Phillip Tomporowski, an exercise psychologist and associate professor at the University of Georgia. They may even end up quitting. Says Tomporowski, "For every child who gets into sports and is very active, there are many more who are dropouts and have a negative history with physical activity." So even if our children take P.E. or participate in organized sports, they might not be getting nearly the amount of exercise at school that we think they are.

When kids want to take a break from studying and burn off some steam and calories, many parents don't allow it. Over and over, parents told us their house rule is "homework first." So kids remain captive to homework, stealthily taking breaks to IM friends or play games on their computer so they look like they're still studying.

Unfortunately, even when kids are done working, they're not likely to spend much time running around. After hours bent over their books, the last thing most kids want to do is go out and play. Often, it's too late anyway. As Joshua, a high school student in Pembroke, Georgia, says, "Homework should be outlawed! It's a main reason why kids are getting fat. By the time they get through with their homework, it is dark and some kids don't like going outside in the dark!"

So what do they do? Like many of us, they collapse on the couch. "After I'm done, the only thing I want to do is watch TV or go on the computer," says Allison, the ninth-grader from Brooklyn, New York. "I don't feel like reading because that's a majority of my homework. I don't want to do anything that resembles homework. All I want to do is relax and rest my brain." Perhaps if kids weren't so depleted by homework, they might not feel the need to spend what little free time is left zoning out in front of a screen.

Connecting the Dots

Whether our children spend hours in front of the tube or hours in front of their books, their bodies react the same way to the inactivity. Yet while there have been literally thousands of studies confirming that too much television leads to weight gain, researchers have never investigated homework overload in the same way. We believe it's because homework is such a sacred cow that it's never really occurred to most researchers that it could be a cause of obesity.

Once we brought it up, however, every single expert we interviewed agreed that there was a connection. "More youngsters today have more opportunities to be inactive, including doing more homework," says Professor Malina. "And being sedentary is bad for a kid's health, period." Dr. Howard Taras, a professor of pediatrics at the University of California, a practicing pediatrician in San Diego, and former chairperson of the American Academy of Pediatrics' Committee on School Heath, agrees: "You know, now that you mention it, I'm surprised that homework doesn't come up more often in the pediatrician's office. Too much of it could definitely be a barrier to lots of healthy habits, including exercise and sleep."

Pediatric obesity expert Melinda Sothern is even more adamant. "Giving children hours of homework when they should be outside playing can lead—and probably has led—to the obesity epidemic," she says. "To place children in a situation in which they can't get enough physical activity is to doom them to ill health. It's not just the parents' problem—it's a public health issue."

She believes that "no one's looked at whether there's a correlation between how many hours of homework kids do and obesity because no one wants to find it." She might be right. After all, as we know all too well, it's hard to challenge society's assumption that homework is always such a positive thing.

But the truth is, we don't need a study to connect the dots. Common sense tells us that excessive homework causes the same problems that excessive television watching does—and that the studies that have been done on television apply to homework as well. For example, according to a 2001 analysis of data from a national survey of more than four thousand children between the ages of eight and sixteen, published in the journal *Archives of Pediatrics and Adolescent Medicine,* kids who watch more than four hours of TV each day had the highest rates of obesity, while those watching one hour or less had the lowest. It doesn't take a rocket scientist—or an obesity researcher—to figure out that kids who sit and study for the same number of hours are in the same ever-expanding boat.

In fact, it comes down to a simple math problem. "If a child spends two hours doing homework, he's burning a hundred calories at most," says Sothern. "But if he played tag or rode his bike instead, he would burn at least four times that much." So when a child replaces physical activity with assignments, he's not expending 300 calories he could be.

Over a five-day school week, that adds up to 1,500 calories. Since 3,500 extra calories equal a pound, this could lead to almost a half-pound gain per week. Over the 180 days in an average school year, a child could pack on more than 15 additional pounds this way.

THE WEIGHT OF THE WORLD ON THEIR SHOULDERS

Another reason kids arrive home exhausted: the huge load of books overflowing their backpacks. According to a 2004 study of 3,498 middle schoolers published in the *Journal of Pediatric Orthopedics*, some haul backpacks equivalent to 43 percent of their body weight. The Children's Spine Foundation recommends that kids carry loads that total no more than 15 percent. No wonder 64 percent of the kids reported back pain—yet another factor that can discourage a child from engaging in physical activity. Although most schools don't address this issue, they should. Research shows that adults with severe back problems often suffered from back pain as children.

Many parents are worried, and rightly so. According to a large 2003 national survey conducted by the Opinion Research Corporation for the nonprofit National Association for Sport and Physical Education, while 42 percent of parents blame TV as the main reason their kids aren't active, 28 percent point the finger at too much homework. More than one-fifth of the parents we surveyed and interviewed report that homework always or often prevents their child from being physically active.

Homework puts my fifth-grader at a disadvantage physically. He's had to skip basketball practice because of assignments and he's not in as good shape as he should be.

Jackie, mother of a fourth- and a fifth-grader in Buffalo, New York

We've had to cut out ballet and gymnastics because my daughters never had time to complete their homework. By the time my girls are done with everything, there are not enough hours in the day left for them to play outside.

   Leslie, mother of a sixth- and a seventh-grader in Clayton,
   North Carolina

As a nurse, I know kids need to exercise. We're seeing cardiac issues in children as young as ten and there's been a huge increase in diabetes. So it really bothers me when my boys can't get out and exercise because they're spending all their time doing homework. I don't like the fact that they sit all day in school and then come home and sit again to do their homework in the evening.

   Maureen, a pediatric nurse and mother of seventh-grade
   twins in Florence, Kentucky

On the weekends, all of the fourth-graders are inside completing their writing assignment called a reading response, which is always due on Monday. A first draft is required which takes most of Saturday and a final report is done on Sunday. Our phone starts ringing about 4 or 5 P.M. for some play dates, but sometimes it's too late. I think my son has gained five pounds this winter from lack of exercise.

   Jody, mother of a fourth-grader in New York City

The kids themselves are frustrated and angry:

My homework always interferes with exercise, playing hockey or football behind the school, not to mention playing cello. I don't want to sit around doing homework, but I have to.

   Nathan, an eighth-grader in Oaklyn, New Jersey

I hate homework! I haven't gone biking in a year and I don't have time to play any sports!!
Anonymous fifth-grade girl

The doctors want me to get a lot of exercise to help me lose weight. But trying to fit in exercise and basketball practice is really difficult because I start my homework around 4 and it takes me until 9 P.M. I don't feel like shooting hoops after that.
Nina, a tenth-grader from San Jose, California, who is enrolled in a pediatric weight-loss program

America is the fattest country, right? So to help kids get over this, the schools give us so much homework that we can't play outside and exercise. It just doesn't make sense.
Mark, a seventh-grader from Pelham, New York

The Playground Paradox

We agree with that seventh-grader, particularly since physical activity isn't important just for our children's physical health, but also for their proper brain development. Paradoxically, children who give up time at the playground to study might also be giving up a proven opportunity to improve their cognitive functioning—as well as their grades and test scores, especially in math and reading.

While study after study shows that homework has no or little effect on kids' overall achievement until high school, a review of 850 studies by the CDC showed that physical activity has a positive impact on everything from grade point average, scores on standardized tests, and grades in specific courses to concentration, memory, and classroom behavior, according to Professor Malina, one of the coauthors of the review, which was published in the *Journal of Pediatrics* in June 2005.

Since human beings are made to exercise, it's not surprising that brain development would be tied to physical activity, say experts. What worries them is how sitting and studying for long periods, along with other sedentary activities, could be affecting our kids' intellectual abilities. "What's happening now is quite different than what's happened to children throughout the millennia," says Catherine Davis, a clinical health psychologist and assistant professor of pediatrics at the Georgia Prevention Institute of the Medical College of Georgia, where she has been researching how exercise affects cognition in children. "If you take a little rat who is happily running around in his natural environment and you put him in a cage where he can't run around, you're really changing his environment and development. These kids have become lab rats and it's scary to think of what might happen to them. We've taken them from being spontaneously active creatures to adopting a sedentary lifestyle, and it seems to be affecting their metabolism, their weight, and perhaps their neural development. The medical consequences are serious. But if this lifestyle also affects our children's ability to achieve, then it's going to affect our society as a whole. It may be that being inactive will handicap our society's ability to progress."

Kids who are fit also have fewer health problems. This means they're likely to be absent less often, points out Sothern, which might indirectly improve their academic performance. And as we've known for a long time, exercise also reduces stress and increases self-esteem—all additional reasons to think twice before allowing your child to be a homework potato each and every night.

Here is just some of what the studies show:

- In a 1998 study of 546 kids between ages six and twelve published in *Pediatric Exercise Science*, those who engaged in five hours of physical activity per week had better math scores than the control group who engaged in physical activity for just forty minutes per week—even though the first group spent 14 percent less time in class.

- A gigantic 2002 study of 353,000 fifth-graders, 322,000 seventh-graders, and 279,000 ninth-graders conducted by the California Department of Education discovered that students who scored higher on a state-mandated fitness test also scored higher on the SAT-9 standardized reading and math tests.
- High school students who often exercised achieved better grades than those who didn't, found a 2001 study published in the journal *Adolescence.* They also were less depressed, had less drug use, and enjoyed better relationships with their parents.
- Decreasing time spent on academics so that physical activity could be increased had no negative effects on academic achievement, according to the CDC review.

Why does physical activity have such a powerful influence over a child's brain power? "We have clear evidence that the brain is developing at incredible rates for the first ten years of life, then slows down some but keeps developing until the early twenties—and physical activity is critical for that development," says Professor Tomporowski, who has been researching the link between physical activity and cognitive function since the early 1980s. Although scientists aren't sure exactly why, physical activity seems to directly stimulate neurogenesis, the growth of new brain cells and the connections between them. This improves concentration, memory, and many other aspects of learning.

Exercise also has a significant impact on the development of the brain's frontal lobe, which controls what scientists call executive function or a child's decision-making abilities. "This has a direct effect on problem-solving," says Dr. Davis. "When a child is given a word problem, for example, he has to use executive function to strategize how to solve it and how to switch strategies if the method isn't working." Research now shows that a child's executive functioning is not fully mature until the early twenties or even later. So it's essential that kids get everything they need throughout childhood to encourage proper brain development—and physical activity is at the top of the list.

KIDS KNOW WHAT THEY NEED

71 percent of students believe that "I perform better in school when I get exercise," according to a 2002 national student poll by Action for Healthy Kids.

Executive function is also linked to self-control and being able to delay gratification. Kids with better executive function are able to control the urge to get up, talk to their friends, or disrupt class, and are better able to sit still long enough to do their schoolwork. Of course, such impulse control is also helpful in other aspects of life, such as resisting peer pressure to do drugs.

Dr. Davis is also looking for evidence that exercise can improve ADHD. "In children with ADHD, the specific kind of cognitive function that's impaired is actually executive function. So we would expect that a child would be better able to be behaved when he has better executive function." One study conducted at the University of Buffalo found that kids with ADHD showed a significant improvement in executive function after eight weeks of forty minutes of vigorous activity after school each day.

So although more studies are needed, it's a mistake when parents force ADHD kids to forgo afterschool sports or active play for homework, says David Goodman, an ADHD specialist and professor of psychiatry and behavioral sciences at Johns Hopkins University. "Sitting still and paying attention all day in class is even more stressful for kids who have ADHD than for those who don't. Exercising after school allows them to burn off some of their hyperactivity and concentrate better." Some parents worry that if their child doesn't start his homework as soon as he arrives home, his daily dose of medication will wear off in the early evening before he's done. But Dr. Goodman says that a child's doctor can adjust the dose or possibly prescribe a booster dose that will last until late evening, making concentrating on homework—or anything else the child is interested in—easier.

Coping Any Way They Can

In order to deal with the constant stress of homework, most kids have adopted coping behaviors—and some of them aren't healthy ones. For example, the stress and tedium of homework can bring on lots of snacking. When Hillary, now an eleventh-grader in Cupertino, California, switched schools in sixth grade, she gained one hundred pounds in four years. "It started with the anxiety of making new friends, but the increased homework put her over the edge," says her mom, Grace. Hillary has since lost forty pounds through a pediatric weight-loss program. But she still can't face up to four hours of assignments each night without the comfort of food. "When she does her homework, she has all these little snacks on her bed," reports her mom. "When she watches TV, she's not aware of what she eats. When she does homework, it's the same thing. I think she's eating to comfort herself. It's her way of self-medicating."

This is true for many kids of all sizes, says pediatric obesity expert Melinda Sothern. "These kids aren't able to use exercise to raise their levels of those feel-good brain chemicals called endorphins. So they grab the nearest junk food, which does the same thing—but with negative consequences."

After they're finally done with their assignments, many kids are drained and eager to escape the drudgery. "They think, 'I deserve to veg in front of the TV because I've been working at school all day,'" says Sothern. "Adults do the same thing when they come home from work. 'Why should I walk? I'm gonna lay on this sofa. I'm exhausted.' Well, these kids are mentally exhausted. And it's very hard to turn them around."

One mom reports watching helplessly while her nine-year-old son has gotten fatter and fatter from the stress of extra homework to prepare for fourth-grade standardized tests. "He has no time to exercise," she says. "He has breakdowns when it's homework time and overeats from stress. When he's done, all he wants to do is zone out with his TV and Nintendo."

TOO TIRED TO MOVE

More than one-quarter of kids aged eleven to seventeen say that they're too tired to exercise, according to a 2006 poll by the National Sleep Foundation.

Unfortunately, these escape routes can become addictive. Kids could be building bad habits that last a lifetime. "The more kids cope with stress by eating, watching TV, playing video games, or surfing the net, the more they reinforce those behaviors," says pediatric obesity expert Kris von Almen. "If you lay down the template at six, and do the same thing day after day, by age ten, that's all you know how to do."

Some teens even abuse prescription drugs to cope with homework overload. According to Dr. Goodman, there's a growing black market for Ritalin, Adderall, and other ADHD drugs. Kids without the disorder buy pills from friends with prescriptions to improve their concentration and get through mountains of work. Even worse, some turn to illegal substances to relieve the unrelenting pressure. As one high school junior from Hollywood told us, "I think one of the reasons kids do drugs is to forget about their stressful week, to blow off steam from a really hard test."

No Rest for the Weary

Our children are also very, very tired. When we were kids, we begged our parents to extend our bedtimes. These days, our children get to stay up late—whether they like it or not—in order to finish their assignments. More than half of the hundreds of kids who took our survey reported that homework interfered with their sleep. As one eighth-grader from Urbana, Illinois, with a nightly average of four hours of homework told us, "I'm often up until ten or eleven o'clock doing homework and it really takes a toll on me. I feel wiped out all week."

HOW MUCH REST KIDS REALLY NEED

Children between the ages of five and twelve need 10 to 11 hours of sleep each night, teens need 9.25 hours, and as any parent knows, many kids need more. But according to the National Sleep Foundation's 2004 Sleep in America Poll, many kids are seriously sleep deprived. In fact, 54 percent of first- through fifth-graders sleep just

9 to 10 hours each night, and 17 percent sleep less than 9 hours. And according to the Foundation's 2006 poll, 80 percent of teens don't get the recommended amount of sleep. At least 28 percent fall asleep in school and 22 percent fall asleep doing homework. Even small sleep deficits add up quickly. Getting just one hour less each night means missing out on more than a half night's sleep each week.

Even when our children are in bed, they might not be resting peacefully. Lots of parents reported to us that their elementary, middle, and even high schoolers have a hard time falling asleep, anxious that they haven't studied hard enough for a test or done well enough on an essay. "Before my daughter started getting four hours of homework a night, she never had trouble falling asleep," says Jenny, a Virginia mother whose sixth-grader is often overcome with bedtime panic that she's forgotten something essential. Even when kids do shut their eyes, homework could still prevent a good night's sleep. "The stress of homework could certainly have an effect," says sleep researcher Howard Taras. "When your mind is working and working on something and then you go to sleep, you can't help some of the anxiety overtaking your dreams."

Still, many parents allow kids to stay up late to complete assignments. But here's a wake-up call: Chronic sleep loss increases a child's risk of depression, impaired motor function, and even obesity (a fatigued body doesn't produce enough leptin, a hormone that controls appetite). Meanwhile, one Columbia University study of elementary school children found higher levels of the stress hormone cortisol in those who stayed up past 9 P.M. This raised their blood pressure and heart rate, weakened their immune systems, and made it more difficult for them to concentrate when challenged.

Perhaps most ironically, losing sleep to finish assignments can have major academic consequences:

- In a 2004 study of more than two thousand students published in the journal *Child Development,* sixth-graders who got consistently less sleep also had lower grades. A 2006 National Sleep Foundation Poll also found that kids in grades six through twelve who got insufficient sleep were more likely to get lower grades, while 80 percent of those who got the optimal amount achieved As and Bs in school.

- Getting less than the recommended number of hours on a regular basis has a negative effect on school performance and various cognitive abilities, according to a 2005 review of twenty-one studies published in the *Journal of School Health.* "Too little or poor sleep can even be a contributing factor in learning and attention disorders," says Dr. Taras, the lead reviewer.

- Even a few days of staying up late to finish that science project can have consequences. When normally high-achieving six- to twelve-year-olds were limited to just eight hours of sleep each night over a period of one week as part of a Brown Medical School experiment in 2005, they immediately started exhibiting attention problems, had trouble recalling old material, learning new lessons, and completing high-quality work.

Help for the Homework Potato

If children need one hour of exercise each day and ten to eleven hours of sleep each night, yet are burdened with several hours of homework, something has to give. "It should be homework, not their health," says Rochelle Feldman, a pediatrician in Canyon County, California.

Fortunately, as soon as parents stop allowing homework to crowd out sleep and physical activity, their children's health will begin to improve. For example, according to Sothern, studies show that in just eight to twelve weeks of increased physical activity kids can lower not only their weight but their risk factors for heart disease and diabetes.

And if kids start moving, they can still reap the brain development benefits of exercise. In a four-year study of 240 children, Dr. Catherine Davis of the Medical College of Georgia found that overweight elementary school children were able to boost their executive functioning abilities with just forty minutes of vigorous physical activity after school each day, compared to a nonexercising control group who did not improve.

We think a child's health is best served by keeping homework to a minimum. But even if you can't cut your child's workload, you can still help guarantee he gets enough exercise by breaking the "homework first rule." Make sure kids have an opportunity to play actively for at least thirty minutes (an hour is even better) immediately after school, says Dr. Sothern. She suggests kids run around the playground, go to a martial arts or dance class, walk the dog, or even shoot indoor hoops with a Nerf ball if it's raining—whatever they enjoy that will get their hearts pumping.

This might seem risky. Many parents we talked to were worried that if kids were allowed to play first, it would be too difficult to settle them down to study later. But just the opposite is true. "When kids come home and sit right down to work, they struggle because they've got to get their ya yas out, as we say in Louisiana," explains Dr. Sothern. "They need to burn off all that energy that's making them crazy, and when they engage in physical activity, it releases endorphins that make them feel good, which helps increase their level of concentration when they start work."

Kids will absorb what they are studying more effectively as well. "It's been proven by lots of research that kids learn better after they have a break where they have a free choice of active play," says child psychologist and author Lawrence Cohen.

In addition, "When kids get a chance to go outside, they'll start games with their brothers and sisters or other active kids," predicts Sothern.

"Then on the weekends, when they would normally play video games, they will play with their active friends instead. As they get fitter, they'll want to play actively even more. I've seen this happen many times."

Proper sleep is just as essential as physical activity and should not be replaced by homework. "If your kid needs to stay up late two or three nights during the school year, that's fine," says Dr. Taras. "But if it's happening two or three times a week, parents need to give their kids permission to put the work down and go to bed." Luckily, any academic effects of homework-induced sleep deprivation can usually be reversed as soon as a child starts getting enough rest.

It would be nice if we could count on the schools to make our children's health a priority. But as schools feel compelled to cut physical education and pile on assignments, we need to start counting on ourselves.

5

"I Hate School!"

WHEN LEARNING BECOMES DRUDGERY

We know that homework is stressing out our kids. But many of us are still unprepared for the nightly anguish they express when they have to face their assignments.

In first grade, my son got ten minutes each night, which sounded reasonable to me. But he couldn't stand to do it because he was wiped out. Maybe he's immature, I thought. Then I heard other moms saying their kids were having crying fits and tantrums, and that ten minutes of homework was stretching to forty-five.

Cymry, mother of a first-grader in Tucson, Arizona

My daughter just can't face more work after being in school all day. She has a terrible time just thinking about the fact that there is homework waiting in her backpack. Lately, she's taken to saying, "I wish I were dead."

Barbara, mother of a fourth-grader in Westchester, New York

When my third- and fifth-graders begin a long evening of home-work, the first thing they say is "I hate school! I wish they never invented it."

Tami, a former teacher and mother of three in San Antonio, Texas

Why is just the thought of doing homework unbearable to some kids? A look inside today's classrooms, especially in the early grades, can reveal the answer. In an effort to push children academically, schools are pushing them beyond what's developmentally appropriate in both their class work and homework. In fact, homework is just the tip of an iceberg of school pressure that's been weighing on our children all day long, squashing their spirits and their love of learning.

All around the country, children step on the academic fast track as early as preschool. To many parents, that sounds so promising, not to mention necessary. We've all heard teachers say, "Well, kids need to know their letters by the end of preschool or they won't be ready to read in kindergarten." Or, "Well, we have to give homework in first grade to pre-pare them for all the homework in second grade." Or, "Kids need to learn how to take finals for high school, so we're giving them in middle school now." Or, "Kids are going to be working hard in college so they better learn how to do it in high school." Children are expected to master skills in earlier and earlier grades to meet government standards, or just to live up to the school's own "rigorous" ones. As one third-grade teacher told us, "I now teach my students the same geometry I took myself in junior high."

Of course, the schools aren't completely to blame. Not wanting our children to fall behind, many of us have jumped onto the accelerated learning bandwagon with both feet, convinced it will help turn our kids into superachievers, or at least keep up with the others. But warp-speed learning isn't always good for our children's emotional health—or even their education.

In fact, this new academic acceleration is one big—and dangerous—experiment. In the past fifty years we've all learned enough about how children develop to understand that many kids are literally not up to these tasks—and shouldn't have to be. "The evidence shows very clearly that kids learn different skills at different times, just like they learn to walk and talk at different times," says Steve Nelson, head of the progressive Calhoun School in New York City. "Yet those who make up these strict curriculums and standardized tests act as though they think kids should all be at the same developmental level at the same time." That's just not realistic—or healthy. When kids of any age are forced to perform tasks before they're developmentally ready, it can open up a Pandora's box of serious problems. But education policy makers have simply been ignoring these issues.

While some kids thrive on intense challenge, psychologists worry that we could be setting up others for the types of humiliating failures that can color a student's entire school career. Even worse, instead of instilling a love of learning, we could be instilling an enduring hatred of school. Accelerated schoolwork combined with homework overload could be the one-two punch that knocks some kids right out of the learning arena. It's happening already.

Welcome to Kindergrind

Chances are, your early school experiences were radically different from those of your child. Today, many youngsters are expected to *enter* kindergarten already knowing their letters and numbers. As a result, some preschool programs have abolished naps to allow for more instructional time. According to the *American School Board Journal*, one Maryland superintendent of schools told that state's legislature, "Nap time needs to go away. We need to get rid of all the baby school stuff they used to do."

Kindergarten has also changed dramatically. These days, it's a far cry from the learning-through-playing environment that German educator Friedrich Froebel envisioned in 1837 when he created kindergarten, which means "children's garden." Olga Jarrett, the associate professor of early childhood education at Georgia State, has seen many disturbing changes in the last decade. "Gone are the block and dress-up areas, circle time and show-and-tell in many schools. Instead, the kids receive formal instruction for most of the day." And since many kindergartens have expanded from a half- to a full-day program, little kids are sometimes sitting still for twice as long as they used to.

"I feel bad for the kids," says Lori, a kindergarten teacher at a public school in Sorrento, Florida, a small town about twenty-two miles from Orlando. "Kindergarten is so strict. I can't even describe how intense it is. Kids are expected to read when they leave kindergarten. It's changed our whole curriculum. We don't have snack in the afternoon, we have one recess a day, and that's maybe for ten minutes. By the afternoon, the kids are saying, 'I'm hungry, I'm tired.' But our schedule doesn't include time for snack, for play, for rest."

And the pressure doesn't lift at the end of the school day. Homework for kindergarteners, once unthinkable, is widespread. "Five years ago, I wouldn't have dreamed of giving my kindergarteners homework," says Lori. "These kids are already in school for many hours a day, and that's really hard for them. But there are very high expectations in this school, and they have to do it. In the beginning of the year, the kids are so excited. But that excitement goes away pretty quickly."

Sorrento, Florida, isn't the only place with a bunch of disillusioned five-year-olds. Kindergarteners in Detroit have no more time to play.

Teachers at one charter school there report that the kids spend their days filling in workbooks, listening to the teacher lecture, taking weekly standardized tests to measure their progress in reading and writing, and doing more work when they get home.

In San Diego, some kindergarteners are a bit luckier. Recently, after three years of trying to push their pupils up to an unrealistically high reading standard, the teachers rebelled against the school board. "They wanted the kids to climb seven reading levels in one year," says Trish, a kindergarten teacher there. But when the teachers cited research that proved that those kids who were slow to read in first grade pulled even with their peers by fourth, the board backed down. Says Trish, "Now, expectations are more realistic and the pressure is off."

Still, Trish is worried about the changes she sees in kindergarten classrooms around the country. "While we still have a half hour of recess, other schools have cut it down or eliminated it completely. I know there are principals out there who think that the less time outside, the less time socializing, the better the academic achievement—but it's just not true. You get burned-out kids. That's what's happening in some places and it's wrong."

"The demands in kindergarten are becoming extraordinary," says pediatrician and researcher Howard Taras. "I think that kids are being asked to do too much at an early age." In fact, all through elementary school and even through high school, kids in the same class are bound to be at many different developmental levels—not just academically, but physically and emotionally. A child's maturity in these areas has a major impact on how he or she learns.

That's why the one-size-fits-all, your-child-is-five-so-he-must-be-ready-to-read assumption simply doesn't make sense. But that hasn't stopped the government from insisting on it. The great majority of states now have "readiness" standards that spell out what children must know and be able to do before entering kindergarten. Many of those standards focus on literacy skills at the expense of social, emotional, and even motor skills. In reaction, the National Association for the Education of Young Children has issued this warning statement: " 'Readiness' does not happen at the same time or in the same way for all children. For example, one child may develop language skills rapidly, while being slower to gain social competence. Definitions of 'readiness' must consider these variations."

On top of this, some teachers aren't trained in child development. Even those who are don't have much choice in how and what they teach. Lori, the kindergarten teacher from Florida, has taken workshops on brain development and knows that many of her students simply aren't developmentally ready to master the tasks the school has set for them. "There are huge discrepancies in their abilities to read," she says. Yet she's required to push them, anyway.

Although children can learn to parrot the alphabet or count—and will do so to please teachers and parents—that doesn't mean they've absorbed the skill, says clinical child psychologist Kate McReynolds. "When a young child is asked to master purely intellectual tasks that are abstracted from the physical, concrete world, they have no meaning for him." That's why any noticeable academic boost usually fades in a few years, and later learners quickly catch up.

At the same time, the emphasis on early academics is shoving aside what kids *do* need: time to engage in active play and socializing, which is actually the way they learn best. With so many schools cutting out recess (some new ones are even being built without playgrounds), some experts are not just worried that kids won't get enough exercise. They're also concerned that they won't get enough practice sharing, communicating, and learning to get along with others. Children from preschool through high school need to interact with other kids to hone these skills. But sitting at their desks for many hours each day and then again in the evening leaves them little time to do so. This, too, can have long-term ramifications.

How the Fast Track Slows Kids Down

These are just a few of the reasons why rushing kids academically doesn't work. In fact, as researchers have known for a while, it often has the *opposite* effect. Here's what some of the studies show:

- Research presented at a 1996 national Head Start conference demonstrated that kids attending developmentally appropriate kindergarten through second-grade classes scored higher in reading and mathematics than those in academically oriented classes.
- According to a study of children at more than sixty schools published in the spring 2002 volume of the journal *Early Childhood Research and Practice,* by the end of fourth grade, those kids who had attended academically oriented preschools earned significantly *lower* grades than those who had attended more old-fashioned, "child-initiated" preschool classes, where the emphasis was on play.
- In Finland, kids don't begin formal schooling until age seven. At first, they are a bit behind students in other countries. By age fifteen, however, Finnish kids outperform students from every nation in reading skills, such as retrieving information and interpreting texts, while those from the United States barely make the average, according to the 2000 Program for International Student Assessment published by the U.S. Department of Education. Finnish students are also among the highest scorers in mathematic and scientific literacy, while U.S. students score below average.

Astoundingly, education policy makers aren't paying much attention to this research. In fact, some suggest that the reason schools haven't gotten better results is that they don't start academics early enough!

Child development experts are so worried about this trend that in

December 2005, more than sixty of them, including psychiatrists Kyle Pruett of Yale, Alvin Poussaint of Harvard Medical School, and Stanley Greenspan of George Washington University, signed a statement written by the nonprofit group Alliance for Childhood that reads in part: "The current emphasis on teaching reading through formal instruction to five-year-olds is not working, leading many concerned parents and policy makers to assume that reading instruction must start sooner—at three or four. But that assumption is based on a narrow and thus flawed approach to child development, early education, and the development of literacy. The key to developing literacy—and all other skills—is to pace the learning so that it is consistent with the child's development, enabling him or her to succeed at the early stages. Ensure this initial success and the child's natural love of learning blooms. Doom him to failure in the beginning by making inappropriate demands and he may well be unable to overcome the resulting sense of inadequacy."

"If pushed beyond their developmental limits, children are going to feel stupid," says child psychologist Lawrence Cohen. "And as soon as you feel stupid, you're not very effective at learning anything." Says Robin, the Richlands, North Carolina, mother of a first-grader, "It breaks my heart to hear my baby say 'School is hard . . . it'll be better in second grade' when I know it'll probably be worse."

Reading and math aren't the only areas in which we expect too much of our small children. As any parent knows, little kids have little attention spans. We can't force a child to sit still in a restaurant before he's developmentally ready (and sometimes, not even then). So why do we expect him to be able to sit still at school for hours, then come home and do it again for homework?

"Many kids are simply not developmentally ready to sit still all day—especially those who have been in daycare centers where there was a lot of free play," explains pediatrician Howard Taras. Kids have a great need to be physically active, says exercise psychologist Phillip Tomporowski. "If you glue them to their seats, it increases the likelihood that they'll become frustrated and act out." So no one should be surprised when the order to sit still and learn leads to behavioral problems. According to early childhood education professor Olga Jarrett, "When kids are not allowed a chance to be playful, that playfulness tends to come out in negative, disruptive ways."

POPPING PILLS TO SIT STILL

According to a report published in the *Journal of the American Medical Association*, the number of preschoolers being prescribed Ritalin, Adderall, and other medications for ADHD has more than doubled in the last decade. Yet the drug is not FDA approved for use in kids under six years old. We wonder: Would so many kids be on medication if they weren't required to stay in their seats for long periods? As psychiatrist David Goodman says, "I certainly wouldn't endorse medicating a kid whose daytime structure is so noxious that he can't possibly perform at the level expected. That's not the appropriate use of medication."

Still, many schools have lost their patience with young children's developmental inability to adapt to today's classroom. If disciplinary measures or medication don't work, the youngsters are often shown the door. According to a 2005 survey done by the Yale Child Study Center of almost five thousand preschool classrooms around the country, three-and four-year-olds are being expelled at record rates—three times more than all students in kindergarten through grade 12 combined. Kindergarteners aren't far behind. In Connecticut in 2002, schools suspended or expelled 901 kindergarteners for fighting, defiance, or temper tantrums, almost double the number of two years before. In Ohio in 2003, more than two hundred kindergarteners were expelled or suspended in the Greater Cincinnati area alone.

We find this trend extremely sad—and we don't need the experts to tell us it's a terrible idea, although plenty did. "Behavioral problems are a sign that a child is stressed and needs help," says Dr. Taras, who cowrote the American Academy of Pediatrics guidelines on expulsions. "To take punitive action is wrong."

As kids move into the elementary and middle grades, they might be able to stay in their seats longer. But the academic demands only increase. "I have elementary school children coming in who are highly stressed and miserable," says pediatrician Rochelle Feldman. "They feel like failures at the beginning of school. One of the most important things you need to do for kids is establish school as a great place to be, that learning is fun and that they can feel successful there. That is actually the main task of the first three grades. So you're taking a tremendous risk with issues of self-esteem and self-confidence if you make it drudgery instead of fun."

The Test Must Go On

Many kids also grow to dislike school because much of the work isn't challenging *enough* or it's hard but boring at the same time. There's a lot of rote learning during the school day, especially with the endless prepping for standardized tests. "My kids began kindergarten with a passion for learning, only to be turned off," says Deanne, the Houston mother of four, including two sons in fourth and seventh grades. "They would get crammed full of facts just so they could spit them back out for the test. Despite the fact that they were in the gifted and talented program, I began to hear daily complaints about how boring school was, and that homework was even more boring. The problem was that they weren't being given the opportunity for exploration and discovery, where real learning takes place."

Finally, concerned that her children's school was destroying their love of learning, Deanne decided to homeschool them. She didn't feel she had much choice. "My children had really begun to hate school."

It isn't only that there's a great deal of rote learning. In many cases, subjects that once injected variety into the school day, such as music, art, or science, have been cut because they're not on the No Child Left Behind (NCLB) tests. According to a 2006 survey by the Center on Education Policy, 71 percent of the country's school districts have reduced or eliminated music, art, social studies, and/or science to make more time for reading and math. "Learning through play and discovery has taken a backseat," says Sara, the second-grade teacher in Waterbury, Connecticut. "We just hammer the kids with reading, writing, and math."

In addition, teachers are often ordered to use "pacing guides," which require them to cover a certain amount of material and then move on, whether or not the kids have mastered it. There's no extra time to linger on an interesting subject. Sometimes, there's not even time for questions or to go over concepts the class is struggling with. But many teachers feel they have no choice.

"There's no more creative process in teaching," says Tami, a former elementary public school teacher who taught kindergarten, first, second, and fifth grades for a combined thirteen years in San Antonio. "I knew I could do so much more for the kids. But the format of the Texas tests is difficult, and I couldn't cheat the kids out of the practice they needed." Now, however, she sees an even bigger downside of the day-in, day-out practice her own children have to go through. "Often, my son, who's in fifth grade, and my daughter, who's in third, both cry about going to school before bed and in the morning," says Tami. "My son has to take Pepto-Bismol because he gets nauseated. My daughter will fake sickness in order to stay home or come home from school."

Although she believes the teachers are doing their best, she blames her kids' feelings on the fact that today's school is all about testing, all the time. As Tami wrote in an editorial for her local paper, "I'm enraged with the slogan No Child Left Behind. My children *are* left behind. They will pass the test and go on to the next grade. But they are left with a yearning not for learning or reading but to get out of school. This is not what I want for my children."

The tests themselves can be a grueling experience because kids are usually well aware of how much is riding on them. In Rockingham County, North Carolina, elementary and middle schoolers are tested to determine whether they will be promoted to the next grade. And each year, up to twenty test booklets have to be discarded per day because children have thrown up on them, according to an article in *American School Board Journal*. "They cry. They have to be removed. The stress is so much on the test that they can't handle it," says Dianne Campbell, the district's director of testing and accountability, in the article. "As the tests start, they literally fall apart. It would break your heart."

You'd think vomit-covered test booklets might make school officials reconsider whether kids are really developmentally ready to handle such stress. But, no: The tests must go on, despite dire consequences to our kids and the way testing requires them to be taught. "Teachers are given little discretion over how to deal with differences in learners since all must pass the tests at the same levels," writes Kenneth Goodman, professor emeritus of Language, Reading and Culture at the University of Arizona, in the journal *Substance*. "That means that children who pull down the group and can't keep up or can't get a high enough score on the tests will be forced to repeat the grade and eventually forced out of school." He predicts that half of today's elementary public school children will drop out before they finish twelfth grade. It sounds unbelievable. But in fact, we're already part-way there. Studies show that the current dropout rate hovers between 15 and 20 percent, while some researchers believe it's even higher. And according to a 2004 study by the Urban Institute, a nonpartisan think tank, nearly one-third of current public high school students won't graduate.

According to Goodman, research shows that students who are held back a grade are unlikely to stay until graduation. Unfortunately, even children who excel academically are sometimes not promoted because of test scores. "My son didn't pass the Florida Comprehensive Assessment Test, so he had to repeat third grade even though he was getting straight As," says Debby from Lehigh Acres, Florida. As this year's test date draws closer, "he has dark circles under his eyes, cries, and calls himself stupid." She explains that he works nonstop. "My third-grader starts his home-work at 3:30. At 6:00, he has dinner, sometimes with his books and pen-cil still in hand. Then he works on his homework until bedtime, and if he isn't finished, he will arise at 5:30 A.M. to complete it." And he's still afraid of failing again. That's one reason why Professor Goodman says that NCLB should really be called "No Child Left Unscarred."

We think it's no coincidence that as such academic pressures have increased, so have the number of children with mental health issues. Consider these statistics:

- According to researchers at Stanford University School of Medi-cine, the number of seven- to seventeen-year-olds who visited the doctor for depression more than doubled from 1995 to 2002, when a staggering 3.22 million kids were treated.
- A 1999 Surgeon General's Report found that 13 percent of kids aged nine to seventeen suffer from anxiety disorders; another 1999 survey of nine- to twelve-year-olds by Mount Sinai School of Med-icine found that 31 percent of them "worried a lot" and 47 percent had insomnia.

Of course, today's kids are stressed over many things besides school, ranging from terrorism to peer problems to the high divorce rate. But schools certainly aren't helping. Instead of serving as a haven from outside tensions, many ramp them up. According to an online poll of almost nine hundred children by KidsHealth.com, nine- to thirteen-year-olds said they were more stressed by academics than by bullying, peer pressure, or family problems.

Some school officials are worried. By the time kids are in high school, the pressures can take their toll. "We're concerned because we've seen an increase in students who are falling apart," says Paul Richards, the principal of Needham High School in Needham, Massachusetts. "These kids are like professional students, spending so much time on their academics that other things suffer, and they simply don't have the coping skills to deal with the stress. As a result, many more students today are exhibiting significant health problems—everything from cutting to mental breakdowns to suicide."

The Cycle Continues with Homework

When kids get home from school, things are no better. Although it's clear that the sheer quantity of homework has become overwhelming, for many elementary school kids, even a little is too much. "Educators are not paying attention to the fact that until kids are eight or nine, they simply do not have a long enough attention span to handle anything academic past 3 or 4 in the afternoon," says pediatrician Rochelle Feldman. "Some kids can. Most kids can't. So assigning homework to them is a waste of time because it's not going to accomplish better learning. If anything, it might impair learning for those kids who really can't focus in the late afternoon and early evening."

In addition, according to research, the frontal cortex of a child's brain, which controls organization and multitasking, doesn't develop fully until the late teens or early twenties. Yet by the time kids are in middle school, homework requires them to juggle assignments from many different teachers. "These kids work like devils to keep up and it's such a struggle because their brains aren't there yet," explains Dr. McReynolds. "Parents and teachers might think children are lazy or stubborn when they forget to bring a book home or remember all their assignments. But even asking high schoolers to assume that adult level of planning and organization is placing a very great demand on them. Most simply aren't ready for it."

This is not just an organization problem. Moving from one unrelated subject to the next makes learning more difficult. "One minute you have to study math, the next Spanish, then you have to turn to history," says Kalman Heller, a child and family psychologist in Wayland, Massachusetts, with almost forty years of experience. "Each requires a completely different learning process, and making the transition successfully enough to actually absorb all the information is something even adults have trouble with, let alone children."

Whipped and Weary

If kids are not able to overcome their developmental limitations or deal with the stress, they're treated with little sympathy. Schools often make children complete the work at recess (if they still have recess), turning homework into punishment—not exactly the association we'd like them to have. Other schools go further. "The teachers do things to make you feel badly if you don't finish your homework," says Marcia, the mother of three in San Francisco. "My sixth-grader gets a demerit and a parent has to sign the uncompleted work."

A demerit seems mild compared to the penalty at a charter school in another part of California, where elementary school kids have between two and three hours of homework each night. As one mother of a ten-year-old reports, "If you forget any part of an assignment, you're outcast from the rest of the students. You're made to wear your uniform backwards with your shirt inside out, and you have to write thirty letters to all the other kids in your class about why you forgot your homework. Then you have to stay in during recess to finish while the other kids play. They call it being porched."

Of course, some kids also get lots of pressure and punishment from their parents, who might think that's the only way to motivate them. Many parents told us they penalized kids for incomplete homework or low grades by taking away privileges or grounding them. Punishments from teachers or parents might work in the short term by instilling fear. But what happened to instilling a love of learning?

Other kids drive themselves—but that doesn't mean they're enjoying the learning process. "All my daughter cares about is her grades," says one mother of a sixth-grader. "For her, it's not 'this new Greek unit is really interesting.' It's all about the number of points she can get. She just crams in the information, then drops it like a stone as soon as the unit is finished. She isn't having fun, so good grades are her only reward. I'm worried that it won't be enough."

She's right to be concerned. "Even superhigh achievers can be turned off to school," says Dr. Cohen. "Some kids burn out and develop an attitude of 'I don't care because it's just too stressful and overwhelming.' Others become defiant and take that extra negative step of never doing anything that remotely resembles schoolwork unless they absolutely have to. For example, when it comes to reading, you might be able to force them to read their assignments. But they're never going to pick up a book on their own because that represents torture to them."

This is happening earlier and earlier. "My first-grader used to love books and being read to," says Robin from Richlands, North Carolina. "But now she has to read so much for homework that she rarely picks up a book that's not assigned." Over time, kids become even more hardened against reading. "I love books and it kills me that my son doesn't," says one mother of a high schooler. "He associates reading with homework, so he doesn't find it enjoyable. It feels too much like a punishment."

For some kids, homework has poisoned the entire learning process. "My seventh-grader says that learning is no fun anymore," reports a college professor from New York City. "To an academic, hearing your child say 'It's no fun' is like being stabbed. You want kids to think that learning is fun. Instead, my daughter looks at her schoolwork as forced child labor." Not surprisingly, this makes it difficult for parents to introduce any kind of educational experience into their children's lives. "I want my children to learn why we learn and how it applies to real life, whether it's counting money or figuring out what they need for a recipe," says one mother of two elementary school kids. "But they'll say, don't talk to me about that, it's too much like homework." Tami, the former teacher and mom from San Antonio, can't even get her third- or fifth-grader to play educational computer games. "They'll say: Is that math? Is that reading? I don't want to do any more of that."

By the time they reach high school, some kids are tired of learning anything at all—and their parents are worried. "What I fear most is that my son is going to crash and burn," says the mother of a high school junior from Raleigh, North Carolina. "I fear that he's going to say 'Enough is enough, I've had enough of this work and staying up late, and I don't want to do it anymore.' I just hope that doesn't happen before he gets his college education."

Is this where today's kindergartener who is struggling with reading is headed? What about today's third-grader who is buried under mounds of math sheets and spelling lists? Or the ninth-grader who has no time to read for pleasure—and wouldn't want to anyway because it reminds her too much of homework?

If so, *what for*? Judging by the United States' lackluster test results compared to other countries (not the best benchmark, but the only one we have), pushing children harder and faster has never produced the superkids we hoped for. And it looks as though it never will.

PART TWO

Ending Homework Hell

6

Homework Deconstructed

BRAIN WORK OR BUSYWORK?

As you've probably guessed by now, we don't believe there's much value in most homework. Still, most of our kids bring home backpacks stuffed with assignments, so it's a good idea to learn how to do some homework triage.

Remember: Teachers receive little training in devising truly educational and meaningful assignments, and many of them are not even required to be certified in their subjects. As you'll see, there's a lot of bad homework out there. Could some common types of assignments actually be doing your child's education more harm than good?

For example, does assigning fifty math problems really accomplish any more than assigning five? Is it really necessary to take notes every time you read a novel? Is memorizing lists of words really the best way to increase vocabulary—especially when it takes away from reading time? Is laboriously coloring in a map really the best way to teach a child about a particular region of the world? Does memorizing endless names, dates, and events really teach history? And what is the real purpose behind those devilish dioramas? This is what most of our kids are doing night after night, but is this really "quality" homework? And do kids retain what they learn this way?

Even teachers sometimes give assignments a bad grade. When researchers funded by the Consortium on Chicago School Research asked teachers to evaluate the quality of 1,400 math and writing assignments given to third-, sixth-, and eighth-graders from twelve different schools, the teachers said they believed that fewer than 30 percent of the assignments were "even minimally challenging." Translation: More than 70 percent of the assignments were busywork. Even scarier, they were talking about *in-class* assignments. As we've learned, homework assignments are often given much less thought and preparation.

Ideally, homework would be individualized for each student's abilities. After all, there's only a small chance that a "one-size-fits-all" assignment will accurately target the learning needs, abilities, and home environment of more than a few kids at a time. "Kids are all different and the adults helping them are all different," says Deborah Meier, faculty member of NYU's Steinhardt School of Education, author of *The Power of Their Ideas: Lessons from America from a Small School in Harlem,* and a MacArthur Fellowship recipient. "If the homework doesn't reflect that, you've already stacked the deck against the kids for whom it is going to be a problem. When the homework only fits certain kids, you increase what you might call the homework gap."

Unfortunately, few teachers have the time to individualize assignments given today's class sizes, the limited hours they get to prepare lessons, and the many nonteaching duties pressed upon them. As a result, many teachers settle for creating assignments aimed at the average kid in the class. Too often, this means handing out prefab worksheets that have been copied so many times that kids can barely read them or that were inherited from the teacher before who inherited them from the teacher before that. Sometimes it means "fun" projects that involve little teacher planning but lots of crafts supplies and parent participation. Worst of all, it can mean worksheets produced by outside organizations such as Kentucky Fried Chicken that were handed out to third-graders in Brooklyn, New York, complete with the question "Why might Kentucky Fried Chicken call its food 'finger licking good'?"

This chapter will help you sift through your child's nightly load and decide whether he should tackle all of his assignments or maybe, just maybe, let a few of them slide. Then, in the chapters that follow, we'll help you write effective notes to the teacher explaining why you decided to have your child skip a particular assignment—or all the assignments that night. We'll discuss how to meet with your child's teachers to deal with an ongoing homework problem. And, if you're up to it, we'll show you how to work with your child's teachers, school administrators, and even your school district to try to implement saner homework policies for the future.

Homework Triage 101

According to the parents we interviewed and surveyed, close to half of elementary and middle school parents help their children decide what order to do their assignments in. The usual advice is to get the hardest, most time-consuming ones out of the way first. Instead, we suggest advising kids to start with the assignments that have the most educational value, such as reading or those that involve original thinking, when they're freshest. Then, depending on how much time they've already spent, their energy levels, and their remaining enthusiasm, you can decide whether it's worth tackling those others that are more questionable in value.

The first step in performing homework triage on your child's assignments is to learn how to recognize the good, the bad, and the ugly. Of course, some of the bad ones are pretty obvious, as these parents quickly discerned:

> *In the third grade, my son's class was given one hundred math problems one night. Most children either didn't finish, or stayed up two or three hours after bedtime in order to finish.*
>
> Dennis, the father of a third-grader in Tucson, Arizona

> *My son had to do a bunch of math problems, and instead of photocopying the work sheets, the teacher made each student copy each problem out longhand before solving it.*
>
> Ross, the father of a fourth-grader in Elgin, Illinois

> *This year, my fourth-grader was asked to spell a number of words the way she thought they were spelled, and then she had to come up with two other spellings of each word even if she had already written down the correct spelling. It seems like lunacy to intentionally misspell words.*
>
> Bijou, the mother of a fourth-grader in New York City

> *If my children do their assigned reading, they get a reward. For instance, if they read for thirty minutes each night for a month, they get a free pizza. This sounds good. But I find that my kids, who normally read for the sheer joy of it, have now begun to read by the clock. All the pleasure of it has been sucked away.*
>
> Carol, the mother of a fifth- and a second-grader from Oakland, Maine

Other assignments seem worthwhile until you examine them carefully. We've collected some of the most common masqueraders in this chapter. They're grouped by type rather than grade since teachers tend to use the same basic formats for all age levels. Although most of the sample assignments are from elementary or middle school, many of the general principles apply to high school homework, as well.

Fill out your reading log with author, title, number of pages read, and how long you spent reading.

These days, beginning as early as kindergarten, most kids are expected to dutifully log all the books they read. Reading logs can be an effective diagnostic tool if the teacher takes the time to read each child's log carefully, talk to him about what he's reading, and thus get an understanding of his reading preferences, says Kylene Beers, a senior reading researcher at the School Development Program at Yale University and author of *When Kids Can't Read, What Teachers Can Do*. But few teachers have time for that. Chances are, your child's teacher uses the log simply as a way of checking to be sure you enforce the reading requirement or as a record of what's been read.

This might seem harmless. But for most kids, filling out a reading log is tedious. To create each log entry, kids usually have to write the title of the book, write the name of the author and illustrator, write the name of the publisher, and write down the number of pages they read. (Even reading the instructions is monotonous—why would it make kids excited about reading?) Sometimes, kindergarteners who can barely form their letters have to write all that information more than once, a frustrating endeavor. As Mary Leonhardt, author of *99 Ways to Get Your Kids to Do Their Homework (and Not Hate It)*, and an English teacher for more than thirty years, comments, "It's ridiculous to make a child write a book title five times. There's no purpose to that at all."

Second, it probably takes a six-year-old longer to write all that information than it does to read the book itself or listen to it being read aloud.

We bet your child could even read a second book in the time it takes him to record the information.

In addition, this type of assignment interferes with family time. If you're the kind of family who always reads before bed, now you either have to bring that reading log into bed with you and make your final good-night activity getting your kid to fill it out, or else you have to remind him to do it while he's eating breakfast. Reading logs also spur some parents to encourage their kids to tell white lies. If your child didn't read at all for some reason or forgot to keep track of the number of pages, there's still that empty space on the log that needs to be filled in. Many parents we surveyed admitted to fudging the truth.

It's not long before the log has turned what used to be a fun, educational family activity into something that turns kids off to reading. Some parents report that their youngsters resist reading extra books because they don't want to have to record them—not a great way to kick off a lifelong love of reading!

Instead, teachers should encourage kids and families to read for pleasure without imposing any time limits and without asking them to fill out paperwork. Remember that the important thing is for your child to read, whether it's novels, manuals, newspapers, comics, magazines, fan fiction, blogs, cereal boxes, e-mail, or the regular mail.

TYPICAL ASSIGNMENT

Circle all the words on this page that begin with the letter A. Then write them out.

On the surface, this might seem like a fun game that helps early readers recognize letters. And, if you haven't had plastic letters stuck on your refrigerator for years, don't have lots of books in your home, and haven't been taking your child to the library or the local bookstore on a regular basis, then an *optional* assignment giving kids this kind of exposure isn't harmful, says Beers.

Like reading logs, however, these kinds of tasks are boring and take the joy away from beginning to read. Kids get excited when they recognize words and letters. But this is not the way to do it. "Circling letters on a worksheet is just a waste of time," says Susan Ohanian, a teacher who has taught struggling readers and an author of numerous books on education. "It sends out a wrong notion of what reading is. It's not about circling letters, it's about getting involved with stories that engage kids and bring them together with their parents. I might have the kids do that kind of worksheet in class. But sending them home with such an assignment is very isolating and can be frustrating instead of enjoyable. That's not what reading is about at all."

OVERWHELMING INSTRUCTIONS

It's got to stop. As early as kindergarten, kids are getting weekly homework packets that list so many tasks, they need a daily planner to keep track. Teachers tell us all the time that the purpose of homework, especially in the elementary years, is to teach kids responsibility. But that becomes impossible when there's no way that young children can read and understand the directions—let alone map out their week to make sure they get it all done. Parents have to manage this kind of homework every step of the way. This seems a peculiar method for helping children learn to take responsibility.

Take a look at this actual list of weekly homework instructions from a kindergarten teacher at a public school in Pennsylvania, reproduced verbatim here. We wish we could say this is an aberration—but in fact, it's pretty typical of what we've found. Just reading these lengthy to-do lists is disheartening. Imagine how they make our kids feel.

1. *Buddy Book* Home Reading Log: Every night your child should pick a "buddy" to read the book to him/her then remember something about the book to tell the class the next day during our snack time "Book Talk." You or your child should write the title of the book on our monthly "Buddy Book Reading Log" found on the back of the Read-To-Me form. The person who reads the book to the child should sign/initial their name. Keep the form in the "buddy book" baggie.

2. *The Read-To-Me Home Reading Project* is sent home at the be-ginning of each month. You should record all the books you read to your child. Your child should also write down any books he/she "reads" to you, including any books we make in school and prac-tice reading to our small group. Place an asterisk next to any book your child reads to you. Place "tally marks" next to a title that is read over and over. Every month your child will earn a bookmark, a pencil, or a similar reward for reading at home. Keep the form in the "buddy book" baggie.

3. Your child's *Book Treasure Box* is a place to keep every book we make in school that comes home. Please find a place to keep it so your child can easily find it and use it. As his/her book collection grows, encourage your child to read one book to you every day for practice at home. Titles may be added to our monthly Read-To-Me form that is on the back of the "Buddy Book" read-ing log.

4. *Family Homework* is sent home on Monday (or the first school day of the week) and should be completed and returned on Fri-day (or Thursday, if there is no school on Friday). Your child earns a sticker on our classroom homework chart.

5. *Letter Printing Homework* is sent home on Monday to practice what we learned in our handwriting lesson in our small group.

Your child should practice printing the letter, in pencil, and return the paper the following day.

Letter Guessing Homework—On the back of the "Letter Printing Homework" your child should draw a picture of something that begins with that letter sound then should guess how the word is spelled. After your child writes down his/her letter guesses, you should write the word correctly under the child's writing to show him/her how close he/she came to spelling it correctly.

6. *Story Bit Retelling* Homework will sometimes be sent home on Tuesday or Wednesday. We will read a book out loud one day then the children will retell the story and review some words in our small group the next day. That night your child will bring home a "story bit" stapled to the homework paper to remind him/her about something from the story. A grownup should write down the child's thoughts and return the paper the following day.

7. *Math Homework* is sent home on Thursday. Your child should do the worksheet and return the paper the following day.

8. A Math "Home Link" is sent home on Thursday. Each Home Link suggests math activities for family members and children to do together sometime during the week. These informal activities promote interest in real math and help young children develop their thinking skills. It is not necessary to return the paper.

9. *Show and Tell Guessing Game:* Every child is expected to take part in our Guessing Game on Friday. On Thursday night, your child should hide an item in a bag that begins with the "*Letter of the Week.*" Please help your child think of 3 clues so the class will be able to form a mental picture to help them guess the hidden object.

All we can say is: Phew!

TYPICAL ASSIGNMENT

Read Chapter 5 in the book we are discussing and identify the following quotes from the book's characters, find the following vocabulary words, circle them, look them up in the dictionary and write their definitions, and make a timeline of the events.

Your child's teacher wants all the students in her class to read the same chapter so that the class can discuss it the next day. Sounds reasonable. After all, you can't have a discussion if the students don't do the reading. From the teacher's viewpoint, the best way to ensure that the reading is done is to assign a list of fact-based questions.

We could probably fill an entire book with the reasons why reading like this is a bad idea. Here are just a few: This type of assignment makes kids read just to find the answers to those questions. In addition, structuring a child's reading by telling him what to look for in the chapter, and interrupting it to find specific vocabulary words or statements, often ruins the entire experience.

In fact, the whole emphasis on memorizing the "facts" of a novel can make reading even great books downright unpleasant. "How would you like it if you were watching a movie and someone interrupted you every ten minutes and asked you questions about what you were seeing?" asks professor of psychology William Crain. "It takes away from the whole enjoyment, from getting enthralled and absorbed. Reading is a very personal affair. To have to answer questions that someone else imposes on you ruins all the pleasure." A child can't get lost in a wonderful story because then she might miss the answer to one of the questions. When the child is told what to read for and what to look for, "she reads the book at an arm's distance," adds Yale's Kylene Beers. "She only reads it to talk about the facts."

Jonathan, a tenth-grader from a Morgan Hills, California, public school, doesn't want to read this way, but he feels he has no choice. "We're reading *To Kill a Mockingbird* right now," he told us. "On the last reading check quiz, the questions were all about exact names and dates in the book. I didn't really know these facts because I try to read for the overall picture and theme of the book instead of just the answers to specific questions. I would rather be thinking about how the themes of the novel relate to our lives—but that's not what we're tested on."

No wonder so many kids say they hate the very books their parents loved at their age. "Having to take notes on *The Catcher in the Rye* in eighth grade really ruined it for me," says Allison from Brooklyn. "And then we had this test where we had to identify which character had said what." Compounding the problem, kids have so much other homework, they often don't get to read for pleasure at all. Again, if we're hoping to encourage a love of reading, this type of assignment won't do it.

To top it off, answering the questions doesn't guarantee that a child has actually read the book. As Mary Leonhardt explains, "Teachers have the illusion that if you give a quiz on a book then you know that the student read it. But a lot of kids don't read the book. When all the students are supposed to read the same book, many ask their friends about it."

Instead of assigning limiting Q&As, Madeleine Ray, a longtime faculty member at New York City's Bank Street School of Education, believes that literature should be taught in a more open-ended manner. Her method is designed for middle school, although it could apply to any age group except the very youngest: "Give kids a book in a baggie with Post-its. Tell them to read it in two weeks and to jot down any questions or thoughts they have on the Post-its and stick them on the relevant pages. Then, when they've all read the book, which often is before the two weeks is up, the teacher's first question should be: 'What was your take on this book?' They'll answer, 'I liked it, I didn't, it reminded me of . . .' That will become the fodder for discussion, because it's their responses to the work, not the teacher's. When a teacher gives a kid her list of questions, it's from her reading of the book, not from the kids'. Her reading of the book is irrelevant. What's important is how the kid responds to the book. And if a kid didn't finish the book, that's also fodder for discussion. I'd ask, Did you get bored? Let's find out why and where."

Some reading experts even believe that not all the students in a class are best served by reading the same book at the same time. Of course, one reason teachers assign the same book to every child is that it's easier to hold class discussions. The trouble is, there probably isn't one book that all thirty students will love. Just as you've surely passed your favorite novel on to a friend only to hear that it does nothing for her, no school-assigned book can possibly speak to every child. Of course, most kids will plod through whether the book resonates for them or not. But if they've discovered SparkNotes or CliffsNotes, they might take that shortcut.

We believe it would be better to just allow children to read the books they choose. If our goal is to raise literate children, we need to raise children who want to laze around with a good book—a book that they can't put down because it's so fantastic.

Mary Leonhardt believes that kids learn more from reading than any other activity. But, as she explains, "Not all kids enjoy *Ethan Frome* or *Great Expectations*." So she allows students to choose their own books, and "they read like crazy," says Leonhardt, recommending their favorites to the other kids. "Books just sweep my class." There are no tests on the reading. Instead, she just requires students to read two hundred pages a week, and reports that almost all of them do. They also keep reading journals. But, she says, "If a student hates keeping a reading journal, I ask them to talk with me about the book instead, and write me a story or an article or a memoir." The result: She's produced class after class of book-loving kids. They might not remember which character said a particular phrase on page 42, but they're able to think critically about a book's content and voice their opinions. And she knows they'll keep reading forever.

RELAX AND UNDERLINE A GOOD BOOK?

Here's an example of a real fifth-grade assignment (reproduced verbatim) on the novel *Bridge to Terabithia* by Katherine Paterson. This book is beloved by many kids, but probably not the ones in this class.

1. Find and underline these vocabulary words: *obsessed, consolidated, speculation, surplus.* Look each up and write a definition in the margin of your book.

2. What is a foundling? Why does Jess daydream about being a foundling?

3. What is Jess really angry about concerning Christmas?

4. Underline all the angry, harsh words spoken in the Aarons' household on Christmas.

5. What things does Jess do at Christmas to make his younger sisters happy? Why does he do these things?

6. What is Jess's father like? Think of three adjectives to describe him. Underline and then write down a specific example from the text to back up your adjective.

7. Underline and write down an example of Jess's mother's rudeness to him and her favoritism toward the girls.

8. Why does it feel "like Christmas again" to Jess at the end of the chapter?

As Sophia, a student in the class, recalls, "I probably would have loved that book, but we've been taught to read the teacher's questions in advance, and they gave away what was going to happen next. I couldn't get into the story because we were supposed to be looking for all those vocabulary words and the answers to the questions. It ruined it."

TYPICAL ASSIGNMENT

Tonight, read Chapter 5 and STOP.

Why this doesn't work: How would you like to stop at the best part of the book? A better approach is to tell kids to read as much as they want and encourage them to pick up another book when they're done.

TYPICAL ASSIGNMENT

Study a list of spelling words for a test.

This might *seem* like the best way to learn to spell large numbers of words. After all, we don't want our kids to be dependent on spell-check. And we learned spelling this way ourselves. (Could that be why *we're* so dependent on spell-check?)

Spelling lists and spelling tests are a time-honored tradition. However, every educator we interviewed agreed that they are not actually the best ways to produce great spellers. The main problem, according to Dr. Beers, the reading researcher at Yale, is that spelling lists presume that all kids are ready to learn the same letter patterns at the same time. "In a class of thirty children, it's likely that you'll have students at four or five different spelling levels," she explains. "Each level requires different words that focus on different spelling patterns."

For many kids, the words are too easy, so writing them out numerous times over the course of the week is busywork. "Every week my third-grader is expected to learn twenty spelling words by writing them several times and putting certain phonic markings over various letters," says Gay from Hawaii. "It is terribly tedious, which has really affected her motivation, and has taught her nothing. In fact, it has made her overgeneralize certain spelling rules."

Other kids aren't ready for the same words or even spelling rules yet.

Those children might *seem* to learn the words. But "if the child isn't at the right developmental stage, he's just memorizing," says Beers. "The child might be able to parrot the list for Friday's test. But the words are not internalized or assimilated and are forgotten by Monday." In fact, says Beers, if you want to create strong spellers, "parents should encourage teachers to offer spelling instruction that fits each child's developmental needs while giving the child a lot of time for reading and writing."

LEARNING FROM HISTORY

Dr. Joseph Mayer Rice, a physician, studied the success of spelling drills for 33,000 fourth- to eighth-graders. Rice found no link between the time spent on drills and students' performance on spelling tests and he concluded that what he dubbed the "spelling grind" was futile. And this was in the late 1800s.

TYPICAL ASSIGNMENT

A spelling scramble or maze

Many spelling books feature a variety of games using words: Unscramble the letters to reveal the word; follow a maze to find the word; do the crosswords to figure out the word, and so on. But these types of exercises have nothing to do with learning how to spell. "They should be completely disassociated from the spelling list and never be part of spelling homework," says Dr. Beers. Some can even be detrimental: "When kids see a word scrambled, some might continue to see it that way," she explains. As for mazes and puzzles, if your child loves doing them at home or during free choice time at school, great. Lots of adults enjoy doing them, too—just not as a mandatory assignment that claims to be educational.

Look up all the words on your English vocabulary list and write a sentence using each of them.

Most kids also get some kind of vocabulary list every week. We all want our kids to be articulate and many parents are concerned about the SATs. But is memorizing endless definitions the answer?

"Memorizing vocabulary words makes me crazy," says Mary Leonhardt. "There's all kinds of research that shows kids acquire vocabulary best through wide reading, and they acquire it in a much more sophisticated way than they do when they're just memorizing definitions." The problem with vocabulary lists is that they fail to put the words into context for kids. As Beers explains, "When you just memorize a word without learning it in context, the word doesn't have anything to hook on to." So the word doesn't get stored in long-term memory, and can be forgotten soon after the quiz.

Research also shows that less is more when it comes to vocabulary. It's preferable for children to really absorb five to ten words each week instead of memorizing twenty to twenty-five words they might not retain.

In addition, with the list method, kids often learn only one or two of a vocabulary word's many definitions. They might be able to recognize the word on an SAT test—and even that isn't certain—but it won't be part of their working vocabulary, at least not with all the nuances.

That's why Deanne Rohde, an elementary school principal in San Diego, doesn't like those vocabulary workbooks that so many kids drag home night after night. Instead, she suggests students read, read, read and talk, talk, talk. Reading independently and discussing books—or current events, or school, or anything else—with adults automatically increases a child's vocabulary with words he'll actually remember because he's learned them in context and they have meaning. "Independent reading and rich conversations are strong components of a vocabulary program," explains Beers. "The more limited a vocabulary a child has, the more he needs to hear or read the word before the meaning is cemented."

When children are reading, teachers should encourage them to "jot down the words they think are cool," adds Beers. "You want them falling in love with words—words like 'hors d'oeuvres' that look funny and so intrigue them." In addition, learning about Latin and Greek roots helps kids see connections between words and gives them real tools for figuring out their meanings.

TYPICAL ASSIGNMENT

Color in all the groups of five/the objects beginning with "A"/ the map.

Lots of homework assignments these days have some sort of art component to them. Teachers seem to believe that because most kids love to draw and color, it's a great way to engage them. However, clinical child psychologist Kate McReynolds calls these kinds of assignments "falsely meaningful. Teachers think that they are making the homework more interesting by making kids color pictures. But some children find this an added burden . . . it's boring *and* there's the extra work of coloring pictures!" After all, coloring on your own is one thing, but it becomes a lot less fun when you're obligated to do it and you know that the finished product will be judged.

And some kids don't even like to color at all. "My kindergartener doesn't want to do her homework if it involves coloring, such as color all the pictures of things that start with the letter *A*," says Abby, whose daughter goes to a public school in Fairbanks, Alaska. "There's no point to it that I can see—it just adds lots of time to the assignment without any educational value. My daughter does not enjoy coloring unless she can draw her own picture."

In fact, many of those carefully colored worksheets are being done by parents, as we discovered from our surveys and interviews. As one mom from Mesquite, Texas, put it, "I do the coloring so the kids can do the more important stuff."

Older kids are often given more complex assignments, such as drawing a freehand map of a country, filling in a number of required characteristics, and then coloring the mountains, oceans, and forests with specified colors and required types of pencils or markers. Is such coloring work necessary? "It sounds like academic infantilism to require middle-grade students to color the rivers blue and the land green," says former teacher and education author Susan Ohanian. She says there might be some value in requiring students to figure out the minimum number of colors a map designer needs so that adjoining states or countries end up in different shades. But we've never heard of any mapping assignment that involved that kind of strategizing.

If your child enjoys a chance to color, is there any harm? Sure, she might have a good time. But she probably won't learn much about the subject of the assignment, and she will lose valuable time she could be spending on better things. And, if she really likes to color, she'd be better off choosing her own art projects. After all, artists don't spend their time painting by numbers.

TYPICAL ASSIGNMENT

Doing independent research—before a child is independent.

We all want our kids to be independent learners, and mastering research skills is key. But few children are equipped to handle research in first grade, and that's when some teachers start sending home such assignments. In some cases, research must be done on the Internet, yet six-year-olds often can't comprehend the information they download, and many of us don't allow our young children to surf unsupervised. As a result, such "independent" research inevitably turns into parent-dependent research, with us doing most or all of the work.

When June's first-grader was told to research and write a biography of a civil rights crusader, the Brooklyn, New York, mom knew right away that there was no way her son could do it on his own. In order to turn in the assignment, "I figured that I would have to do all the research, explain it all at a level he could comprehend, and then try to put it into a context he could relate to," she says. "But six-year-olds don't understand the issues behind civil rights. Their big issue is: I want more candy." June decided not to have her son do the project. "What's he learning if I do the research and tell him what to say? So we didn't turn it in. And you know what? Nothing happened." In fact, the teacher, who had inherited this assignment, saw June's point. She ended up reevaluating the project and decided not to assign it the following year.

Even when kids are older, the research might still be beyond them *and* their parents. As one father told us, "My seventh-grader got an assignment to investigate Julius Caesar with some incredibly inane questions, like 'Why did Julius Caesar wear his hair the way he did?' and 'What sports did Julius Caesar play as a child?' After my daughter got completely frustrated researching it on the Internet, I spent hours trying to find the answers to those questions. The teacher hadn't given the kids any text to work from and no Web site was provided. They were truly on their own. My daughter was falling on her face when we gave up."

Kids are just too young for such independent research projects before high school, says Emma, an eighth-grade social studies teacher in Croton, New York, who believes such assignments are an easy way out for some teachers. "Young, inexperienced teachers assign homework to teach what they can't teach," she says. "If I can't teach it, I don't assign it."

Research skills need to be age appropriate and taught in the classroom, says Thelma Farley, executive director and founder of the Beacon

Day School, a year-round, K-through-8 school in Oakland, California. "That way, the teacher can help with all of the steps. You don't want kids coming home and saying, 'I have to do a paper on supernovas. Where do I start, Mom?' Research is a process, and the teacher needs to break it down into doable chunks that kids handle on their own. For example, the first day, the teacher might discuss what constitutes a researchable idea. The next day, he might have the kids work on thesis statements." At home, kids might gather additional materials, interview people, or polish a paper that a teacher has already reviewed. "But before eighth grade, kids shouldn't be doing the original work at home," she insists. "That must be done under the teacher's direction."

TYPICAL ASSIGNMENT

Solve fifty math problems.

Almost every math teacher we surveyed claimed to be against assigning an excessive number of math problems, a practice they've charmingly dubbed "drill and kill." So why are our kids still bringing them home by the dozens?

Lori, a teacher from Mission, South Dakota, sums up the opinion of many teachers we surveyed when she says, "Excessive amounts of drill and practice are ineffective because they overwhelm and discourage, not to mention cut into precious family time." In fact, research suggests that assigning more than five math problems for homework can actually hurt a student's comprehension—and for some very good reasons.

First of all, as the U.S. Department of Education itself asserts, five problems is all it takes to demonstrate whether a child understands how to do them—or not. "A common mistake, particularly among beginning teachers, is to assign too much homework," writes Nancy Paulu in *Help-*

ing Your Students with Homework: A Guide for Teachers, published by the government's Office of Educational Research and Improvement. "It can be hard to resist doing so if parents push for more homework and assume that the best teachers assign the most homework. (This is not necessarily the case.) Most often, however, a math teacher can tell after checking five algebraic equations whether students have mastered the necessary concepts." Although the guide singles out algebra, it's clear that the five-problem rule applies to all areas of math.

If a child comprehends a mathematical concept solidly enough to solve five problems correctly, there's no need to practice more. "A child who clearly demonstrates the ability to do addition or subtraction does not need to complete forty-five problems just because it's a homework assignment," says Emily, a first-grade teacher and department chair in Valhalla, New York. "That's clearly not useful or meaningful for that child."

And if a kid doesn't get a concept, doing additional problems is a particularly bad idea. "If a child does the first five wrong, what's he going to accomplish by doing the next forty-five wrong?" asks Deanne Rohde, the principal from San Diego. "He'll just cement the wrong way of doing it into his brain." Then the incorrect method will have to be unlearned before the child can progress.

Of course, repetition can be a good way of mastering skills, provided the concept is already in place and instant recall is required. As Paul Yellin, national director of the Student Success program at the All Kinds of Minds Institute, explains, "Repetition helps things become automatic. Sometimes kids have learned the skill, but need to do a few to really nail it. Neurologically, you need to pave that path you've created. Kids need to get to the point where the skill is automatic, and practice does that, especially if a child is struggling."

But this technique works best when the problems are spread out over time rather than dumped on a student all at once, says Steve Nelson, the head of the Calhoun School. "We know that concepts are reinforced by intermittent learning," he explains. "If a teacher wants her class to solve fifty division problems to be sure they get the concept, she'd be better off assigning two problems a night over twenty-five nights, with perhaps a night in between each time." That way, kids aren't overwhelmed with work—but they do get lots of practice. Better still, any difficulties can be addressed promptly, and by the end, the teacher can be sure the concept has really sunk in.

And, of course, endless practice sheets should never be used as a substitute for going over material sufficiently in class. Before a teacher sends home even two math problems, says former teacher and education author Susan Ohanian, she should be sure that the kids have a firm grasp on the skills they need to solve them. "When I was teaching, I thought it was my job to make sure my students learned math facts in class. If they're worth knowing, then it's worth my time going over them in class until the children learn them, understand them, and retain them."

TYPICAL ASSIGNMENT

Read pages 62 to 66 in your science (or social studies) textbook, then answer the questions at the end.

In both social studies and science (assuming they haven't been cut from your school's curriculum in order to focus solely on standardized tests subjects), the typical homework is to read the textbook and answer factual questions. Unfortunately, this rarely engages kids, and it's unlikely to help them remember facts.

"If a homework assignment extends the learning and makes kids really think about the topic, then it can be valuable," says Beers. But asking kids to answer questions at the end of a chapter simply encourages them to "skim and scan" as they've learned to do with other reading assignments. And when kids are reading solely to find particular facts, they're not delving deeper. "Even good students don't read the chapter. They hunt in the text for the answers," says Andrea Libresco, associate professor of Curriculum and Teaching at Hofstra University School of Education. "Worse, such assignments ignore a kid's biggest question, which is, Why should I care about this topic? Teachers are at fault for training our kids to find disparate pieces of information to which they make no emotional connection." Without that connection, little true learning is going on. As Gilly, a seventh-grade history teacher from New York City, puts it, "Reading a textbook chapter and answering questions at the end is a waste of students' time. They don't remember anything they 'learned,' and they don't even practice good study habits."

As kids get older, some copy answers from one another. Erin, a high school teacher from Brandon, Florida, observes, "One person does the work and everyone else copies before school. I am amazed at the ease with which students pass their work around. Many do not even bother to rephrase statements to make answers seem less copied."

So, how did we get to this point? According to Professor Libresco, teachers were probably taught social studies and science the same way when they were children. So they are just continuing an unfortunate tradition of "if it's Tuesday, it's page 27, so answer these questions, do this worksheet." And today, many teachers are supplied with so-called pacing guides that plan every lesson down to the minute. If the teacher doesn't finish the lesson, it must be finished at home—without her guidance—and a new one started the next day. Unfortunately, with this method, kids don't get much chance to practice their analytical skills. Do they even remember the facts? Try asking a student to repeat them a month after the unit test and you'll get your answer.

Cardboard, Glue, and Pasta:
The Homework Hall of Shame

Dioramas, posters, game boards, models—all those "fun" homework projects that require arts and crafts skills, special supplies, and plenty of parent participation deserve a special category. Most of us hate these assignments with a passion, and it's little wonder why. (Note: We're not talking about project-based learning, a hands-on educational approach that has been shown to be a more effective way of learning in the classroom than lectures.) Not surprisingly, when we asked parents to submit their kids' worst assignments ever, we were deluged with responses. The thinking behind many of these assignments remains mysterious, but here are some of the most outrageous.

> My sixth-grader's science teacher gave her an assignment to build a volcano using things around the house, with strict instructions not to purchase anything, not even the board it was to rest on! After I picked myself up off of the floor from laughing, we headed to the local party-supply store. Guess what? All of the modeling clay was sold out. That told me that the other parents had gotten to it first! We spent $88 for that volcano. Sure, it was pretty and she got a good grade, but give me a break!
>
> Kim, a mother of one from Downey, California

> My first-grader had to cut out fifty paper pennies from a sheet to count with. This was torture since he barely had the fine motor skills to use a pair of scissors. Finally, after much frustration and tears, we just gave him fifty real pennies to count.
>
> Elaine, a mother of two from Hastings, New York

> In third grade, my son was assigned a research report on a region in Texas, then given a list of topics to choose from, such as animal life,

rocks and minerals, and native trees. My child was assigned the Northern Plains and Lakes region, and he picked rocks and minerals. Of course, he had no way of knowing he would be unable to locate any facts about rocks and minerals for this specific region. We spent hours online trying to get information and couldn't find anything. Then the teacher refused to let him pick a new topic. What should have been a fun, educational project evolved into a major disaster. He hasn't felt quite the same way about science projects since then, and science is one of his favorite subjects.

Deanne, a mother of four from Houston

In elementary school, my daughter had to do fifty-two arithmetic problems, translate them into an alphanumeric code, and then plot them on a graph to look like Abraham Lincoln. I had my child stop the assignment and wrote a note to the teacher saying she would not do it as it was pointless.

Marion, a mother of two from River Forest, Illinois

Recently, my daughter had a project where she had to observe the moon for forty nights in a row, draw a picture of her observations, and write an analogy each night. Isn't forty nights a bit much? We live in a house surrounded by trees and had to walk a few blocks to see the moon, and by the time it came out, my kid was tired and just wanted to relax. Instead, she needed to get her coat and shoes on and go for a walk she didn't want to take. A lot of the other moms told me that they just stayed up late the night before it was due and looked up the moon phases on the computer.

Barbara, a mother of a fourth-grader from Westchester, New York

The prize for worst homework assignment ever was when my daughter's seventh-grade Spanish teacher made the kids bake sixty

*decorated cookies celebrating the Day of the Dead. He gave the
assignment one day before it was due, and based a big part of the
kids' grades on it! He even screamed at my kid in class because I had
the nerve to call him at home to ask about it. I don't know what this
guy had in mind, but he had no idea what shopping, cooking, deco-
rating, and schlepping boxes of cookies to school involved for a kid
already carrying a thirty-pound backpack.*

Catherine, a mother of one from Brooklyn, New York

*My eighth-grader had a math project in which she had to purchase
and paint a 12 × 12 piece of plywood, nail one hundred special-
sized nails into it at precise intervals at the same depth, then take
six different colors of embroidery thread and weave it between the
nails in a geometric pattern. This is math?*

Anonymous

Of course, we have to assume that teachers either believe in these
projects or are pushed to assign them by administrators who do. But just
what is the purpose behind them? Here's what one middle school director at a New York City private school told us: "Some kids might not necessarily write such a great essay. But when they come in with this fairly
humble, goofy-looking shoe box with some figures in it and you ask
them to discuss the relationship between Scout and Atticus in *To Kill a
Mockingbird*, it's pretty remarkable what they can say," he explains.
"These kinds of creative activities are frustrating for some kids, I grant
you. But for others, it gives them another window in."

This *sounds* good. But aren't there other ways to help kids express
themselves that don't involve a family weekend with a glue gun? Teachers
tend to think that these "creative" projects are fun and a great opportunity for the family to work together. In fact, there's nothing that can

drain all the joy out of baking a cake, drawing a picture, or building a model faster than being rushed through it and then graded on it.

The misery starts with the frantic search for supplies, which are often expensive. "We always end up spending at least forty dollars at the crafts store," says one mom. "I can afford it. But what if you can't?" Of course, you're lucky if you can find the correct supplies at all. "Last year in eighth grade, my son needed Styrofoam balls of a certain size for a science project," says a mom from Needham, Massachusetts. "I went to the art store, but they were all sold out, and we couldn't find them at any other stores. The teacher didn't bother making sure you could actually get them. It was very stressful."

And there's sometimes little leeway. "Last night, we had to sign a form from the teacher acknowledging we knew that our son had been 'unprepared' for class," says Debbie, the mother of a sixth-grader. "This was because we had bought an 11×17 piece of posterboard, and the teacher wanted a larger size! We had to run out at 6:30 P.M., delaying dinner, to get the right size. He bought extras so he could bail out his friends whose parents didn't have cars. Otherwise they would be penalized and given a failing grade for the semester."

Parents who can't afford the time to find the correct size Styrofoam balls or posterboard are often in a bind. Many schools don't take into account the needs of working or single parents who don't have unlimited hours to participate in these projects. Karen, from Pelham, New York, had to spend hours and hours over one weekend driving her second-grade twins from one location to another for a school community project. "It involved crayon rubbings of local monuments, collecting bus and train schedules, and gathering leaves. They had to interview local merchants and get restaurant menus. I did not feel they learned anything useful *at all* and this was complete Mom homework. It was totally too much to ask of a parent with more than one child."

Of course, we'd say it's still "totally too much to ask" even if you have just one child. "The most complex projects always pop up with the worst possible timing," says Lauren, a mother of third- and sixth-grade boys in San Mateo, California. "When my older son got his first diorama assignment in third grade, he naturally forgot to mention it until a few days before it was due. It also included a book report, and the book he'd chosen was *The Blob That Ate My School,* which didn't have a single easy, simple scene to depict. This occurred during a week where I had a huge, stressful client project, and my younger son had started having nightmares, so I wasn't getting much sleep. Then, on the day we came home armed with modeling clay, felt, and a glue gun which I wasn't sure how to work, the plumbing in the house we were renting backed up, spewing a stream of sewage all over our driveway. Naturally, this was fascinating to two little boys, and it was almost impossible to drag them inside so I could start the older one cutting and gluing."

Ironically, learning firsthand about the sewage system was probably more educational than depicting a scene from *The Blob That Ate My School.* "I fail to see what creating a diorama teaches my son about the book he's reporting on, or about the period in history that his class is studying," says Lauren. A songwriter, Lauren got her revenge by producing an amusing parody called "There's Always a Diorama" on her latest CD, *Psycho Super Mom.*

Some educators agree that the purpose behind many of these projects is obscure at best. "Children spend a lot of time creating projects without understanding the purpose or goal of the learning experience," says Gigi Morales David, an early childhood education specialist and visiting instructor at the University of North Florida's College of Education. "I do not think that projects should be assigned unless there is a clear link to learning objectives." But often, it seems, the teacher forgets to include that part in the instructions.

In California, for example, building a model of a mission (an early Spanish settlement) is a standard fourth-grade project. So standard, in fact, that local crafts stores sell prefabricated mission-building kits. Many kids take advantage of these kits, which teach them little more than how to follow the directions in the box (unless their parents are doing the building, in which case, they're not even learning that).

Other times, teachers seem to fall in love with the artsy-ness of a project—and its ability to pretty up a classroom for an open house—at the expense of any academic point. "If my children are asked to create one more cereal box book report, I'm going to homeschool them (just kidding . . . sort of)," says Peg, the mother of first- and fourth-grade sons in Montclair, New Jersey. She explains: "You take a cereal box and the child is supposed to paste a different component of the report on each panel. The front has to have a catchy 'cereal' type name for the book; for *The Grapes of Wrath,* maybe you'd put "Dust Bowl-E-Os," with some kind of slogan, such as 'If the Joads had any money, they would have loved this cereal!' Then the back usually has to be some kind of activity, similar to what you'd find on the back of a cereal box. Let's say a Subsistence Word Search. The sides might include the ingredient panel, such as a list of characters with their descriptions or a plot summary. I'm sure that when the first cereal box book report was assigned, it was novel and refreshing. But at this point, it's tired and kids spend most of their time squeezing items onto the box and trying to make them legible, instead of actually thinking about the book. It's a classic case of form completely eclipsing function."

But if you thought any of the above projects were outlandish, just take a look at this assignment (reproduced verbatim) that fifth-graders at a Brooklyn, New York, private school faced after reading a cookbook. We award it our unofficial Grand Prize. It involves lots of people, lots of food, lots of cooking, lots of cleanup—and, oh yes, lots of arts and crafts supplies, disposable plates, and eating utensils. A video camera is optional. Note that the purpose of the project is never mentioned—and we're still trying to figure it out.

HOW TO PREPARE AN EXCELLENT PROJECT BASED UPON A COOKBOOK

You cannot simply make one dish from the book, bring it in, and expect to get an Excellent on your project. You must do more than that! You could do one of the following:

1. You could prepare a whole meal at home using a number of recipes from the cookbook. Take pictures during the meal and make a poster documenting the food you made and ate, and who got to eat them. You could put quotations on your poster of what the people said about the food you made.
2. You could prepare a recipe to bring into class the night before the project is due, and have someone video-tape or take photographs of you in the different stages of making it. Ahead of time you could make a poster with captions explaining the different stages, then tape/glue the photos on once you have taken them.

WHATEVER YOU DO: If you do bring in food to share, make sure there is enough for everyone in your group (10 plus the teacher!) and make sure that you bring napkins, plates, spoons, or whichever utensils will be needed. This is your responsibility!

The Parent Trap

The real problem with projects like these is that we often end up doing part or all of them for our kids. Educators are always saying that the goal of homework is to teach responsibility and self-reliance. "Projects should be done by students, not parents," says Jolinda, a fourth-grade teacher in Minneapolis. "It's hard to control who produces the output when big, complicated projects are assigned for homework. The parent tends to take over and the child learns little from the experience other than the parent is vested in the project looking perfect."

Of course, it's hard not to supervise when your child comes home with something like that cookbook assignment. But if we refused to get so overinvolved, teachers would have to scale back their expectations to what our kids could actually achieve on their own.

Still, try telling that to a parent whose kid has an assignment to build a scene from *To Kill a Mockingbird* in a shoe box or a mobile of the solar system that counts toward the final grade. As soon as we see that assignment sheet, many of us feel driven to do whatever it takes to help our kids compete. "Almost all these projects do require substantial parent involvement if you want your kids to turn in something comparable to everyone else's kids," says Wendy, a mother of eight kids between babyhood and age fourteen in Stamford, Connecticut. "You really need to assist your child in planning, outlining, drafting, editing, and preparing each project, or your child will be at a disadvantage to other children whose parents get more actively involved. For two working parents with a large family like us, this does become a burden. Worse, it creates an expectation by the child that you, not he or she, will be project manager, which is not consistent with the learning process."

This can lead to taking things way too personally for anyone's good. When Ginny's fourth-grader had to create a game based on a story the class was reading, Ginny, a mom from Hillsborough, New Jersey, read the book, typed up a synopsis, and figured out how to set up the game. Her daughter's only job: to help Mom glue stuff to the game board. "Needless to say, after having been so involved, I was disappointed when the final grade was only an 85. I thought surely after many hours of work, we would get an A."

These complex assignments also encourage parents to get involved for all the wrong reasons. "If my son were to walk into school with something he created on his own, he'd be down on himself when he compared his project to the other kids' projects," says one mom of a fourth-grader from Maryland. "It would be ego threatening. I help him because I want him to feel proud of the finished product."

Children might be relieved to be rescued from a daunting task, but we question whether they'll ever be proud of work that they know isn't truly theirs. More likely, they'll come away feeling dishonest and convinced that quality work can be completed only by adults, says Karen DeBord, an associate professor of child development at North Carolina State University. Deep down, we know this, too. Instead of doing our kids' projects, we should be teaching them to be proud of their own work. It's time that teachers acknowledged what a project by a ten-year-old really looks like—and that it's better because it's authentic. It's sad that we've let our fears overcome our better parenting instincts and our confidence in our kids.

Of course, there is educational value to many projects, such as those for science fairs. But the best way to make sure the child is actually learning from them is to make sure that the child is actually *doing* them—and the best way to achieve that is to have all project work done at school. That way the teachers can be the ones to answer kids' questions, keep them on track, make sure they have the right supplies, and yes, even unjam the glue gun. If the kids are doing a group project, teachers will also be able to make sure everyone is doing their part for the team (and parents won't be responsible for refereeing the kids and driving them back and forth).

Teachers will also be sure that they're getting a student's genuine work—not that of an obsessed parent. And, if we're so inclined, we'll be able to recapture the joys of baking cookies or building models or even doing science experiments as a family without the stress and worry of being graded on them.

7

The Real Way to Help with Homework

What's the best way to help your child with homework? The advice in books, articles, and at back-to-school nights is always the same: To guarantee success, all you have to do is provide a quiet, well-lit spot to study, a wholesome snack, the proper school supplies; make yourself available to answer the occasional question; and sit your child down at the same time each day. If she has trouble getting started (or finished), you just need to put your foot down and she will buckle down—problem solved.

Of course, it's not nearly as simple as that. And worse, should these strategies fail miserably—as they so often do—we end up blaming ourselves and our children. If only they weren't so lazy or stubborn. If only we were better at making and enforcing rules. If only we could provide that perfect homework environment, then our children would happily do endless hours of work without complaint.

The truth is, our failure to fulfill this fantasy is neither our fault nor our children's fault.

Homework overload is not a parenting problem. It's a school problem that has been dumped in our laps. If teachers can't get to all the material they're supposed to during the day, or if administrators want to make their school appear "rigorous," or if the school believes parental involvement is a must, or if standardized tests are around the corner, teachers often feel they have no choice but to pile on the assignments. Then the dismissal bell rings, and we're left to deal with the resulting mess: overwhelmed, exhausted children whose problems can't be fixed with a tasty snack or color-coded file folders.

Every night, our families are put in the untenable situation of having little choice about how to spend our free time. While the schools might never have intended for homework to eat up so many of our hours together, that's the inevitable result of assigning such huge quantities. If school administrators would only think about it, they could see what havoc they're creating. But too often they turn a blind eye to the ways in which homework overload is hurting our families. That way, they don't have to do anything about it and it remains our problem.

Because our schools refuse to think enough about homework, it's often *all* we get to think about. As good parents, we want to support our schools. So to get the homework done, we turn our homes into second classrooms, ourselves into taskmasters and surrogate teachers, and our children into stressed-out miniadults. But we haven't just handed over our evenings to homework. We've handed over our power to decide what's best for our kids—sometimes to teachers who are still relatively young and don't have children themselves. From what we can see, the schools aren't making such sound decisions. It's time for us to make those sound decisions, and to stop enabling a broken homework system.

Going with Your Gut

Here's a radical thought: It's time to trust your own instincts. Don't let the schools tell you that you have to accept things the way they are. If you see your child is suffering because too much homework is sapping his energy and breaking his spirit, something *is* wrong. If you're giving up precious family time for hour upon hour of assignments—time you'll never get back—something *is* wrong. If the time you have left over is marred by irritating discussions or arguments over when, where, and how homework is going to get done, something *is* wrong. If it feels like homework has taken over your family's life, something *is* wrong—and it's okay to do something about it. The solution is to say enough is enough. In the following chapters, we'll give you some ideas about how to do that.

We're not going to kid you—depending on how far you decide to go, it might not be easy. If you just use our strategies to put an end to the occasional onerous assignment, that's one thing. If you decide to put an end to most of them, as Sara, one of the authors of this book, did, that's quite another. (We'll tell you how she accomplished this in the following chapters.) We think that any effort will be worth it in the end. But it's got to be up to you.

Of course, it's scary to buck the system—especially when our children are involved. If we don't do something about it, however, the situation is probably not going to get any better in the coming years—and it could get worse. After all, schools often claim (and might even sincerely believe) that most parents want more homework, not less. If we remain silent, they have no reason to think otherwise. Do we really want to look back and realize that large chunks of our kids' childhoods were stolen by unworthy homework while we stood by?

While the schools have to focus on children as students, we know that, as parents, we have to focus on them as whole human beings. The goals of the school might be to make sure that they achieve a certain reading level or pass standardized tests. But we know in our hearts that this is the short view. Our goal is to raise happy, healthy, well-rounded, well-educated children who go on to lead successful, productive lives. To do that, we need to make sure our kids are getting enough physical activity, sleep, and dinners with the family; plenty of time for friends, outside interests, and reading for pleasure; and even a little time to wind down in front of the TV. We need to make sure our kids are having a real childhood and learning early to maintain some balance in their lives. The schools certainly aren't going to help them achieve that.

Sometimes it's as simple as saying, stop for tonight. "My second-grader's teacher wanted the kids to write vocabulary words and draw pictures of them," says Marcia, a mother of three in San Francisco. "My daughter couldn't draw a spoon, and it got really late and there was lots of crying. So I told her, just put it away and play. She said, 'What?' That was really what she needed to hear. She was just so frustrated and burnt and angry, it wasn't worth it. Sometimes they've had enough. We have ways of taking care of ourselves as adults. Kids need to learn to take care of themselves, too. They need to learn to recognize that they need a break."

Sometimes, it's not as simple as issuing a one-night stop-work order. If homework overload has begun to affect your child psychologically or physically, you might have to talk to the school about how to reduce the burden *every* night. If you make the request in the right way (as we'll discuss in the next chapters), you might find the school is very responsive.

Karen, a divorced mom of three, successfully put the brakes on her kids' runaway homework without any effect on their grades. She'd moved her family from the San Francisco area to Missoula, Montana, nine years earlier for the more relaxed lifestyle. But it was hard to relax with the amount of homework her kids received from the local public school (three hours for her sixth-grader, close to two hours for her fourth-grader, and forty-five minutes for her first-grader each night). Karen soon felt forced to make unhappy trade-offs to get the assignments done. "Playing board games or talking about the news, reading together, laughing, rolling on the floor, fort building, fishing, skiing, sledding. Name something and we have given it up for homework." When her sixth-grader started hating school, she decided to take action.

After discussions with her daughter's teacher failed to change things, Karen requested a meeting with the principal, the teacher, and the school counselor, whom she'd poured her heart out to. "The counselor had a little more authority than I did and she talked about my daughter feeling badly about herself and school." What happened? After a long conversation and quite a bit of prodding, the teacher and principal agreed that Karen could decide when her children had done enough homework and that no points would be deducted for failing to complete it. Now her children concentrate on the more worthwhile homework, such as reading, and skip the busywork. That allows them to spend more time as a family—and get the broad education that Karen wants for them. "There are many ways our family learns things that aren't necessarily homework," she says. "There's a lot to be learned from music, drama, natural science—we're in beautiful country here."

Across the nation, a New Jersey mother of a third-grader with learning issues took a less drastic but still effective step to relieve the homework burden for her own child. She realized that her son's required reading was such a struggle that it was turning him off to books altogether. But instead of panicking that her child would never learn how to read, she trusted her instincts and decided to take a temporary break. "I finally wised up and signed up for Netflix, the DVD-by-mail service. For twenty minutes most nights, we would crawl into bed and watch classic movies in little bits and pieces. Was it really too much to ask for twenty minutes of pleasure in my company instead of twenty minutes of reading and extended work? Should it be so difficult to carve out twenty minutes a day of enjoyment with his mother?"

She was not surprised to find that their movie watching had no negative effect on her son's reading and a positive effect on their relationship. "Did I take something away from him? No. I added something for him to look forward to. And if I lost him some speed on the learning curve, then shoot me. At the very least, he'll have memories of me that aren't drill, drill, drill."

We have to stop being afraid of our children getting bad grades, says clinical psychologist Kalman Heller. "I'm not talking about kids failing. But for some parents, a B is a bad grade." This is especially true in elementary and middle school, where grades really have little effect on a child's later success unless he or she will be applying for highly competitive public or private high schools. Even then, says Heller, "Parents need to put school in perspective. The skills required to be a successful student are often not the skills required to be a successful human being in the workforce or in one's personal life, with the narrow exception of an academic career. In the end, personal success is the most important, anyway."

We must not let the schools' needs and misguided goals override our best instincts when it comes to our children's health, either. As Maureen, the pediatric nurse and mother of four from Kentucky, says, "We're not taking care of ourselves in general, and we've got to look at the messages we're sending. We don't want our kids to think it's okay to slack off and not do what they're required to do. But on the other hand, we want them to get the rest that they need. So I tend to be more nurselike in those situations and look at what's best for my child right now—not at what the school wants. If my child is exhausted and can't even make sense out of this anyway, what is he getting out of it? The teachers have been pretty good about it so far."

From the time our children are born, we know that getting enough sleep is crucial. So we shouldn't be willing to sacrifice our common sense for homework's demands. "Too much homework is a direct cause of chronic sleep loss, which is as hazardous to your health as smoking," says Dan Kindlon, the Harvard child psychologist and parent of two. "I ask parents: If you heard that smoking would get your kids better grades, would you let them do it? Of course not."

So what does Kindlon do with his own kids? "It's not easy to tell your kid to go to bed, I don't care what you get on the test. But you have to be willing to have the courage. I'm trying to practice what I preach. I tell my kids, 'Go to bed. I'll send your teacher an e-mail.' And you know what? Most of the time, the teachers understand and don't care." That's certainly what Nancy, one of the authors of this book, has found. When her daughter was in elementary and middle school, she'd often insist on continuing to plow through her piles of work way past her bedtime—and past the point of being productive. "Kids often don't know when to stop and they need your help," Nancy says. "So I'd tell her that's enough for tonight. I'll write your teacher a note saying you did all you could, but needed to go to bed so you could be well rested for tomorrow."

That same sentiment is echoed by Angie, a former elementary school teacher and mother of a fifth- and a second-grader in Baton Rouge. "If I feel that what is being done is less important to my children than sleep, I will send them to bed. Sometimes the best help you can give your child is permission to go to bed."

Putting Homework in Its Place

Every night we promise ourselves that we won't descend into homework hell yet again. Well, why not begin making some changes tonight? They don't have to be major. They could be as small as deciding that you're not going to start up the whole machine by asking your child how much homework she has. This simple step, which coauthor Nancy took when her daughter reached high school, alleviated much of the stress home-work had caused between the two. "I'd still ask about school, but I'd focus on what she was learning or had done in art class that day. I wanted to send her the message that I thought education—and the rest of our lives—were about more than just homework and that I trusted her to get her assignments done. It really worked."

Or, when your child asks for help with her math problems, you could say, "If you're having trouble with them, your teacher should know that." When your child says, "I want to practice my violin/go to my grand-father's birthday party/finish this novel I'm really into, but I've got too much work," you could say, "Let's make a decision about what's most important." When your six-year-old's head is down on the table because she's too worn out to do any more schoolwork, you could say, "C'mon, honey, you've worked hard enough today. Let's do something fun."

In all these cases, you might either want to handle communicating with the teacher yourself or, if your child is old enough, advise her how to do it herself.

But whether you start taking action tonight or not, you need to think hard about your ultimate goal. A few of us might want to eliminate most or all homework. Most of us probably won't be interested in going nearly that far. But almost all of us, we believe, will want to cut out the busywork and make sure that what's left is high quality and worth our child's time.

The quantity part is easy. Why not draw the line when your child reaches a *total* of ten minutes per grade level per night? (That's ten minutes for a first-grader, twenty minutes for a second-grader, thirty minutes for a third-grader, and so on). Remember, after reviewing over 180 studies on homework, this is what Duke University education professor Harris Cooper recommends. In addition, now that you know which types of assignments are busywork, you can make those minutes count even more by encouraging your child to do the most valuable assignments, such as those that involve reading, first.

In Chapter 9, we'll show you how to write an effective note to the teacher if you decide to have your child stop working at a particular time limit. The homework your child is assigned might still not be of high quality, but at least the quantity will be more manageable, and you can salvage some good family time. Of course, if those ten minutes per grade level are pure misery, then you might want to stop before you even get started—especially since research shows it can have a negative impact on achievement in elementary school. We'll show you how to deal with the teacher in this case, too.

And just think: If most of the parents in your child's class stopped the homework clock at ten minutes per grade, no matter how much was completed, then your child's teacher would have to think a lot more carefully about what really must—and can—be done in that time frame. That would solve a huge part of the problem right there.

The ultimate goal: Choose your homework battles with your child wisely (just like every other parenting battle). If you find yourself forcing your six-year-old to labor miserably over circling the long *E* sounds in a word list, you might decide that's not a battle worth having.

Answering Your Kids' Questions—and Your Own

If you do decide to relax your formerly strict homework policy, how do you explain the change to your children? We're the first to admit that there are no easy answers to this or some other questions that will come up. If, like most of us, you've been going along with the whole homework thing every night without question, your child is probably going to be shocked when you change your tune.

The best bet is to have a family meeting and be honest with your child. Admit that what you're doing is not working (believe us, she already knows that part), and that you're going to try something different. Just opening up the discussion with your child can be a big relief for her. "Your children will feel so much better because you're not lying to them or telling them they should feel happy about something they can't feel happy about," says Peter Loffredo, the Brooklyn psychotherapist who has been working with children and families for more than thirty years.

How to begin? "You could say something along the lines of 'Daddy and I have been doing some talking and we feel that you're doing too much homework, and that there are other things that are important that you should have time to do,' " suggests Dr. Heller. " 'So we're going to put some limits on how much time you work each night.' "

If your children are old enough, this is the time to help them look at their homework critically and figure out their priorities, such as reading. "This process is actually very useful in helping a child learn how to make decisions," says Dr. Heller.

He does warn that some kids will be bothered by the thought of going to school without their assignments. If they're upset because they *want* to do all the work, bite your tongue and let them do it since it's obviously important to them. But if they're upset because they fear repercussions from the teacher, reassure them that you'll talk to the teacher and work out the problem. Explains Heller, "You have to tell your child, 'Look, you might get a red mark on your homework because you only did part of it. But that's okay. We're not going to be upset with you.' If your child is still anxious, you should talk to the teacher about putting your child's mind at rest."

But if you allow your children to avoid some homework assignments, aren't you teaching them to be disrespectful to authority? We believe you're teaching them to question it in a healthy way and not blindly follow every rule that's set out for them in life. You're modeling the virtue of standing up for something you believe in. "It's the parent's job to speak up when something is not good for the children and protect them," says Kate McReynolds, the clinical child psychologist at the City

College of New York. "I think kids can understand that we have to take care of ourselves and not do anything that's not good for us. That's a lesson we want our kids to learn in all contexts—especially when they're teenagers and dealing with their peers—that you don't always need to do what someone tells you to do. You want to train them to ask, Is this good for me or is this going to hurt me? That can start with homework in kindergarten."

But what if your children decide that what's good for them is to use all their newfound free time to watch TV or play video games? Tell them that you're not limiting homework so they can spend endless hours with SpongeBob or Tony Hawk. Instead, you're doing it so they can spend time with you and the rest of their family, their friends, or finding out what they love to do in life and doing it. When you relax the rules or allow your children to use their own judgment, it doesn't mean you have to give in to anarchy.

But how can you be sure that your children won't take your change of heart as license never to do another assignment again? They won't—because that's not what you're teaching them to do. You're teaching them to discriminate between what's worth giving up valuable time for and what's not. That's an important life skill. "It's not like you're telling them 'to hell with everything,'" says Dr. Loffredo. "Kids can understand that, Okay, there are some things in life you really have to do."

Even if they *do* decide to blow off all their homework every night, it won't be the end of the world. Instead of strong-arming them—which won't work anyway as they get older—you'll be teaching them a great deal about personal responsibility.

"As a parent, you need to be clear in your own mind about your goals for your student, and you need to communicate them clearly," says veteran teacher Mary Leonhardt. "Then you need to stand back and let your student work independently. You must always take the long-term view. If you have a child who is not doing his homework, ask him if there is anything you can do to help. Listen to your kids. Trust your kids. But never make them do anything. In the long term, there is no benefit. Kids are going to go away to college and you, the parent, will not be there. Students want to succeed, and they need to do it on their own, without parents propping them up."

But will your children still get into college? The short answer is yes. After all, according to Robert Gilpin, a former high school and college teacher, the coauthor of *Time Out: Taking a Break from School to Travel, Work, Study in the U.S. and Abroad,* and founder of an independent college admissions advising firm in Milton, Massachusetts, there are more than 2,500 colleges in the United States, enough to find a great match for every kid.

The long answer, of course, is not quite so easy. If your child is in elementary or middle school and her grades are reduced because she doesn't always complete homework, it's really not going to make any difference in the long run. After all, since most middle schoolers go to their local high school, their early grades have no long-term consequences. The exception: if you live in a place where your child has a choice of high schools and admission is partly based on grades.

High school grades, on the other hand, can count, depending on the kind of college your teenager wants to attend. So, if your high schooler doesn't complete all her homework, and it counts for 30 percent of her grades, then you need to be prepared that they might be lowered. If your teenager's goals are admission to one of the top colleges, then you can't have it both ways. You can certainly strive to change your school's policies (we'll show you how in Chapter 10). But while you're waiting for change, there's no getting around it: She'll have to do all her homework. And that's where you have to decide what's best for you and your family. Talk to your teenager about the consequences of not doing homework and make some decisions together.

But couldn't there be repercussions at school if your family rebels against all the work? There could be. Again, that's where you have to decide for yourself if it's worth it. But, often, there aren't any at all. Parent after parent we interviewed reported being pleasantly surprised by how accommodating teachers could be. And let's say your child has a teacher who refuses to agree or change things, or who thinks you're a bad parent for not enforcing her rules. That doesn't mean you're stuck. You might be able to switch your child to another class that's less homework heavy. Even if you can't, we'll show you how to keep working to get the teacher (or her superiors) to compromise. At the very least, you'll know you tried your best and taught your child a lesson about standing up for himself.

The truth is, if your children are suffering from homework overload and you *don't* do anything, the repercussions to their mental and physical health could be worse than anything the school could dish out. In our opinion, a teacher's disapproval or a bad grade pale in comparison.

In the end, it all comes back to trusting your instincts. That's the real way to help with homework.

8

What You Should Know Before You Talk to the Teacher

By now you know what many of the leading homework researchers say. But before you attempt to reduce your own child's homework load, this chapter will show you how to maximize your chances of success. We recommend taking the following steps early in the school year, ideally before homework issues crop up. You might be able to prevent some problems before they even start.

Even if it's the middle of the year, however, and you're already embroiled in a homework crisis, take a look at these suggestions *before* you contact the teacher. Often, simply taking the time to plan out a strategy will really pay off. One Brooklyn mother was upset by the large quantity of homework her kindergartener was getting. But before approaching the teacher, she decided to find out what her school's policy was. When she called the kindergarten coordinator at her school district's office, she was informed that the policy actually forbade assigning any homework to kindergarteners at all. "The coordinator then contacted the principal, who must not have been aware that the kindergarten teachers were giving homework, because he immediately put a stop to it," she reports. "Not long after, the school also held a parent meeting where the coordinator explained the philosophy behind not giving homework to young kids. I couldn't believe my success."

Sometimes it's as simple as that, sometimes not. Here's what to keep in mind while planning your own strategy, and how to make your efforts as productive as possible.

Before There's a Problem

1. FIGURE OUT YOUR OWN GOALS AND LIMITS.

Before you can discuss homework problems with the teacher, you need to be clear about your own philosophy. We think it's safe to assume that we all want the same thing—happy, well-adjusted kids who are polite, bright, able to think for themselves, and who have a few passions. You have to decide for yourself how homework fits into that goal. How much is too much for your family? What is it you want to fix? The quantity of homework? The amount you have to help? Perhaps you'll be able to come to an understanding with the teacher and lessen your child's load without affecting his grades. But what if he is penalized? What are your priorities?

2. FIND OUT IF YOUR SCHOOL HAS A HOMEWORK POLICY.

Is your school or district one of the 35 percent that actually has a policy? If so, and it follows the guidelines of ten minutes per grade per night, it will be easier to justify drawing the line when your child has worked for the prescribed period. "If a child is coming home with scads more homework than the policy suggests, it provides parents an entree into a discussion," says homework researcher Harris Cooper. "It legitimizes the concern and that's important."

Sometimes, if the policy is being ignored, a simple phone call might even solve the problem, as it did for the mother who discovered her kindergartener wasn't supposed to be getting homework at all. In other cases, your school might have a policy that allows for—or even encourages—an unreasonable amount of homework. For example, it's not unusual to find a middle school policy stating that parents can anticipate two to two and a half hours for seventh graders. Knowing the policy in advance, even when it's one you disagree with, is useful and shouldn't deter you from talking to your child's teacher. If you tactfully bring up the ten-minutes-per-grade guidelines and other supporting research with the teacher, you might find she's actually on your side. At the very least, it will help the teacher understand why the quantity of homework is so overwhelming for the kids in general. If the teacher is still unsympathetic, Chapter 10 will show you how to work with other parents to push for a better policy at your school.

Finally, if your school doesn't have a policy at all, then you'll know that homework is up to the individual teacher. The fact that she has flexibility gives you a better shot at reaching an understanding about what constitutes a reasonable amount, at least for your family.

3. FIND OUT ABOUT THE TEACHERS' PERSONAL HOMEWORK POLICIES.

At most back-to-school nights, teachers talk at length about their homework policies, outlining their expectations, including the amount and purpose of homework and how the parent should be involved—helping, not helping, vouching that it was done by signing off on it, and so on. They usually tell you how they want to be approached if a problem should arise.

If you're tempted to speak out at this meeting, choose your words wisely. It's best to raise the homework issue when there's enough time to discuss it. However, if the teacher doesn't mention anything about weekend or vacation homework, you might want to bring up the fact that your family looks forward to spending uninterrupted time together and that you hope she'll take that into consideration before assigning work that is due on Mondays or after vacations. You might also ask her to schedule a homework forum for parents and teachers where everyone can explore the topic further.

At back-to-school night, the teachers will also probably say something like, "Please let me hear about any problems," or "The homework shouldn't take longer than [X] minutes." You should take them at their word and notify them immediately if homework starts to cause trouble. As Colleen, a mom from Atlanta, reports, "At meet-the-teacher night, my son's fourth-grade teacher made it very clear that homework was important, but that if there were occasions when the homework just could not get done, not to stress about it, that she'd rather the kids get a good night sleep than stay up late to finish homework. That meant a lot to me."

Remember, you're not helping anyone if you remain silent. Letty, a sixth-grade teacher from Alexandria, Virginia, represents many teachers when she says, "Please do not keep a child up all night trying to figure out a complicated assignment. Write me a note asking me to review the concept. I will respond accordingly."

4.   BUILD UP GOODWILL BETWEEN YOU AND YOUR CHILD'S TEACHER.
Most teachers are stretched to the breaking point. Imagine spending every day in a room with too many children who haven't had enough recess, or P.E., or music, or art, or rest time—nearly all of them clamoring for attention. Imagine that you have to deal with students at different levels, prepare them for standardized tests, and deal with disciplinary problems, too. Chances are that your child's teacher is trying to do the best she can with a difficult job.

So, if you have the time and the inclination, volunteer in the classroom or otherwise help out as much as possible. And, when the teacher does something you really like, there's no harm (and a lot of good) in sending her a note to tell her you appreciate her. Says Ann, a mother of three from Morro Bay, California, "My husband and I are both educators and we like positive feedback ourselves, so we give it to our kids' teachers. If a project or assignment is good, we tell the teacher."

Your efforts will pay off. If most of your interactions have been positive, when you do have a concern, you'll be seen as an ally instead of an adversary. Lauren, a mom of three who helped found a Montessori school in Edison, New Jersey, recommends getting to know the teacher in any way you can. "Once you do, you'll probably realize she's not an ogre. Even if she is one, if you have an established relationship, she's much less likely to give you and your child a hard time."

5. COME TO A MEETING OF MINDS.

Clinical psychologist Kalman Heller, who works with families and schools, suggests that if you don't like what you hear about homework at back-to-school night, set up a meeting with the teacher to better understand her expectations and to express your own. That way, you might be able to come to an agreement about homework *before* any problems arise—even if the teacher already has a firm policy.

At the meeting, even if you've already heard your teacher's philosophy on homework, ask her to briefly explain it again. Showing that you want to understand her point of view communicates respect. Dr. Heller suggests asking: "What's your view on homework? How much time do you expect my child to spend doing it each night? What are the goals of your assignments?"

Now it's your turn to tell the teacher about your expectations, your family's circumstances (for example, you're a single parent with long work hours, or your child participates in lots of after-school activities that are important to her), and what your family can and cannot do. Ideally, this will be the beginning of a real discussion. The goal is to have an equal say in the process instead of remaining silent and accepting whatever the teacher says as though it's written in indelible ink.

There will be times, of course, when a teacher's expectations are totally unreasonable. Dr. Heller advises, "If one of your middle schooler's five subject teachers says, 'Well, I expect a child to spend thirty minutes on homework for my class,' the parent could say, 'Well, I haven't spoken to all the teachers yet, but if you all say the same thing, that's two-and-a-half hours a night for my twelve-year-old and I think that's way too much.'" Ask the teacher what she thinks is a reasonable amount for a child that age. You can be straightforward and assertive without being strident and self-righteous. For example, you can say, "We find that all our child can handle is sixty minutes a night, and after that, homework becomes stressful and unproductive. We would like your support in drawing the line at an hour."

These limitations help all kinds of kids, says Dr. Heller. "If the child is the neglectful type who fools around, she has to deal with the consequences of not doing her assignments. If the child has learning or attention difficulties, or extracurricular activities, that's all she can get done and what she'll be able to turn in."

6.   DON'T WAIT FOR YOUR SCHEDULED PARENT/TEACHER CONFERENCE.

If you have a lot of concerns about homework, don't save them until your parent/teacher conference. Usually, the teacher has allotted a short amount of time to each parent and has already set her agenda. If you try to discuss homework there, the conversation will necessarily get short shrift. Instead, meet early in the year about homework—or as soon as you have a concern. If it does come up for the first time at the conference, ask to set up another meeting where you can discuss it without being rushed.

7. **F**IGURE OUT WHO CAN HELP YOU SOLVE THE PROBLEM.

In elementary school, that's easy: The first person to approach is almost always your child's teacher. But by middle and high school, your child probably has several teachers, so you need to know where to start. If it seems as though most of the homework is coming from one teacher, then start by meeting with just that teacher. If the problem is a lack of coordination among several teachers, then you might want to start with the school counselor. Linda Eby, a middle school counselor from Gresham, Oregon, says, "The counselor is the thread that runs through the team of teachers and can work it out with all of them. If there's a problem, the middle school counselor is the best person to call." If your school doesn't employ a counselor, call the principal's office to find out whom you should contact.

8. **B**RING TOGETHER YOUR ALLIES.

Chances are, you know a lot of like-minded parents. (If you don't, share this book with others.) Pull together a list of contact information for all the parents of your child's classmates. Then when she comes home with an assignment that you're not going to make her do (such as counting, sorting, and listing all her Halloween candy after getting home from trick-or-treating—an actual second-grade assignment), you'll be able to dash off an e-mail to other parents. That way, your child might not be the only one to come in without the assignment done and other parents might not feel compelled to finish it after their kids have gone to sleep.

When There's Already a Problem

Many parents are intimidated by the prospect of negotiating about homework with their children's teachers. But it might not be as hard as you think. Some parents simply ask for changes and get them. Other parents at your child's school might even have gotten concessions you don't know about, paving the way for you. (Teachers and administrators are often reluctant to spread the word that their "rules" are actually flexible.)

As our own personal experiences have shown, when we set aside our feelings of self-doubt and reach out to our kids' teachers in a constructive way, we are often pleasantly surprised. As psychologist Kalman Heller puts it, "My experience has been that when parents really try to create a collaborative relationship, most teachers are very willing to do that. They appreciate the fact that the parents have come in, and most of them understand the need to have a balanced life at home and the challenges that today's families face. Teachers will usually be reasonable if they're approached in a reasonable and respectful manner and you show them that you want to work with them."

In fact, Sara, one of the authors of this book, and her husband, Joe, met with almost all of her children's elementary and middle school teachers to discuss homework overload or other problems with assignments. Most of them were responsive and cut back on homework not only for Sara's kids but often for the whole class, as well. The response from one of her son's middle school English/history teachers was typical. She was a new teacher, very young and enthusiastic, and her homework alone took the fastest kids more than an hour. With three other teachers also assigning homework, the nightly load often easily surpassed two hours. When Sara and her husband, Joe, expressed their concerns, the teacher said that the amount of homework was not up to her, and that she was just following school policy. So Sara mentioned that two of her son's other teachers—both of whom had middle schoolers themselves—gave much less homework and never assigned weekend or vacation homework. Sara and Joe talked with her about their shared goals and how there might be more flexibility in the school policy than she thought, and she agreed to seek the advice of the more experienced teachers. By the next week, she had decreased the amount of work she assigned by about two-thirds.

That's not to say that such discussions are always that easy (we'll get to that later), that everything was solved with that one meeting, or that the workload wasn't still too much. But many parents we interviewed who sought to change things for their children encountered teachers who were equally responsive.

Below are some key points to keep in mind. One caveat: Most of the following advice applies to elementary and middle school kids. By high school, your child will probably want to talk to the teacher herself—at least when it comes to why she didn't do a homework assignment. If she doesn't feel capable of doing that, you can nudge her in that direction by staging a few mock conversations with her. Your goal is to teach your child to stick up for herself; and solving her own homework problems—with your support and advice—will help her build confidence.

1. ACT IMMEDIATELY.

It's best to deal with problems as soon as they emerge from your child's backpack. If your child brings home a math sheet with forty problems and you think five is enough, do something (we have several suggestions in the next chapter). If you don't, chances are that the same situation will keep cropping up and your child's frustration will only increase.

2. DON'T PRETEND THERE IS NO PROBLEM.

If your child is having homework troubles, don't suffer in silence. One of the reasons we're in this predicament is because parents complain to one another but often don't let the teacher know. Then, the lone parent who's willing to talk to the teacher gets the reputation of being difficult, and it's easy for the teacher to say that no one else is having problems. Be confident that if you think there's something wrong, other people do, too. And even if your child *is* the only one having the problem, it doesn't make it any less of one. The teacher should still know about it and you should deal with it together.

3. MAKE SURE HOMEWORK IS THE CAUSE.

For everyone's sake, you have to be sure that homework is really to blame and that there's not something else going on. You want to be able to tell the teacher that you've really examined the issue and eliminated the culprits she's going to ask about: yes, you do have a quiet place for your child to do homework and you've provided those colored pencils and folders; yes, you do give your child a snack; no, your child doesn't have a learning issue but can't focus because there's just way too much work every night; yes, your child does have a learning issue but the homework isn't helping and you have better strategies to deal with it. As homework researcher Harris Cooper explains, "If you can say, 'I've done the reality check and looked for culpability elsewhere, but my kid is still doing three hours of homework, and it's causing big problems,' then you've got a strong case."

4. FIND OUT WHEN AND HOW YOUR TEACHER PREFERS TO BE APPROACHED.

Is it before school or after? Is it by phone, e-mail, a note sent in with your child, or a face-to-face meeting? When we surveyed teachers, we got a wide variety of replies:

> The best way is to call or e-mail, understanding that they will most likely have to leave a message and that it may take twenty-four hours to return the call (teachers do not sit at an empty desk with a phone all day). I am often with students from the minute I get to campus until the minute I leave. Students have to be my top priority. If I have three kids who stayed after school to get help with their homework, they take priority over a phone call from a parent involving only one student. That may not be ideal, but it's the real-

ity of teachers having to serve a hundred and eighty kids. The worst way to approach a teacher is during class, right before class, or right after class. Again, my attention must remain with the thirty-five students in front of me, not the parent of just one student!

Marion, a seventh-grade science teacher

I would love to be approached personally. When the parents come to me, I want there to be a solution. I want them to say, "Hey, this is what's happening. What do you think we can do?" I prefer face-to-face contact because a lot of times people can misinterpret something in an e-mail. But when you hear a person's tone of voice, usually it's much nicer than what you're reading on paper. If it's face to face and smiles are happening, then something can get done.

Trish, a kindergarten teacher in San Diego

The best ways are via e-mail or in person, but it all depends on timing. A parent who makes an appointment or e-mails a nonthreatening "how can we solve this problem?" message is great. A parent who arrives on my doorstep two minutes before classes start will only make me mad. Similarly, if they're attacking ("You give too much work!"), then I'll get defensive and it is hard to have a productive discussion.

Michelle, a computer teacher in Mountain View, California

DON'T TELL ON THE TEACHER—UNLESS YOU HAVE TO

One point every single teacher agreed on: Don't go to the principal first. Start by going to the teacher. Why? If you don't let the teacher know there's a problem, she can't fix it, and it's easier to get a problem fixed through direct communication. If you go to the principal or a counselor, the first thing she's going to ask you is whether you talked to the teacher. If you say "no," she'll either tell you to go talk to the teacher or she'll go to the teacher herself. If that happens, then you've put the teacher on the defensive and you'll have to spend time smoothing things over later. Plus, it's the principal's job, at least initially, to support the teacher, just as it's your job to advocate for your child. That's not to say you won't ever end up going over the teacher's head. But save that for when you've exhausted every possibility with the teacher or for when you're trying to change overall policy.

If the teacher doesn't have a preference, or if your concern is anything more than minor, we suggest a face-to-face meeting. "A teacher has a much harder time saying no when you are sitting there in front of her," says John, a dad from Ocean Springs, Mississippi, who has gone to bat for his kids several times. "And, taking the time to come to the school shows the teacher that you care."

In addition, it's much easier to be persuasive and convey how you really feel in person. A letter is pretty one-sided. Even if the teacher responds (and she might not), there's still no give-and-take, and it's easy to misunderstand each other. To reach a teacher, it's not enough to tell her what's bothering you; you have to show her that you're interested in her opinion, too. That's easiest to do when you're sitting right across from her.

A telephone conversation is second best. While you can't read body language, there's still a two-way conversation and both you and the teacher can hear each other's intonation.

E-mail is a distant third. No matter how hard you try, it takes a lot of work for an e-mail not to feel abrupt. "In an e-mail, emotions can be misconstrued, especially when you throw in an exclamation point here or there," says Mary Pat McCartney, an elementary school counselor in Prince William County, Virginia, and elementary vice president of the American School Counselor Association. "The problem can sometimes come off as worse than it really is, or not as important as it is, which is just as bad."

Whenever you're tempted to fire off an e-mail complaint to a teacher, restrain yourself from hitting the Send button. Wait as long as you possibly can, so you have the distance you need to see whether it makes the point you want without alienating the recipient.

5. Don't wing it.

We can't emphasize enough how important it is to prepare for your meeting with the teacher. It's probably going to be a little different from any other parent/teacher conference you've ever had. Instead of sitting and listening to the teacher tell you about your child's strengths and weaknesses, you're going to be leading the discussion and asserting your own opinions. But in order to do that effectively, you must follow some key strategies.

- **Think about who's going to do the talking.** If you feel really agitated or angry or upset and you have a partner who can attend the meeting, let him or her do the talking, at least in the beginning. As Susie, from Cupertino, California, says, "When it comes to my kids, I'm kind of like a mama bear. So I have my husband talk to the teachers." If you don't have a partner, vent to one of your friends first so you don't let loose on the teacher.
- **Stick to the "I" voice as much as possible and stay away from using "you."** "I see Matthew miserably sitting at the table and working for a solid three hours every night" will probably be better received than "You assign too much homework and you're making my child miserable." It keeps you from sounding accusatory (plus, it's really

hard to argue with people who preface every statement with an "I" because they are simply stating their own experience).

- **Don't expect to make a convert.** No matter how well you present the antihomework research, you're no more likely to alter the teacher's entire philosophy in one conversation than you are to change someone from a Democrat to a Republican (or vice versa) over dinner. "To change the paradigm is big," says Stanford professor Denise Clark Pope, who conducts workshops around the country for schools interested in reducing student stress. She reports that when she polled the teachers at one workshop, only half were willing to alter their opinions about homework—even after hearing the research on it. So instead of arguing over the general merits of homework, stick to how it's affecting your child specifically.

- **Jot down your thoughts.** If you work best from notes, make a few beforehand. That way, you'll be sure not to leave anything important unsaid. It might help you listen better to whatever the teacher has to say, since you won't have to constantly think about what you're going to say next.

- **Remember your purpose.** Your purpose is to stop the frustration you and your child are feeling. Your purpose is not to intimidate the teacher or appear more knowledgeable, and this is probably your biggest challenge. If the teacher seems receptive to reading more on the topic, you can offer to pass on some materials. Remember, the teacher believes that homework is *her* area of expertise. You will be most successful if you make it clear that you just want to help the teacher understand *your* area of expertise—your child. To that end, you want to paint a picture of how homework affects your home: how your child feels when she's doing homework, how much or little you have to be involved, if your child has tantrums, if you have to cajole, threaten, punish, bribe, and so on.

Once she understands what it's like for your family, she'll want to
help.

- **It doesn't hurt to acknowledge that you feel emotional.** You can
even say something like, "You know, this is a very emotional topic
for us. It's very hard for us to watch our child feel so frustrated and
beaten down. It's taking a big toll on his self-esteem and we're sad-
dened by this."

- **Enlist outside help if you need it.** If your child works with a tutor,
learning specialist, doctor, therapist, or anyone else who can lend
support, consider having them attend a meeting with you or at
least write a letter about your child. Such professionals lend weight
and demonstrate that this is a problem that the school needs to
take seriously. They can also help you figure out how best to present your specific concerns, says Dr. Kalman Heller, especially if
things get rough. "Many times, I've gone in and helped negotiate
with those teachers who are a little more difficult to deal with."

Now that you (hopefully) feel better prepared to talk to your child's
teacher, it's time to get into the nitty-gritty of what you should actually
say when a specific crisis comes up.

9

When There's a Problem

HOW TO BE YOUR CHILD'S BEST ADVOCATE

What will you do when your kids come home tonight with more work than they can handle or yet another homework disaster? This chapter will give you step-by-step strategies to deal with teachers effectively and get results, starting tomorrow. Sara, one of the authors of this book, employed nearly every one of them for her own kids from the time her first child entered first grade and almost always met with success. Inspired by her, her coauthor, Nancy, also started writing notes to teachers whenever her daughter's homework became too much, and to her surprise, got the desired results every time. We'll describe the methods that were most effective for them, as well as for dozens of other parents we interviewed.

While trying to change the opinion of your child's teachers might sound scary, tiring, and time-consuming (and sometimes it is), we believe reclaiming our family's evenings is worth the effort. Many times, all you need to do to solve a problem is let the teacher know there *is* a problem (and be willing to persevere), as these parents found.

"I approached my son's third-grade teacher with a lot of trepidation," says Ayelet, a mother of four from Berkeley, California. "I did a little research on homework and went in to talk to the teacher about how the work was taking a lot longer than the thirty minutes experts recommended for my son's grade. I had worked myself up into thinking that this was going to be a miserable exchange. And then the teacher said, 'Okay, fine. Have your son work for half an hour and then draw the line.' So that's what I do." Several months later, Ayelet is still drawing the line. But she doesn't have to do it nearly as often since the teacher has reduced the assignments for the entire class. "Yes, the teacher actually cut back on *all* the kids' homework!" reports Ayelet. "And, yes, we're still enforcing the ban when it stretches beyond thirty minutes."

When Lisa, a mother from Arvada, Colorado, requested that her son, who has a learning disability, be allowed to do fewer math problems, it made his teacher rethink her general homework policy. "When the teacher saw how few problems my son had to do to show her that he knew the concepts, she wound up lightening the load for the whole class."

The day after Angie's second-grade son had spent the day at home because he was sick, the Baton Rouge mother and former teacher decided to ask her son's teacher to suspend her policy of making kids who had not completed their homework finish it the next day during recess. "That goes against everything I believe in," reports Angie. "So, I sent the teacher a note that said, 'Please let my second-grade son run around for ten minutes.' I thought she'd ignore me, but she didn't. My son got his recess!"

Unfortunately, it turned out to be a one-time reprieve. But Angie decided not to push it. Her son's teacher, as well as her fifth-grade daughter's teacher, had already responded to requests from her and other parents to reduce their kids' workload. "Now, they will keep my kid in from recess to make up homework if he's been sick, which totally frustrates an energetic boy who needs the activity. But sometimes we must pick our priorities."

Sometimes, the fix isn't quite as easy. Jenny, the mother of a twelve-year-old from Sperryville, Virginia, had to have several meetings with her daughter's teachers about the overwhelming amount of work assigned. "They suggested ways to find more time to do her homework—over lunch, during free-choice time, before school. To me, that was not a solution. It wasn't just the time; it was the amount that was overwhelming. But they said that if I wasn't happy with it, I should find another school." Jenny refused to give up, though. She liked the school in many ways; she just didn't like the amount of outside work. "I kept on calling for more meetings. The final result: Now I'm 'allowed' to write a note saying my daughter has done enough work, and she will not face any negative repercussions (such as having to stay in at break time or doing it later). You could have knocked me over with a feather."

Of course, there is no single method that's perfect for all situations. A lot depends on the chemistry between you and the teacher, the teacher and your child, and, perhaps most important of all, the teacher's personality. When trying to solve their kids' homework problems, coauthor Sara and her husband, Joe, often found that what worked with one teacher didn't always work with the next. If a teacher wasn't amenable to one approach, they'd try another. And, when they got stuck, they'd call on Sara's brother, David Bennett, a professional mediator, to brainstorm. David, who conducts workshops in mediation and negotiation training in Ottawa, Canada, provided many of the communication techniques in this chapter.

On the following pages, we'll cover some of the most common problems involving homework overload and how to deal with them. We've supplied lots of sample e-mails, notes, and dialogues to give you ideas. But they're just that: ideas. Feel free to adapt them to your own situation and style.

Setting the Tone

The key is to establish a respectful, friendly tone with every communication. You have to be able to get across your concerns, find out the teacher's concerns, and figure out how to resolve them together. The actual words you use are not that important—it's your approach that really counts. But try not come across as a know-it-all (although, after reading this book, you will know quite a bit).

We know we don't have to tell you this, but don't forget to start out every communication with some kind of pleasantry. Unless you're face to face, it can be difficult to read your tone. So we firmly believe a sincere compliment or kind word at the beginning will help show that you don't mean to be antagonistic or confrontational. For example, try something like this before getting to the heart of the problem:

> It was so nice to hear you speak at Back-to-School night. We feel lucky that our son is going to have such a thoughtful, kind teacher this year.

or

> We're so glad we got to meet you yesterday when we brought Ariel into school. As you can see, she's a little reticent to leave us, and your warmth quickly won her over.

or

> Elena came home from school today bubbling over with enthusiasm about _____.

or

Antoine was so happy when you shared a little story with him about _____.

PROBLEM: Busywork

EXAMPLE #1: Forty math problems (and it's clear that your child knows how to do them after she completes five)

GOAL: To eliminate time-wasting, boring homework

PROBLEM-SOLVING STEPS

1. Tell your child that you can see that she knows how to solve the problems and that it's okay with you if she stops. When she says she'll get into trouble if she doesn't complete them, tell her that you'll send a note to the teacher with an explanation. Remind your child that you're not asking the teacher to limit homework because your child's not capable of doing it, but because you believe that it's too much of a burden for *any* child that age.

2. Write a little note on the worksheet, such as:

> *Last night was really busy in our house. I hope you don't mind, but I told Grace to stop after she had done five problems because it was clear to me that she knew how to solve them. Please call me if this is a problem.*

3. Follow up before school the next morning by sending an e-mail to the teacher (so that if she reads her e-mail before class, she'll have a heads-up). Also consider asking her to meet with you. The reason for requesting a meeting is that this problem, or one like it, is going to come up again. It's better to deal with the situation up-front. Otherwise, the teacher might feel as though you're always taking matters into your own hands without even consulting her. Here's how the e-mail might read:

[Begin with a comment that's both nice and genuine.]

As I wrote you in a note on her worksheet, Grace will be bringing in her math sheet today with only five problems completed. I told her to stop because it was clear to me that she knew how to do them and the assignment was going to take up a good portion of her free time. I would like to get some guidance from you on to how to handle this in the future. Please let me know a convenient time to meet or talk by phone. I look forward to having an open discussion.

4. At the meeting or in a phone call, you might approach the topic like this:

PARENT: Last night, Grace was assigned forty multiplication problems. I understand that it's important that she learn how to multiply without a calculator. But I'd like to tell you my observations. When faced with those forty problems, Grace didn't even want to get started. So I said, "Why don't you do the first five?" and she did and they were perfect. Given that she understood the first five, I felt that she'd also understand the next thirty-five. So that's why I told her it was okay for her to stop.

TEACHER: The reason I assign forty problems is that, in my experience, forty seems to do the trick for most kids. Some need a little more, some need a little less. But I have to be fair to everyone. So it wouldn't be fair to the others if Grace did only five.

PARENT: I understand your desire to be fair to all the kids. But if I'm hearing you correctly, it seems like your goal is to reinforce the concept.

TEACHER: Yes, that's the goal.

PARENT: Well, five problems seems to be enough to do that for Grace. Doing thirty-five more would just frustrate her. I don't want to see Grace lose her love of math. So could we have her stop at five problems for now and reevaluate this in a few weeks? If it turns out that she's falling behind, we can always change it. That way, we're not committed and neither are you. We don't have to make a big deal out of it. Why don't we just try it for Grace and see whether this works? [Asking for a temporary change is a very good strategy for any problem because no one feels boxed in.]

TEACHER: Okay, I'm willing to try that.

PARENT: Thanks, I really appreciate your understanding.

EXAMPLE #2: Spelling puzzles or mazes, word scrambles

PROBLEM-SOLVING STEPS

1. Tell your child to stop and say you'll write a note to the teacher explaining why.

2. Write a note on top of the worksheet, such as:

We didn't want to tear Malcolm away from the book he is reading to have him do the spelling maze. Can we please make an appointment with you to discuss this further in person or by phone?

3. Follow up before school the next morning with an e-mail, such as:

Last night, we allowed Malcolm to read instead of doing his spelling puzzle. We really value reading and believe that it improves his spelling. Would it be possible for us to substitute reading for the spelling maze and other spelling puzzles? Please let us know a convenient time for us to come in and talk to you. Thanks.

4. At the meeting, be careful not to use your knowledge that these types of activities have little educational value (although you can try to slip in some of the research in a gentle way). That could put the teacher

on the defensive. And it's possible that the way she uses an assignment *does* make it educational, so be willing to listen to what she has to say. Don't tell her your child "hates" an assignment, either. That makes it seem as though you refuse to have your child do work he doesn't like. Instead, try this:

> PARENT: I wanted to talk to you about those word scrambles and spelling mazes you've been assigning. I know a lot of people love to do those things, but I'm not clear on how they teach a child to spell.
>
> TEACHER: Now that you ask, I'm not really sure. But they're in the spelling book and they're the best thing we have, so I assign them.
>
> PARENT: Well, I appreciate your honesty. But for me, that causes a bit of difficulty. I understand that you use them because that's what you have. But if we're not sure what the benefit is, I'd like to have Malcolm skip them and read instead. We're big believers in reading and we're delighted when we see him engrossed in a good book. We see a vast improvement in his spelling and vocabulary this year, and we think it's because he's been reading so much. We're thrilled and would like to keep that going. That way, he's reading, he's using words, and he'll enjoy it. Can we try that for a few weeks?
>
> TEACHER: Well, I think there is a purpose to these kinds of exercises. The kids are working with the words of the week and it gives a lot of exposure to them.
>
> PARENT: Maybe it works for a lot of the kids. But it just doesn't work for my child. I've noticed that Malcolm always gets 100 on the spelling test. But then the following week, he's not spelling the words correctly in his written work. I don't think they're making it into his long-term memory. I've been reading up a little on

spelling recently and it seems that many people believe that one way kids become better spellers is by reading. And that's what I'm noticing in Malcolm. So we really don't want these kinds of exercises to cut into his reading time.

TEACHER: I'm aware of that research, too. Well, if he's comfortable with turning in an incomplete workbook and not getting his homework certificate at the end of the week, I guess it's okay with me.

PARENT: Could he get a certificate that he's read during the spelling exercise time instead? While we're all for internal motivation, it will be pretty discouraging for Malcolm if all the other kids are getting rewards and he isn't.

TEACHER: I'll think about it. But I can't promise anything.

CASE STUDY #1: STARTING THE CONVERSATION

Wendy, a mother of two private school children and former teacher from Highland Park, New Jersey, was tired of watching her six-year-old yawn through his homework and found it more and more difficult to say, "No, you have to do your assignments" when all he wanted to do was play. She met with the teacher, whose only suggestion was that her son take a nap after school so he could stay up later to finish his work. After thinking that over, she wrote this letter, which we've excerpted here.

> *Please know that I am sharing these thoughts about homework with you, but not directing them at you. I would like to get your feedback on all of this.*
>
> *Here is a glimpse of my son's day after school. He gets off the bus at 4:00, and is in the door and unpacked by 4:15. He is a pretty energetic kid. But he is six, after all, and a school day that goes until four o'clock is a long, full day. In order to get enough*

sleep so he is rested, his bedtime is 7:00. Bath time and down-time, which includes reading together for fun before he goes to sleep, needs to get underway at around 6:15. In those two hours in between arriving home and getting into the bedtime routine is dinner, homework and, hopefully, time to play. It is very, very tight and I feel like I am always rushing him and my other child along to stick to a way-too-pressured schedule because every minute counts.

My son doesn't need to nap when he comes home, and he wouldn't even be able to. Kids shouldn't need to do this in order to have the energy to stay up late to do their homework. What he needs to do is go outside and run around and play and get fresh air and exercise. We are overworking our kids and it isn't healthy.

It is sad to see kids overloaded at younger and younger ages. I understand the pressure you are under, and this bothers me just as much. It is bad enough that as adults we must strive more and more to find ways to handle it, but our kids are not able to do that. They are going to burn out before they even reach college at this rate.

When I see my son yawning through his homework, it pains me to have to tell him to keep going even though I know he has had enough for one day, which is why we have begun to pick and choose what he gets done.

Thanks for taking the time to read this.

Wendy

The results: This letter itself didn't solve Wendy's problem, but it opened a dialogue between her and the teacher. They reached an agreement where the teacher said she would support Wendy's judgment in deciding how much homework her son would do each night.

PROBLEM: Your child doesn't understand the material well enough to work on it at home.

EXAMPLE: Forty math problems (and it's clear after your child has done five that he *doesn't* know how to solve them)

GOAL: To alert the teacher that your child needs help and take yourself out of the role of teacher or tutor

PROBLEM-SOLVING STEPS

1. Tell your child that you can see that he doesn't know how to do the problems and that it's okay with you if he stops. When he says he'll get into trouble if he doesn't complete them, tell him that you'll send a note to the teacher with an explanation.

2. Write a little note on the worksheet, such as:

> *I hope you don't mind, but I told Aaron to stop doing the problems after he had completed five because it was clear to me that he was having a lot of trouble with them. Can you please go over the concept with him?*

3. Follow up before school the next morning with an e-mail to the teacher (so that if she reads her e-mail before class, she'll have a heads-up), adding that you would also like to set up a meeting.

> [Begin with a comment that's both nice and genuine.]
> *As I wrote you in a note on his worksheet, Aaron will be bringing in his math sheet today with only five of the problems completed. I told him to stop because it was clear that he didn't know how to do them. It looks as though he needs some help and I don't feel qualified to provide it (AND/OR: and Aaron doesn't respond well when I try to teach him material). I would like to get some guidance from you on how to handle this in the future. Please let me know a convenient time to meet or talk by phone. I look forward to having an open discussion.*

4. At the meeting or in a phone call, you might approach the topic like this:

> **PARENT:** Last night, Aaron brought home a sheet with forty multiplication problems. He really couldn't do any of them without a lot of supervision and help on my part. It's my understanding that homework is supposed to be independent work, so I'd rather he didn't start depending on me for help. It seemed futile to make him sit there for hours to struggle through the other thirty-five. I know he'd have been frustrated, and I'm afraid that if he ended up doing them the wrong way, it would have just reinforced that.
>
> **TEACHER:** The reason I assign forty problems is to give the students lots of practice. If Aaron would just sit down and concentrate, I know he could do them. But if he doesn't get this practice, he's just going to get further and further behind, and he'll never pass the test.
>
> **PARENT:** I understand your concern about the test. Quite frankly, I'm concerned, too. But having Aaron sit there for hours doing problems he doesn't understand doesn't seem to be accomplishing anything. He's just getting more and more upset and he's starting to hate math. He's even getting stomachaches. Can you show him how to do those problems again?
>
> **TEACHER:** Sure, I'm glad you let me know that he's having trouble. He seemed to get it in class.
>
> **PARENT:** And how would you feel about giving him a homework sheet with just five problems? That way, he won't feel so overwhelmed. And if it's clear that he isn't getting the concept, I'd rather he stop at five and learn the correct method from you at school.
>
> **TEACHER:** I'm sorry, but I just can't make up individual sheets for all the students.

PARENT: Well, then how about if I tell Aaron that you give him permission to do just the first five problems? When there's so many, he just gets so overwhelmed that he can't even start.

TEACHER: Well, I can't see how that's going to work. Some of the sheets have forty of the same type of problem. But others have problems that build on each other, and so the children really need to do all of them.

PARENT: So what would you suggest? This is just not working for my child.

TEACHER: Well, I'm not happy about reducing the number of problems for him. But, for now, I'll circle the ones he must do and he can skip the others. If he starts to fall behind, though, we're going to have to talk again.

PARENT: That's fine. I really appreciate your flexibility.

"IT'S JUST NOT WORKING FOR MY CHILD"

Only you know what's going on in your house every night at homework time. So when you bring up your concerns and the teacher insists that all the other kids can handle the homework, the best response is: "Well, it's just not working for my child." In fact, it's the best answer to almost any objection a teacher can raise—and it's a great fallback line when you find the conversation veering out of your control. "The teacher knows she's sending home an assignment that she's chosen for thirty children and that probably won't suit all of them," says Deborah Meier of NYU's Steinhardt School of Education. "That means that the teacher has to trust you when you say that the homework's not working for your child." So it doesn't matter if your kid is the only one in the class who's overburdened (and we doubt that). If the homework doesn't work for your child, a good teacher is obligated to figure out what will. And a good teacher will want to, as well.

PROBLEM: The assignment needs to be adapted to suit your child.

EXAMPLE: Your child loves to create stories, but the physical act of writing gets in the way.

GOAL: To avoid taking the joy out of an educational activity and to foster your child's love of creating and learning

PROBLEM-SOLVING STEPS

1. Tell your child that you can see she's too tired to write, but that you'd be happy to act as her scribe. When she says she'll get into trouble, tell her you'll send a note to the teacher with an explanation.

2. Write something like this on top of the worksheet:

Ayanna was too tired last night to write out a story. She had lots of ideas and was eager to tell a story, so I acted as her scribe.

3. If you get no response from the teacher, then your problem is solved. If the teacher does object, saying she doesn't want you adapting assignments to suit your child's needs, then you should make an appointment to see her. To do that, send an e-mail like this:

Ayanna is often too tired at the end of the day to do certain homework tasks, such as the physical act of writing. So I act as her scribe and make other adjustments. I realize you're not happy with this, so I'd like to get some guidance from you on how to handle this in the future. Please let me know a convenient time to meet or talk by phone. I look forward to having an open discussion.

4. At the meeting or in a phone call, you could say something like this:

> PARENT: I think that the creative writing assignments you've been giving are wonderful and Ayanna loves doing them. One of her favorite things to do is write stories. The problem is that she has trouble getting what's in her head down on paper. Developmentally, she's just not there yet. As soon as she has to write it down herself, she says she doesn't want to be a writer anymore. It's such a shame, so I decided to be her scribe to keep her writing going.
>
> TEACHER: But I want to get the kids to start writing down their own ideas on paper and use the writing techniques they're learning in school.
>
> PARENT: I understand that. I just don't think she's there yet, and it's very important to me that she doesn't lose her joy of creating. If I'm hearing you correctly, your goal is to have the kids practice putting their thoughts on paper. So how about if we have Ayanna write a sentence or two with her thoughts, and then continue to dictate the rest of her story to me? Would do you think?
>
> TEACHER: Sounds like a great idea. I love Ayanna's stories and certainly want her to continue to create them. Thanks for coming in to see me.

"MY CHILD IS STARTING TO HATE SCHOOL."

This is another effective line you can use when you're not getting the results you desire. No good teacher wants to hear that a child who used to love school is starting to hate it or is getting turned off to learning. So this statement should resonate and motivate even a reluctant teacher to find a solution. But take care not to overuse it, or it might lose its impact.

PROBLEM: The teacher hands out punishments for incomplete homework.

EXAMPLES: The teacher holds your child back from recess to finish homework and/or gives out rewards (such as pencils, stickers, candy) only to those children with completed assignments.

GOAL: To avoid punishment or public humiliation of your child due to incomplete homework when you were the one who stepped in and told your child to stop

PROBLEM-SOLVING STEPS

1.　When your child tells you that she was punished by missing recess for not completing her homework, send an e-mail like this:

> *Brittany really enjoys school and her friends and she looks forward to playing with them at recess. When she doesn't finish her homework and has to miss recess, she comes home out of sorts. I'd love to meet or talk by phone with you about this. Please let me know a convenient time.*

2.　At the meeting, try saying something like this:

> **PARENT:** I understand from Brittany that she didn't get to go to recess the other day because she didn't finish her homework the night before. I want to make sure that's what happened and I'm interested in hearing your perspective.

TEACHER: Yes, that's my policy. If you don't finish your work, you don't get to go outside.

PARENT: I guess there are a few issues here. It's important for everyone—kids and adults—to exercise and let out some stress. And I've seen this with Brittany. She needs to get outside and play and looks forward to it every day. If she doesn't get recess, she comes home really cranky and there's no way she can sit down to more schoolwork.

TEACHER: Sorry, but that's my policy.

PARENT: Can we talk about this a little more? It's not just the exercise—although since Brittany is a little overweight, we want her to run around as much as possible. It's also about how badly it's making her feel about herself as a student. She's starting to hate school.

TEACHER: Really? She's a slow worker but a good student. I'm surprised to hear that she feels like this.

PARENT: The kids who can get their homework done quickly and easily never have to miss recess. But the slow workers like Brittany already feel a bit different and this is another way they're stigmatized. I'm sure that's not your intention, but that seems to be the effect on Brittany. And she feels the same way when other kids get rewarded for homework and she doesn't. Instead of motivating her, it does just the opposite.

TEACHER: Oh, I hadn't thought of that. I would never want to stigmatize a child, and I do know that kids need their exercise. I've noticed that when the kids miss recess, they're so wiggly that they can't even concentrate. I guess I'll have to rethink my policy.

PARENT: Great. I'm glad you're so understanding.

CASE STUDY #2: ADDRESSING PROBLEMS PROMPTLY

Gay doesn't let anything slide. Although she's spoken to the teachers many times about her third-grader's homework load at their private school, it keeps creeping up. So every so often, the Hawaii mom jots a note to the teacher on her daughter's worksheet and tells her daughter why she's doing it. "I'll write, 'My daughter spent an hour on her homework today and didn't finish it. I felt she did what she could.' "

Most of the time, there are no negative consequences. But one teacher had a policy of publicly shaming kids who hadn't completed their homework. The teacher would put cards on each kid's desk with the green side showing if the homework was completed and the pink side showing if it was not, allowing everyone to see who had and hadn't turned in their work. "I wrote the teacher and said, 'I don't think my daughter should be embarrassed by having her card flipped to the pink side when I'm the one limiting the time she spends on it.' " To Gay's delight, the teacher agreed.

PROBLEM: Your child receives an assignment or project that requires lots of parent participation and supervision.

EXAMPLES: Your child is asked to bake a cake in the shape of a Roman aqueduct (a real assignment), produce a project that involves lots of hard-to-find supplies and lots of help, or research a subject on the Internet when he isn't old enough to do it alone.

GOAL: To choose how you spend your time with your child and not have the school dictate it by assigning projects to bring you and your child together

PROBLEM-SOLVING STEPS

1. Talk with your children about how important it is that they do

projects on their own so that they can take pride in their own work. Explain that other children might get a lot of help from their parents and bring in something out of the pages of *Architectural Digest, Cook's Illustrated,* or *Popular Science* (depending on the topic), but that you prefer them to do their own work.

2. If you're meeting with the teacher for any reason *before* your child receives his first project assignment, you can mention that you're one of those parents who believes that the work should represent what the child is able to actually do. The teacher's likely response: "Fine. I'm not interested in what the parents can produce." But if the teacher says she expects it to be a joint effort because it brings the family together, feel free to tell her that your family is scrambling to find time together and would like to choose how to spend it—and that these projects actually get in the way. You could also say that you hope the various parts of the task—from gathering supplies to executing the steps—are age appropriate and don't involve box cutters, glue guns, mix masters, ovens, or dangerous chemicals.

If your child has already come home with one of these assignments, try writing a note like one of the following:

> *Abigail was unable to bake a cake in the shape of a Roman aqueduct last night because she would have required a lot of help and I was working the 3–11 shift/the baby was sick/we were having company for dinner/I had my own work to do. I'm sure you thought this would be a fun project and I imagine plenty of families enjoyed it. While I really appreciate your good intentions, I'd like to meet with you to discuss homework that requires family assistance. Please let me know a good time when I can come in and do that.*

> *Jacob's poster is done on typing paper because we didn't have the time (and/or money) to get the posterboard you specified in the instructions. Hope this isn't a problem.*

We read over the list of proposed science fair projects and it looks as though there are only one or two Morgan can do by herself. We assume you want to see the children's own work, not ours, and we just wanted to give you a heads-up that Morgan will be doing her project all by herself. If we're wrong and you're expecting parental involvement in this project, please let us know.

We don't allow Elliott to use the Internet without our direct supervision, so he couldn't do his research last night. We'd like to know whether you've had a session on using the Internet safely. And, can you share any tips to help us with this at home? Thanks.

PROBLEM: There seems to be no coordination among teachers regarding homework.

EXAMPLE: Three tests scheduled on the same day

GOAL: To get the teachers to take into account what others are assigning (About a third of the teachers we interviewed and surveyed revealed that they never coordinated their assignments with other teachers and only a few were always able to coordinate.)

PROBLEM-SOLVING STEPS

1. In this case, you'll need to figure out the correct person to address this problem. It could be the homeroom teacher, a school counselor, a department or division head, the dean, or even the principal. Once you identify the most appropriate person, you might be able to solve this one with a phone call that goes something like this:

> **PARENT:** Hi, I'm Ben's mom. He's in the seventh grade. I wanted to talk to you about a problem that you might not be aware of, but I'm sure you'd want to know about. It seems like somehow the coordination between Ben's different teachers is not very co-

ordinated at all. For example, this week, Ben had three tests on Thursday. And last week, the science project was due on Monday and he had an English paper due on the same day.

COUNSELOR: Wow, that does sound like a lot.

PARENT: Do you have any way of coordinating the assignments so that this doesn't happen?

COUNSELOR: Actually, we have a board in the lounge where the teachers are supposed to list their big assignments and tests.

PARENT: Then I wonder how this could happen. Perhaps the teachers aren't using it as much as they should—because this has been a recurring problem. I realize it may be a pain for them to keep the board up to date. But it's a bigger pain for all these children to have the stress of overlapping assignments. Ben is usually well prepared. But when he had three tests to study for in one night, he didn't feel he could do very well on any of them. That's not helping anyone.

COUNSELOR: You're right. I'll make sure we bring this up at the next staff meeting. Thanks for calling.

If the school doesn't even have an assignment board, suggest one. Should the situation fail to improve, you might have to press the issue in a face-to-face meeting or organize other parents to change things (we'll show you how in Chapter 10).

CASE STUDY #3: REDUCING THE TOTAL FROM SEVERAL TEACHERS

When John's ninth-grader regularly started coming home with no less than five hours of homework from her six teachers each night, the Ocean Springs, Mississippi, dad felt compelled to take action.

"She would arrive home from school at 3:30 and other than thirty minutes to eat dinner, was doing her homework until she went to bed. This was ridiculous." But when John contacted the teachers individually, they each told him, "I assign only forty-five to sixty minutes of homework each night. I don't think it's unreasonable for your daughter to spend an hour on homework."

Not at all happy with this explanation, John decided to take his case to the principal and get all the teachers together at once. "When I got them all in the same room, I made them eat their words," he says. "At first, they gave me the same song-and-dance routine I had heard many times before: If you care about your child's education, you will support us, the homework isn't excessive; if you want your child to learn, you will make her do her homework. Sorry, I replied, but I don't see it that way. They had all said previously that an hour of homework each night was appropriate. So they really couldn't argue with me when I told them to work together to make sure my daughter had only one hour between all of them. They worked it out by each giving an assignment once per week that would take about an hour and wasn't due until the following week. My daughter could then decide which assignment to work on each day so it came out to about an hour each night. I still wasn't happy because I think no homework is appropriate. But I had won a major battle, so I didn't press any further."

PROBLEM: Vacation homework

EXAMPLE: Any assignment given in the few days before a vacation and due a day or two afterward

GOAL: To end vacation homework (you believe that family time and downtime are very important, and that kids need a break without any work hanging over their heads).

PROBLEM-SOLVING STEPS

1. Ideally, it's better to be proactive and approach the teacher about vacation homework at the beginning of the year or at least several weeks before the break. If that's possible, try something like this in a phone call or face-to-face:

> PARENT: I was wondering whether you're planning to assign homework over any of the long weekends or major vacations this year. I'm asking because last year Georgia got homework over Christmas break and it really ruined it. She had to drag her books to her grandparents' house and do homework while the rest of us were playing games and socializing. She didn't even have time for our family tradition of caroling around the neighborhood.
>
> TEACHER: Well, I always assign a project during vacation. It gives the students lots of extra time to work on it—and it's supposed to be fun.
>
> PARENT: It might seem like the extra time is helping the kids, but it often has the opposite effect—at least for my child. It just hangs over her head for the entire vacation. In our family, vacation time is sacred. So we've decided that we're not going to allow Georgia to do any homework during the break. If you must assign a project, could you please give us enough notice so that Georgia can complete hers before the break or do it once she returns?
>
> TEACHER: I've never had a parent object to vacation homework before. Thanks for bringing it to my attention. I'll think about it and let you know.
>
> PARENT: Thanks, I would appreciate that—and I think all the other parents will, too. I'm sure everyone would be happier with a homework-free vacation, and the kids would return refreshed and ready to go back to work.

TEACHER: You're probably right. Like I said, I'll think about it.

PARENT: Okay, thanks.

[But if you didn't have the conversation in advance and you're caught off guard by vacation homework, try this if you happen to be at school for a holiday function or something else before the break:]

PARENT: Hi, what are your plans for Christmas?

TEACHER: Oh, nothing special, just relaxing.

PARENT: It's nice that you're going to have some downtime. You've worked so hard with these kids, I'm sure you really need it. You know, we've really been looking forward to this break, too. I've been trying to clear my desk so we can all have some relaxing family time together. So we were upset to find out that Georgia has an assignment over the break. [Continue the rest of the conversation as above.]

But if you won't have an opportunity to talk to the teacher in advance, here's what you can do: Tell your child why vacations are important, and that you don't want her to do any work while she's on break. When she says she'll get into trouble if she returns without the assignment, tell her that you'll talk to the teacher. Since it's right before vacation, the teacher might not be able to meet with you, so you might have to explain what you're thinking in an e-mail like this.

> *Georgia tells me that she was given an assignment that is due on January 3, the day she returns from the Christmas break. We believe that downtime is really important and we want Georgia to learn how to achieve a little balance in her life. I always try to tie up my loose ends at the office so that I don't have to do any work over the vacation and can return refreshed.*

If you still want her to do the project—just not during vacation, you could say:

> *I'd appreciate it if you could extend the deadline so that Georgia can begin the project the week after the vacation ends.*

Or, if there's enough time, you could offer to have her hand it in before the vacation.

If you don't want her to do the project, you can close the e-mail by writing:

> *Georgia is not going to be able to work on the project during the vacation and I'd like to discuss this with you as early in the New Year as possible. I'm hoping you'll allow Georgia to skip this project to avoid having a homework pileup after the break and allow her to start the New Year refreshed. Thanks for your consideration and have a wonderful holiday.*

SOMETIMES IT'S JUST A MISTAKE

If the homework assignment seems totally out of whack, find out what the teacher intended. One parent from our survey had his child do all one hundred math problems on a worksheet in one night, only to discover that it was meant to be broken up over many nights.

Sometimes a huge assignment isn't a mistake, but e-mailing the teacher as though you assume it is might just get you the desired results, as it did for one parent who wrote the following note:

> *I have a hunch that there might be a miscommunication in this week's homework instructions. My son is quite stressed out by the amount and I'm wondering if you really wanted the kids to do all of the symmetry problems or just choose one or two.*

> *I estimate that it will take him way more than the allotted time per night to complete them all. Could you clarify? Thanks.*
>
> The teacher responded that the child needed to complete only one or two of the problems, as the parent had suggested.

PROBLEM: Homework overload

EXAMPLE: Nightly homework of more than ten minutes per grade level or more than you've decided is reasonable for your child

GOAL: To get the teacher to reduce the amount, at least for your child, to a level your family can live with

PROBLEM-SOLVING STEPS

1. Send the teacher an e-mail asking to meet to discuss homework. If your child has multiple teachers, you have a few options: You could ask to meet with each one individually, all of them at once (this is actually easiest if you have the courage to face a group), just the worst offender, or the person most likely to change policy. Your e-mail could go something like this:

> *It was nice meeting you at Back-to-School night. Sam has been telling us how much she likes her new teacher; it wasn't hard for us to see why. It was also good for us to hear about your homework policy. We'd like to come in and talk to you about it as soon as possible. Just to give you a heads-up, homework is causing a lot of stress in our home and we'd like to sit down with you and figure out a way that we can alleviate it. We look forward to having an open discussion with you.*

2. At the meeting, discuss what your child's homework is doing to

your family and press the teacher to find a solution. Since this is the most important homework conversation you're likely to have, be sure to cover any circumstances that affect how much time you're willing to devote to homework (whether you're a single parent, there are siblings, you work a night job, etc.). You might also want to touch on your child's schedule: what time she arrives home, what time she goes to bed, and all the things she needs and wants to do in between, including play, physical activity, and socializing with family and friends. Many teachers—especially those without children of their own—just don't understand the time crunch the average family faces each night. Of course, this is also the time to explain your own feelings about homework. If you haven't sorted them out, it's best to do so before you sit down to talk.

> PARENT: Sam's been really excited about some of the things you've been doing this year, especially your unit on Egypt. But that's not what I've come here to talk about today. I see you're doing a lot of innovative things in your class, but there's one thing that's a little problematic and I wanted to bring it to your attention.
>
> TEACHER: Oh, what's that?
>
> PARENT: Well, the amount of homework that Sam's getting is causing a lot of stress for her and for our entire family, mainly because it's taking so much time each night.
>
> TEACHER: Well, it's only supposed to take thirty minutes, since she's in third grade and that's how much I assign. Of course, it's going to take some kids more, and some kids less. But that's my general goal. Sometimes, I also assign long-term projects, but I try to give plenty of time so that they aren't too onerous.

[If your goal in this conversation is to draw the line at thirty minutes—or whatever the teacher says the homework is supposed to take—then you can continue the conversation like this:]

PARENT: Well, it's taking Sam way more than thirty minutes each night. If it were limited to thirty minutes, that would be fine. So if that's your goal, perhaps we can talk about how to keep it to that.

TEACHER: As I said, it's thirty minutes, give or take.

PARENT: Well, if it's supposed to take thirty minutes, would it be okay if we told her, "Do whatever you can for thirty minutes— work hard for thirty minutes—and then stop." That would work well for Sam. I've noticed that's Sam's upper limit and anytime she works longer than thirty minutes, it's not worth it because she completely loses her focus and her ability to do things she already knows how to do.

TEACHER: Sure, draw the line. That's fine with me.

[If your goal is to reduce the amount of homework even more for your child, then you can continue the conversation like this:]

PARENT: I understand that thirty minutes is standard for a third-grader, but I want to let you know what life is like at our house on a typical night. I pick up Sam and her little brother from their after-school program at 5:30 on my way home from work. She's supposed to start her homework at afterschool, but that never happens because all she wants to do is play after a long day of sitting, and she wouldn't be able to concentrate on it anyway. We get home about six, and that leaves just two hours until her bedtime at eight to get through dinner, bath, stories, and playing with her brother. There's literally no time for thirty minutes of homework. And at least in Sam's case, by the time I get her to sit down, focus, and do the work, it adds up to way more than a half hour.

TEACHER: I give out the homework packet on Wednesday to provide families with a lot of flexibility. Perhaps she could do most of it on the weekend.

PARENT: Maybe that would work for some families, but it doesn't work for us. We have lots of other things to do on the weekends, including activities with our younger child. As I'm sure you know, we can't leave Sam home alone to do her homework, so any assignment really affects the whole family. Last weekend, for example, we were really looking forward to spending the day together, especially since our weekdays are so rushed. But my husband had to stay home with Sam so she could work while I went to the park with her little brother. When she couldn't go, she cried and cried. The homework took more than two hours and the whole thing ended up ruining our entire day.

TEACHER: Well, that's too bad. But homework is really important.

PARENT: I understand that the homework is important to you. But it's taking the joy out of learning for Sam and causing her— and us—a lot of stress. I've read some research that says that there's little correlation between homework and academic achievement in elementary school. So I'm not sure it's worth all the anxiety and frustration we're experiencing.

TEACHER: I'm sorry that she's so anxious. She's such a good student in school.

PARENT: I'm glad to hear that and we really want to keep it that way. But at the end of a long school day, she's just had it. So this is just not working for Sam. I've thought hard about it, and this is what I'd like to suggest: I'd like Sam to be able to sit down and do what she can each night before she loses her focus and enthusiasm. Some nights that might be thirty minutes and some nights it might be five. But when the homework starts to have a negative effect on her, I'd like to stop her and write a note to you saying that she did her best.

TEACHER: I guess that's okay. But it's going to affect her final marks.

PARENT: Would you consider evaluating her on what she does as opposed to what she doesn't? That way, we can still encourage her to have some balance, and it won't negatively affect her grades and self-esteem?

TEACHER: I'll think about it.

When Teachers Raise Objections

Often, your child's teacher will express concerns of her own, some of which you hadn't expected. The following scenarios might help prepare you:

WHAT TO SAY WHEN . . . THE TEACHER BELIEVES PARENTS SHOULD BE HIGHLY INVOLVED WITH HOMEWORK

TEACHER: I expect parents to help. I think it shows the child that you value education.

PARENT: We show Sasha that we value education in lots of ways— from reading to having conversations at dinner. Of course, I'm happy to help occasionally. But being a teacher is not a role that works well for me. I'm not qualified to teach, and I don't feel comfortable doing it. Plus, it changes the dynamic between me and my child in a very negative way. That's why I'm so glad he has you as a teacher.

You could also add:

PARENT: We also want Sasha to be an independent learner. Helping him with homework has the exact opposite effect and could set up a pattern that will only have to be broken later.

WHAT TO SAY WHEN . . . THE TEACHER SAYS NO ONE ELSE IS COMPLAINING

> TEACHER: No one else is complaining about homework. Maybe the problem is actually something else. Let's figure out what's going on with Ella. Does she have a quiet place to do homework? Does she do it at the same time each night?
>
> PARENT: Yes, she does. But I think it's a bigger problem than that. I'm surprised you haven't gotten other complaints. I've been hearing a lot of grumbling at the bus stop in the morning and several of—
>
> TEACHER [interrupting]: I'm not interested in hearing about what you hear at the bus stop. I have an open-door policy and any parent can come in here anytime if they're having a problem.
>
> PARENT: The only reason I mentioned that other parents are grumbling is because you say you haven't heard from them. I'd think you'd want to know what the perception out there is. If it were me, I'd certainly want to know. But you're right. It doesn't matter what other parents are saying. The truth is, it's not working for my child and that's what I'd like to figure out how to fix.

WHAT TO SAY WHEN . . . THE TEACHER SAYS THAT THE PROBLEM ISN'T THE HOMEWORK LOAD, IT'S AN EMOTIONAL ISSUE (AND YOU'RE SURE IT'S NOT)

> TEACHER: No one else is complaining about homework. I've noticed that Jessie seems anxious about her schoolwork and it might be helpful if I referred her to the school counselor. Maybe she has an emotional issue that's interfering with her ability to do her work.
>
> PARENT: Thanks for your concern and please don't think we're being dismissive of it. But we really believe that Jessie is anxious because

there's just too much expected of kids these days. Sure, plenty of kids can handle the pressure, but plenty are not yet ready for it. We feel pretty confident that when the work expected of Jessie is more in line with what a kid her age can do, that she'll be able to do it without much trouble.

WHAT TO SAY WHEN . . . THE TEACHER SAYS NO

If despite your Herculean efforts and charm, the teacher remains unmoved and inflexible, what do you do? We suggest making one last effort to reopen the conversation like this:

PARENT: Maybe I'm not expressing myself well enough here. Bear with me while I try again. Jane is feeling really anxious, she's spending way too much time on homework, and it's having a negative impact on our whole family [or whatever your concerns are]. I'm worried it's starting to give her a really negative attitude about education in general. Isn't there something we can come up with to help her? What's happening now just isn't working for my child.

TEACHER: Well, now that you put it that way, let's put our heads together and come up with a solution.

WHAT TO SAY WHEN . . . THE TEACHER STILL SAYS NO

Then you have to realize you can't change everyone. At least you've tried. Next, you should take up the matter with the appropriate person in the school hierarchy. You don't need to tell the teacher what you plan to do; it's too combative and she will probably expect it in any case. But since she'll be interacting with your child for several hours each day, try to have a pleasant parting.

PARENT: So let me make sure I'm understanding you correctly. What I'm hearing is that even though the homework is causing a lot of trouble for Erica, you're not prepared to make any changes for her at this point.

TEACHER: Yes. I hold the students to high standards and I expect every one of the students in my class to do all the work. It's only fair.

PARENT: Okay, I'm disappointed that we weren't able to do something to make Erica's experience more positive in school and lessen her anxiety. [Pause here because this comment might actually re-engage the teacher. After all, she doesn't want an unhappy student in her class. But if she doesn't respond, say:] Thank you for your time.

CASE STUDY #4: FINALLY TAKING ACTION

When Gwen, the mother of a public school third-grader from Oakland, California, took our survey in December 2005, her frustration practically jumped off the page—so much so that Sara, one of the authors of this book, decided to call her and see if she could help. As Gwen wrote, "My son is in school 6.5 hours a day learning academics. Life has more to teach than math and reading. I wish school would allow kids time to learn about love, family, playing, and imagination, not to mention allowing downtime to integrate what they've learned during the day. Homework invades the boundaries of family life to an excruciating degree! School doesn't take into account that many kids have after-school activities that they choose and when you add homework on top of that, there's no time left in the day for friends or family. I resent spending the precious few moments a day that I have with my son struggling over homework that, quite honestly, is usually boring and rote."

Although Gwen was obviously fuming, she still had not approached the teacher to express her dissatisfaction—until she talked to Sara, that is. She wasn't sure what to do or whether her concerns were valid. "Our discussion raised my awareness and my thoughts became clear," she says. "At the beginning of the school year, we'd been told to expect only thirty minutes of homework a night. But my son was being assigned thirty minutes of homework, plus thirty minutes of reading, plus questions on that reading. Altogether, it was taking more than an hour and fifteen minutes each night—and that was just too much."

So when Gwen met with her son's teacher, she calmly told her how much time all her son's assignments added up to. At first, the teacher's only response was that the homework and the assigned reading were both really important. Yet, on Sara's advice, Gwen pressed on, saying, "But it's just too much for my son. Isn't there anything we can cut down on?" The results: Gwen's personal appeal swayed the teacher, who replied, "Well, the reading is extremely important so I really want him to concentrate on that. But if the rest of the homework is taking too much time, you can make your own decision." All it had taken was one conversation to align their priorities. Gwen just wished she had done it sooner.

What Gwen didn't realize was what a big effect her concerns had had on the teacher. "Interestingly, from then on, the nonreading part of the homework has been really minimal." Although, during their meeting, the teacher never let on that she was going to change the amount of homework she assigns to the whole class, she did just that. Now instead of assigning four worksheets, she assigns just one. These days, Gwen says, her son has plenty of time to "ride his bike, skateboard, play on stilts, climb trees, build Legos with his brother, play dragons, wrestle with his dad when he comes home from work—and do math and logic puzzles, which he loves."

Gwen came away from this experience feeling empowered and confident. "I now plan to talk with teachers every year about homework, and to educate other parents, too. I'm developing a structure for managing homework and not losing my son to busy-ness. My husband struggles with working too much and is away from our family more than he'd like. I don't want my kids to think that's the way life has to be."

Say Thank You—No Matter What

We know we don't have to tell you this, but after any meeting with the teacher, don't forget to say thank you when you leave and send a follow-up e-mail or note. If you had a great exchange, it's always a good idea to acknowledge it. If you came to some kind of agreement, it's important to reiterate it. And even if nothing good came out of your meeting, you should still express appreciation for the teacher's time. Here are a few examples:

> *Thanks for meeting with us yesterday. We're happy to know that Olivia is active and engaged in your class, and that you were so open to discussing the homework situation. We are extremely satisfied with the solution that, from now on, Olivia will work on her homework for twenty minutes each night, and whatever is unfinished will remain unfinished. Again, we really appreciate your time, your concern, and your willingness to reach a satisfying resolution. We look forward to the rest of the year.*

> *Thanks so much for meeting with us this morning. Although we're disappointed that we don't see eye to eye, we very much appreciated the chance to sit down and chat with you. We think it's very important to keep the lines of communication open and we look forward to revisiting this issue again in the not-too-distant future.*

The Last Resort: Reducing the Homework Load Yourself

Sometimes it just isn't possible to get the teacher (or her supervisors) to make the changes you believe are necessary for your child. This can be truly upsetting. But even if you've gone through all the proper channels to no avail, you can still take action to help your child.

After years of successfully persuading teachers to reduce their children's homework loads and make other changes, coauthor Sara and her husband, Joe, ran into an impasse a few years ago when one teacher just wouldn't budge. Their middle school daughter was overwhelmed with at least twice the nationally recommended amount of homework, and Sara and Joe were surprised and disappointed when one of the teachers couldn't—or wouldn't—agree to even one strategy to alleviate some of the burden.

So they took matters into their own hands. They examined their child's assignments, decided what was valuable, and eliminated the rest. They made their decision knowing that the teacher might be annoyed, and she was. Although she didn't take it out on their child in class, she did lower her grades. Still, Sara and Joe much preferred the teacher's annoyance and a lower grade to the alternative: their daughter's life being ruled by homework.

Did their child's intellectual development suffer? Of course not. And both their children learned a great deal about taking a principled stance, a quality that they have embraced in their own lives.

We want to emphasize that most of the time teachers want to help. But if you've walked out of your last meeting without a satisfactory solution, you might feel you have no choice but to take unilateral action and cut the homework yourself. Of course, you have to inform the teacher. You might want to write something like this:

> *Thank you for meeting with us the other day. We really appreciate the time you took with us and we were happy to have such an open discussion. We are truly disappointed that we could not come to a solution that would meet both your needs for uniformity in the classroom and those of our family to have some time where we can do what we choose, without schoolwork being the major focus.*
>
> *We respect your views that you hold the students in your class-*

room to high standards and that you are uncomfortable with allowing students to complete different assignments or different amounts of homework. While we understand your position, we disagree with it. We think it must be extremely difficult to come up with homework assignments that reach every child in the class or that all students can do within a reasonable amount of time.

At this point, we feel we have no choice but to take the step of unilaterally cutting down Laura's homework. We intend to make sure that she does all of the required reading so that she is able to participate in class discussions and any other work she can get done in [X] minutes, but much of her work will not be completed. We hope to do this in a way that doesn't draw attention to Laura and is not disruptive to your class. We know that none of us wants her to be embarrassed or singled out.

We are confident that, even without doing all of the homework assignments, Laura will gain all the skills necessary to be successful and happy in school and in life. We would really like to meet with you again after we've tried this for a month to discuss this more. Hopefully, at that time, we can come to an understanding of what works for both you and for Laura. Thanks again for your time and consideration, and we'll do our best to make the process as painless as possible for all of us.

CASE STUDY #5: A SMALL RISK WITH HUGE BENEFITS

"I didn't really want to rock the boat or single out my child," says Deborah, a mother of two children in public school in Arlington, Virginia. While she was upset by the heavy homework load her second-grader sat down to each night, she wasn't sure whose problem it was or what to do about it. As she explains, "I wondered who was at fault: my child, me, the teacher?" She was determined to approach the teacher, but wondered about the possible repercussions: "If I challenged her too much, would there be retaliation? Or if I needed a favor, such as wanting a particular teacher the next year, would it be payback time?" Still, she decided she had to take a stand, so as her first step, she wrote to the teacher:

> I am writing to ask you and the other second-grade teacher to reevaluate how much homework you require your students to do each week. The usual homework workload is too much for second-graders. And there is research to back up what I am seeing firsthand.
>
> Is there a big difference in the benefit of having the children do reading, writing, math, and spelling every night compared to every other day or so? Please let me know if there is. Too much homework makes children hate school, decreases all-important playtime for this age (particularly since they only get one very short recess at school), cuts into family time, and limits other types of learning activities.
>
> I have asked the PTA to hold a program to explain the school's policy on homework, how much homework we can expect our children to have at each grade level, and the reasons for that amount of homework. The program will also examine the latest research on homework.
>
> I think you are a wonderful teacher. I would like to hear your comments on this matter. Would you have time to discuss this one day after school?
>
> Deborah

The results: After writing this letter and meeting with the teachers, Deborah was told she could reduce her child's homework load as she saw fit. At the same time, the Arlington school board was examining homework policy for the entire district. With input from Deborah and many other parents, they adopted a brand new—and much saner—policy. Not only have there never been negative consequences for her actions, the benefits have been enormous. "Homework is much more manageable," she says. Deborah moved on to help organize other parents to extend recess in her community's schools and, as this book went to press, the recess campaign ended in victory.

10

Getting the School on Your Side

WORKING TOWARD A SANER HOMEWORK POLICY

If you're like us, you don't want to start at square one again every September. You want to know what to expect concerning your child's homework, you want to know that it's going to be reasonable, you want to know that the school has a policy that it enforces, and you want to know that at least your weekends and vacations are going to be homework-free. You want to know that any work that your children do at home is worth their time and is age appropriate. You want to know that you're not going to have to fight one battle after another—writing notes or meeting with the teacher every single week—to relieve the burden and reclaim your family time.

How are you going to accomplish that? In this chapter, we'll give you a step-by-step guide to changing your school's homework policy or creating a reasonable one if there is none. You can use these same tactics for reinstituting recess, abolishing summer homework, obtaining waivers for standardized tests, or whatever issue concerns you.

Sometimes it's relatively simple. Maybe you live in a community where you can pick up the telephone and call the principal or a school board member, tell them you have a concern, and, next thing you know, it's on the agenda, there's a committee formed, and the problem is addressed and solved. Sound remarkable? That's how public school parents in Arlington, Virginia, handled the issue. Or maybe you live in a community where a new principal lets it be known that he thinks there's a homework problem that needs to be addressed, and you can provide support. That's how a public elementary school in Newton, Massachusetts, reduced the load.

But it's probably not going to be quite so easy. In the pages that follow, we'll show you how to organize other parents and raise the homework issue at your school and at the district level. We'll also give you examples of important changes that other schools and districts have implemented. Some of these new policies are inspiring; others could use improvement. In any case, schools all over the country are tackling the homework problem. Here's how to make sure your school does, too.

Sara, one of the authors of this book, knows from firsthand experience that parents can effect change, even when policy seems ingrained and those in charge seem uninterested. At the private school her children attended in Brooklyn, New York, the homework policy allowed teachers to assign twice the recommended ten minutes per grade, but there was nothing to stop them from assigning even more, and there was little coordination among them. So each year, Sara and her husband, Joe, would e-mail, call, and meet with individual teachers with the immediate goal of reducing the work. In addition, once a year they'd also meet with the school's policy makers, such as the elementary or middle school division head or head of school, to encourage them to reexamine their homework policy in general.

There was lots of research that homework was not as valuable as everyone claimed. Yet the administrators responded that so much homework was assigned because the school was "rigorous" and parents demanded and expected it. The administrators often told Sara and Joe that they were a minority of two, and that they should find a school more aligned with their own philosophy.

Since every other school in the area had the same attitude about homework, this wasn't really an option. Plus, Sara and Joe knew they weren't the only parents feeling this way. Everywhere they went, other parents groused about homework—openly or in whispers. As someone who had spoken up against injustice from the time she was a teenager, and who, as an attorney, had successfully freed several innocent clients from prison and won a pardon from the governor for a battered woman client, Sara was not satisfied to leave things as they were.

Inspired by the success of another mother who had organized a group that pressured the school to develop more services for kids with learning issues, Sara decided to pull together a group of parents to push the school to change its homework policy. At the first meeting, several parents showed up who had, at one time or another, also been told that they were the only parents who had expressed concerns about homework. They set a goal of pressing the school to have an open discussion about homework. At about the same time, Sara's son, Julian, the president of the middle school student council, became fed up with the hours of work he was doing each night. He easily organized his fellow eighth-graders to sign a petition requesting a forum for the students to discuss homework, and within days their request was granted.

It wasn't nearly as easy to schedule a similar homework forum for the parents. The request had to come through the Parents Association (PA), a group that seemed to set its agenda months in advance and whose leaders seemed reluctant to raise such a thorny issue. After repeated requests, the PA finally put homework on the agenda. Knowing that this was their big opportunity, Sara and her group reached out to every parent they knew and packed the meeting. The full house sent a clear message: Homework was not the concern of just a few disgruntled parents.

Parent after parent spoke passionately about how homework was killing their kids' love of learning and school, and how their children were dropping outside activities, fighting with their families, and becoming a little less well rounded every day. Sara's coauthor, Nancy, also a parent at the school, was at the meeting, too. Her daughter, an eighth-grade honors student, was buried under four to five hours of homework each night. Even more alarming than the stress this caused the whole family was the fact that her daughter had started to say that she hated school every single day. Normally not one to speak up, Nancy felt she had to share her distress and despair at this statement. When she did, the middle school director looked even more worried than he had before. Now that she and other parents of honors students were publicly speaking up, he could no longer pretend that homework overload was just an issue with struggling students. When even good students start to hate school, something is wrong.

Faced with this flood of parent concern, the school administrators agreed to solicit more comments from parents, create a homework task force, and hold more meetings. In the meantime, they encouraged parents to take up current complaints with their children's teachers. Many parents walked out feeling that a lot had been accomplished—and it had. But Sara knew this was not the time to let up. Her group organized other parents to send in their comments to the school administration and many of the members volunteered to be on the school's task force—an offer that was uniformly ignored.

As the year began to wind down with no further word, the group repeatedly requested the promised follow-up meeting until it was finally scheduled. There, the school unveiled its new homework policy. It included many of the stipulations that Sara and the other parents had been requesting individually over and over for years. The school appointed a curriculum coordinator to monitor homework levels across subjects, abolished vacation homework, limited weekend homework, got rid of Monday tests, restricted major tests to two per week (never on the same day), established more study hall time, stated that major assignments must be scheduled in advance, and made teachers accountable for the kind of homework they assigned. There was no mention of reducing the nightly amount of homework, something that Sara knew would have to be taken up again the next school year. But the following September, when she read the new homework policy printed in the student handbook, the school had reduced the nightly amounts significantly. It was still too much. But it was a major victory.

Other parents around the country have made similar strides at all types of schools, and you can, too. All you need is some courage, some planning, and some help from other parents.

Putting Together Your Wish List of Policy Changes

Before you can make changes to the way your school handles homework, you have to figure out exactly what changes you want. One thing's for sure: If your school doesn't have a homework policy, it's absolutely essential to establish one. Otherwise, no one will be held accountable for sticking to the changes. As homework researcher Harris Cooper says, "You have to permit flexibility. But what the policy does is chop off the extremes by communicating to teachers that they are not to overdo it."

That said, the rest is up to you. You'll find several excerpts from policies below and more in "Tools for Homework Reform" at the end of this book. You can also find out the latest homework news and what parents are doing around the country at stophomework.com.

When thinking about revamping your own school's policy, don't be afraid to be ambitious. Even if you don't achieve everything you want the first time around, you'll have established a benchmark, and the next time you might succeed in moving the bar further. And it's always possible you'll get what you ask for.

Here are some provisions you might want to consider requesting. All of them appear in actual policies around the country, except for one recommendation of our own in italics. To check out the precise wording used in some admirable policies from around the country, see the Sample Homework Policies at the end of this book.

- No homework before middle school.
- Homework should not exceed ten minutes per night per grade level.
- Differentiate assignments to meet students' needs and students' available resources as appropriate.
- No weekend, school break, or summer vacation homework.
- No tests after a holiday or school break, *or on any Monday.*
- Reading should be paramount. (In Newton, Massachusetts, for example, all assignments revolve around reading. In the younger grades, parents are asked to read to their children. As students get older, reading assignments take priority over any other.)
- Appoint a homework coordinator.
- Schedule major assignments in advance to allow for more student planning.
- Avoid assignments that require adult help.
- No grading of homework.
- Assign homework only when you feel the assignment is valuable. A night off is better than homework that serves no useful purpose.
- There will be two weeks a year where homework is suspended and students are encouraged to read. (A school in New Brunswick, Canada, instituted this policy after a trial run in 2006.)

IT'S A START

Some schools have made small changes, rather than sweeping ones, to bring a little relief and balance back into their students' lives. Here are a few examples:

NO-HOMEWORK WEDNESDAYS

At Tenacre Country Day School, which serves K–6 students in Wellesley, Massachusetts, assignments are never given on Wednesdays, leaving the night free for families to spend as they wish. "Everyone takes a breath in the middle of the week," says Chris Eliot, the head of the school. "Parents know that they don't have to be hounding their children about homework. It eases the teachers' load as well. And we've noticed no reduction in the quantity, quality, or rigor of our curriculum."

NO-HOMEWORK WEEKENDS

The Castilleja School in Palo Alto, California, prides itself on providing "a rigorous college preparatory education for young women in grades six through twelve." But that rigor was causing many students a lot of anxiety. So when Denise Clark Pope, the founder of Stressed Out Students (SOS), a program affiliated with Stanford University's School of Education, offered to help, they readily agreed. Working with students, parents, teachers, and administrators, SOS assists middle and high schools in coming up with an action plan to reduce academic pressure and develop healthier attitudes toward homework, among other things. After going through the program, administrators carved out five homework-free weekends a year, plus an additional weekend for seniors. Tests can't be scheduled and projects and essays can't be due until the Wednesday following a homework-free weekend.

NO-HOMEWORK VACATIONS

After complaints from parents and school counselors, and after see-ing more students than ever suffering from stress-related illnesses, Needham High School, a public school in Needham, Massachusetts, has been experimenting with ways to take the pressure down a couple of notches, says principal Paul Richards. They've eliminated all homework during Thanksgiving and Spring Break, as well as on religious holidays, and reduced the number of required books for summer reading. Once a year, the town also celebrates "Needham Unplugged," a night where schools assign no homework and all reli-gious, sports, civic, and government groups agree to forgo activities, explains Jon Mattleman, the founder and director of the Needham Youth Commission.

Enlisting the Parents in Your Child's Class

Here's an easy way to start getting the homework problem noticed at your school. The very next time you're irked, e-mail or call a few—or more—of the parents from your child's class and find out if they're irked, too. Chances are, they're also fuming over those fifty long-division prob-lems. If five of you (or even two, for that matter), register a complaint with the teacher, perhaps she'll reexamine the kinds of assignments she sends home in general.

If you don't have time to call other parents, here's an e-mail you could send, based on one written by a New York City mother of a third-grader attending public school:

Dear Fellow Third-Grade Parents,
    I would really appreciate any feedback at all you can give me and my husband about the following homework issue.

The assignment that requires writing a paragraph for each spelling word is, for us, so burdensome that it is affecting our precious family time together as well as what we consider to be essential time for James to unwind and relax after a very busy week. It is taking us literally hours to complete. I think that many of us (myself included) might be reluctant to speak out for fear of putting our kids in a bad light or being regarded as a whiny parent. But I feel a need to break at least my own silence.

I would love James to learn how to write a paragraph properly, but I feel that this should happen in the classroom, not at home. Creative writing is hugely important not only for future academic success but also for the sheer enjoyment of language. How sad it would be for this early experience with writing to diminish or even kill that joy!

This is not a criticism of Ms. Smith, who strikes me as lovely and genuine. I'm sure she's been taught to use these methods, and other teachers might well give the same assignment. But that doesn't mean that it's helpful or of educational value. My understanding— which may not be correct—is that the curriculum is mandatory but that teachers have some discretion when it comes to homework assignments. Perhaps if enough of us asked her to ease up on this a bit, she would be open to it.

Anyone else have thoughts on this? Please feel free to respond either to the group or just to me if that's more comfortable. Thanks for your input.

Best regards,
Kris

The result: Although it was difficult opening up to other parents, this mother was rewarded. A few parents responded. But even better, her letter started a buzz about the homework overload in this class. By Christmas, several parents refused to have their kids do the holiday homework. By the spring, the teacher had cut back considerably.

Often, galvanizing just a few other parents to add their voices to yours will be enough to make the teacher rethink her personal homework policy—at least temporarily. Unfortunately, the effects can be short-lived. So you might have to repeat this step every month or two until it sticks.

If you want to create a more permanent change that will help your child this year and beyond, you have to employ the same strategy on a larger scale. Your goal: to change the school policy or create one where none exists.

Two's Company, Three's a Committee

In order to make an impression on the school administration or school board, it can be useful to form a committee. It gives your concerns credence, and when you name yourselves something like "The Parents Coalition for Homework Reform," it commands more respect.

The first step is to reach out beyond your circle of friends and find other parents at the school who are upset about the homework situation. These other parents might not be aware of the research on homework (although you'll definitely tell them). But almost every parent has some homework complaint, so your meeting will probably be well attended. And once parents hear that the beliefs they've always held about homework are based on smoke and mirrors, they will likely be even more upset and want to take action.

Remember: There is strength in numbers. But the numbers don't have to be large. If you end up with six or seven parents on your committee, that's more than enough.

To begin, you have to take a leadership role. Does your school allow nonsanctioned school groups to meet at the school? If yes, reserve a room, set a date and time, and send out an e-mail or flyer announcing your meeting. If you're not allowed to meet on school grounds, do you have room in your house to host an untold number of people? If yes, great. If not, choose a local gathering spot—the playground, coffee shop, or community center. If you're meeting in a place you don't have to reserve, you can be a lot more flexible about the date and time.

To spread the word about scheduling a meeting, you could send out an e-mail and post a flyer like the ones that follow. Note: Some schools have strict policies regarding the use of their e-mail list. Familiarize yourself with the rules before you make a faux pas. If you have just a few e-mail addresses, don't worry. E-mail has a way of being passed from person to person.

Many schools also have rules about posting flyers on school bulletin boards. If you can't post yours (or even if you can), pass it out at the bus stop, the playground, outside the school grounds, or the local coffee shop. You can even get your kids to help.

Dear Fellow Parent,

Do you know these facts about homework? A review of more than 180 homework studies reveals that there is little correlation between homework and achievement in elementary school, and only a moderate correlation in middle school. Even in high school, research shows that too much homework is counterproductive.

So why are our kids overloaded with homework each night?

I'm interested in getting a group of parents together to talk about homework and take some kind of action. If you're interested in attending a meeting, please send me an e-mail, and let me know which of the following dates and times work best for you. [Suggest a few possibilities here, and be sure to include both early-morning and evening options.]

If you can't attend a meeting but would like to help in some

other way, or if you have any thoughts you'd like to share, please let
me know that as well.

Thanks and please forward this e-mail to any other parent you
know in the school. I have only a limited list of e-mail addresses.

Best,
Lucinda

To create a flyer, you can use the same text as the e-mail. Just don't forget to include a contact address, the date, time, and place of the meeting, and a big bold headline (such as "What Do You Think About Homework?") to catch people's attention.

Another way to gather parents together is to stand up at Back-to-School Night, a PTA meeting, or any other well-attended function, and say something like this:

Hi, I'm Sara and I have two children in this school, a son in the
eighth grade and a daughter in the fifth. I'm really concerned
about the amount of homework I'm seeing this year. My kids seem
overburdened and burnt out, and I'm not happy about it. I'm
interested in forming a parent committee on homework to see how
other parents are feeling on this issue. I don't know whether my
opinion is held by most other parents. But, either way, it'd be great
to get a public discussion going. If you're interested in working
with me, please see me after this meeting or sign up on a sheet
I left at the door.

The next step is to confirm the date and time of the meeting. You'll want to send out an e-mail like this:

Dear Friend,

You are one of many people who expressed interest in meeting
to talk about homework. The majority of the people who responded

*preferred meeting on [X] date at [X] time. If you can't make it,
please call me or send me an e-mail with any of your concerns so
I can be sure that they're addressed. If you know of anyone else
who might want to attend the meeting, please pass on this e-mail.
I look forward to seeing you.*

Regards,
Michael

GETTING YOUR COMMITTEE GOING

The first meeting is always important. This is where you'll meet people you'll be working with and figure out who's going to do what. You'll want to be organized but at the same time you have to be flexible. You should run the first meeting, though that doesn't mean you have to be in charge forever. If someone steps up who is a better organizer—or speaker or note taker or petition writer—delegate, delegate, delegate.

Just as important, consider the politics in your community. Should you make a courtesy call to the head of the PTA or school board to solicit her advice and support? Are you the person who should phone her—or does someone else in your group have a better connection? Making the most of personal relationships will help smooth the way for you.

WHAT TO PREPARE

1. **A copy of your school's homework policy.** Find out if your school has a policy and, if so, be sure to bring a copy with you.

2. **A fact sheet.** Now that you've read this book, you're an expert on the topic. But for those who aren't as well versed, bring along a fact sheet detailing all the research on homework. To make it easy, you can copy the

one in Tools for Homework Reform. Make sure to add your contact information at the bottom.

3. **An agenda.** This is optional. But most people like to know what they're going to discuss and it will help keep the meeting on track. The three main items should be an introduction, a discussion of the problem, and planning for future action.

RUNNING THE MEETING

Briefly introduce yourself and have everyone else do so as well. Then say a little about your family's problem, mention a few key bits of the research, and propose how you'd like to change things. Try to come across as measured, thoughtful, and focused. Limit your remarks to two or three minutes (you'd be surprised at how much you can say without rushing in that amount of time). You could say something like this:

> *Both my children are working way harder than I think is healthy and they don't have enough time to pursue their own interests anymore. I also see way more homework being assigned in fifth grade this year than when my son was in the same grade three years ago, so I have a feeling that it's been ratcheted up. I've done a lot of reading on the subject and I've brought along a fact sheet outlining a lot of the important research. In case you haven't had a chance to read it, the highlight is that studies show that most homework has very little value, teachers don't study homework in their training programs, and depending on what grade your kid is in, homework can even be detrimental to learning and achievement. Every year, this school gives a workshop for parents on how to manage homework. But, as far as I know, and even though I've requested one*

several times, there has never been a workshop to discuss how par-
ents feel about homework and how it's working for them and their
children. So one of the things I hope this committee will want to do
is push the school to look at its policy and change it.

Next, open up the meeting to discussion (otherwise known as Vent-ing Time). Sara discovered that parents who showed up at her ad hoc homework committee wanted to spend a lot of time sharing their frustrations about the workload and the school. While she sometimes felt eager to move the meeting along and figure out a plan of action, it was important for everyone to have a chance to talk about what was bothering them. You'll probably find that many parents have been feeling all alone in their homework woes. So be prepared for your committee to act as a de facto support group. This is exactly what you want. If people feel more connected, they'll be more willing to work together. Be patient while they tell their tales.

PREPARING A PLAN OF ACTION

The big question: What will your committee do about all this? As a group of parents, you don't have the power to change the school's homework policy. Your mission is to convince those who *do* have the power that it's a change many parents want and that they should want it as well.

If your school already has a good homework policy, but the teachers haven't been following it, you need to prompt them to do so. Most of the time, all this involves is getting a small group of parents to meet with the principal (or whoever is in charge of the policy) to present evidence that the policy has been violated and to *gently* remind the school why it should be enforced.

If your school has a bad homework policy (or has no policy at all), you'll want to get homework on the agenda at the next PTA or school board meeting, and/or arrange a homework forum where parents can speak out at your school. Or, if there's one person in your school who can implement change on her own (say, the principal), then start by meeting with her.

Either way, you'll need volunteers for a few tasks. You could give your committee a head start by doing a few of these before you even meet. Otherwise, get started now.

ACTION STEPS

1. **Look at other homework policies.** Then decide as a committee which elements you'd like to see in your school's policy. This way, you'll be informed and can say with confidence that other schools have adopted what you desire.

2. **Assemble the evidence.** Solicit stories of homework overload from parents, do a simple survey, or ask parents to keep a homework log for a week (we'll get to all the how-tos in a moment).

3. **Launch a letter and telephone campaign.** Get your committee members (and all their friends) to inundate school officials with a flood of homework concerns and what you'd like to see in your school's policy. It's really important that other parents, the class parent, the parent representative to the Parent Teacher Association, the PTA president, teachers, administrators, school psychologists and guidance counselors, school board members, and anyone else you can think of know that homework is a hot topic that needs to be discussed ASAP. You can be working at many different levels at once—from the most local (the teacher) to the broadest (the school board).

Here are two notes for inspiration, the first from an elementary school parent to the members of a public school board, the other from a middle school parent to a private school principal:

Dear School Board Members,

I'm writing to let you know that we feel completely overwhelmed by homework these days and that it's really taking a toll on our family and our child. By the time Hannah, my third-grader, gets home from afterschool, it's 5:45. We have dinner at 6:00 and her bedtime is at 8:00. Add in bathtime and her bedtime routine—which includes reading and singing—and you can see that there's no time for anything else but homework. In the little time we have with Hannah during the evening, we'd much rather be doing things of our own choosing than prodding her through an array of worksheets. I think it's time for the school board to reexamine this district's homework policy. It's been five years since it was last revised and it's not too soon for the community to have this discussion.

> *Sincerely,*
>
> *Joseph*

Dear Principal,

Our family experience with homework has been one of great frustration and overwhelming exhaustion in the form of stress and sleep deprivation. If I am painting a dramatic picture, it is only because homework has become a "dirty word" in our home. Our lives revolve around how much homework comes home every night. On most nights, Sienna, our seventh-grader, must begin her homework in the car on the drive home. After a quick supper, she is banished to a quiet area where she must struggle with anywhere from three to five hours of work per night. As parents, we are the taskmasters that must keep her focused on her work. We are the homeschooling instructors who must be available to help her through the difficult assignments. We are the sounding boards, reviewers, and editors of her finished work. Half of our weekends are occupied with work or studying for upcoming tests or projects.

Sienna has a passion for acting and she would love to be in the school play but that is not an option if she wants to keep her grades from sliding. My strong belief and indeed my experience is that there simply are not enough hours in the day or night to satisfactorily complete the given assignments, do the required reading and study for tests, and have any time left for downtime and recreation.

Unfortunately, up until now, this has been a closet issue as parents and students alike have been loath to admit that they have a problem handling the workload. I would welcome an open forum and dialogue among parents, teachers, and administrators to address homework. But most important, since homework is work that comes home and includes family involvement outside of the school, I would like to suggest that a homework task force be formed and parents be included. I would volunteer my services to this task force. And, is there something you can do in the interim to relieve the stress in our household?

> *Sincerely,*
> *Kathy*

In addition, get your campaign going by urging other parents to participate by sending an e-mail like this:

Our homework committee has been meeting for the past two months. We've found that homework is a big concern in the community. As a committee, we've decided that it's time for the school to revisit/revise/create a homework policy.

We think it would be really effective if as many parents as possible communicated their feelings on the subject to the adminis-

tration. We're asking for a parents' forum on homework [or a task force or a survey of parents]. Of course, you can ask for whatever you want. But we urge you to make your views known to the principal [or appropriate person]. His e-mail is <principal@aol.com>. It's best if you write your own heartfelt note. But if nothing else, it would be great if you could write something as simple as that you think that there's too much homework and you're looking forward to having a chance to discuss the issue.

If possible, please let me know if you write a letter, so that we can tally the number of parents who have. Thanks for your support.

Even a deluge of form letters will be very effective. If the principal or school board receives fifty letters (probably ten is enough), you can bet they'll address the issue.

4. **Gather signatures on a petition.** If letter writing is too great an effort or if you're told that the agenda of the next PTA or school board meeting is too full to add an item about homework, try a petition. Usually, a long list of signatures on a page, or multiple phone calls from different parents, is enough to make someone respond. (If you still can't get it on the agenda, try standing up at the next meeting during the question-and-answer period and making a brief statement, and then asking for it to be put on the agenda.) Here's a sample petition:

We, the undersigned parents, respectfully request that the issue of homework be placed on the agenda of the next meeting of the school board. We also request that plenty of time be allotted for discussion of this important topic.

_____   _____   _____

Your Name   Your Signature   Date

5. **Create a survey.** Ideally, your child's school would want to survey parents about how much homework their kids are doing and how they feel about it. But if not, or if you don't want to wait until the lumbering bureaucracy gets around to it, it's easy to do a simple survey on your own, and very worthwhile. (You can even post it online. There are several Web sites, such as SurveyMonkey.com, that will walk you through the steps and host your survey at low cost.) People who might not want to stand up at a meeting and admit that homework is a problem in their house will often be happy to fill out an anonymous survey. So it's a useful way to reach more parents than you otherwise might.

Here is a simple but effective survey. We've included three more extensive surveys in the Tools section, including two used by public school districts and one that we created and posted online.

SIMPLE HOMEWORK SURVEY

How much time does your child spend on homework each night? We'd like to know. We're the new Parents Coalition for Homework Reform at this school. Please take the time to fill out the following survey and return it to _____ by Friday. You can remain anonymous. Thanks for your time.

Your name (optional):_____

Your child's age: _____

Your child's grade: _____

Your child's sex:_____

Your child's teacher(s): _____

How much time does your child spend on homework each weeknight (Monday–Thursday)? Please circle the amount listed below. The numbers are in minutes.

   0–10   10–20   20–30   30–40   40–50   50–60   60–75

   75–90   90–105   105–120   120–150   150–180   More than 180

How much total time does your child spend on homework each weekend (Friday–Sunday)? Please circle the amount listed below. The numbers are in minutes.

0–10   10–20   20–30   30–40   40–50   50–60   60–75

75–90   90–105   105–120   120–150   150–180   More than 180

Any additional comments on homework: _____

6. **Ask parents to fill out a homework log.** Request that parents track the amount of time kids spend on assignments for two weeks straight (older kids can fill out the log themselves). Assuming people are honest (some underestimate because they don't like to admit how long homework takes), logs will give you an accurate picture of how long kids are working on an average night. Here's a sample:

HOMEWORK LOG

For the two weeks beginning on October 15 (including Friday, Saturday, and Sunday), please log the number of minutes your child spends on homework each day. And, if you're up for it, please give us a few details about the assignment itself: how many math problems are on the worksheet, how long the reading assignment is, etc.

You may fill out the log anonymously if you wish.

Please write your comments about homework as well. We'd really like to get a sense of how parents are feeling about the work their children are doing.

Thanks for taking the time to do this. Please return this to _____ by November 5.

Your name (optional):_____

Your child's age: _____

Your child's grade: _____

Your child's sex:_____

Your child's teacher: _____

DATE	SUBJECT	TIME SPENT	TYPE OF ASSIGNMENT

Additional comments: _____

Once you have collected the surveys and/or logs and tallied the results, you'll have great anecdotal data to use at any meeting or forum on homework. "This data speaks volumes to teachers and usually results in action to reduce loads," says Mark Wertheimer, vice principal of the Classical Academy in Colorado Springs.

7. **Write a letter to your local paper.** Don't forget the power of the media. If you write a letter to the editor or an op-ed piece for your local newspaper (or simply call the paper and ask them to cover the issue), the school board or administration is going to have to take notice. Here's one of our favorites by Richard Krawiec, a father of two sons from North Carolina, which was published in the *Raleigh News and Observer* on January 2, 2006:

THE HOMEWORK THAT ATE CHRISTMAS BREAK

It has already been a long school year for my eighth grader. Good, but long. He likes his teachers, he's excited about what he's learning, but it has been a year full of so much homework, he has shown signs of burnout. I'd already had to stop his music lessons, cut back on his after school sports, eliminate family game time, prohibit him from visiting with friends, playing on the computer, or watching TV during the school week because there simply wasn't time for him to do anything he wanted. We'd had to cut back our family holiday rituals this past month from forty-five minutes a night to fifteen, so he would have time to finish his schoolwork. He spent so much time on his studies every night he rarely even had one hour for himself. There were days this past semester when he had as little as fifteen minutes to relax before he had to go to bed. I know. I timed him. In one course alone he had forty-two graded assignments the first quarter of the year. That's just in one course. Where the teacher, who had about 140 students, found the time to correct close to six thousand assignments in the first forty-five days of school, I have no idea.

So I was really looking forward to Christmas vacation, when my child could finally get a break, recharge his batteries, relax, play, be a kid again. Truth be told, I was looking forward to getting a little more free time for myself, too. I was exhausted from completing the "assignments" of my own two jobs, cooking meals every day, cleaning the house, doing laundry, squeezing in time to write, and trying to check over my son's homework—which, to be honest, I simply did not have the time or energy to do as thoroughly as I desired. A break for him, would be a break for me, too.

When vacation started, the Friday before Christmas, I asked my son if he wanted to help me bake cookies for the neighbors, an activity we enjoyed doing together every year. "I can't," he said, "I really should get some of this homework done."

"Homework?" I asked, amazed. "On vacation?"

I looked over my son's assignments. He had to read a 300-page book and write a comprehensive thesis essay on it. He had algebra problems to complete. He was assigned to read scores of pages in one of those textbooks that are so dense and boring each page reads as slowly as four pages in a regular book.

Given the speed at which my child reads, writes, and computes, I estimated that he had a good 25–30 hours of work to look forward to on his "vacation."

It's no wonder, I thought, an increasing number of our academically gifted high school students are downloading papers online, reading CliffsNotes instead of novels, cheating on tests and quizzes. At some point, they reach their limit, they decide that there has to be more to life than schoolwork. They decide it is simply not worth throwing away so much of their childhood time doing work for school.

At some point, we need to recognize that children are just that—children. They should be allowed to have a break, too.

The result: After this op-ed was published, Krawiec noted a big decrease in the amount of homework being assigned. "I have no doubt that my op-ed had something to do with it," he says. "Afterwards, the school administration apparently addressed the issue with the teaching staff."

It would be ideal to get all these strategies going at your first meeting. But it's probably not going to happen. By the time parents are finished venting, you might have only enough time left to schedule the next meeting (which you should do right then and there). This is fine. If you've managed to get your group fired up and ready to take action, you've accomplished a lot. You can continue at the next meeting.

FOLLOWING UP AFTER THIS (AND EVERY OTHER) MEETING

Don't forget to send an e-mail to both those who attended and those who expressed interest but didn't. Explain what happened and what's going to happen next. You have to do this every single time. First, it will serve as an important recap of what you've already accomplished and plan to accomplish, a record of who volunteered (so it will hold people accountable), a reminder of the next meeting date, and a newsletter of sorts for those who couldn't make it (so that you don't have to field individual calls or e-mails). It could go something like this:

> Hi Everyone,
>   We had the first meeting of the homework committee today. Several people spoke about their own experiences with homework and it was great to meet so many people in the same boat. We had such a lively and passionate discussion that the time flew by, so it's really important that we get together again soon.
>   We decided we'd meet in two weeks—on March 25 at 7 P.M. at Judy's house. Her address is 33 Main Street.

> *By that date, Linda volunteered to find out the procedure for*
> *getting this issue raised at the next PTA meeting. Juanita volun-*
> *teered to draft a survey so we can assess how the larger community*
> *is feeling about this issue. Gary volunteered to collect examples of*
> *onerous or meaningless homework assignments from other par-*
> *ents. And Karen volunteered to pull together a list of dates on*
> *which different teachers all assigned big projects or tests due at*
> *the same time. If you have any information that would help or*
> *if you'd like to assist them, please contact them directly. Their*
> *e-mail addresses are:*
>
> *Thanks for your interest and I look forward to seeing you at*
> *our next meeting.*
>
> *Best wishes,*
Charles

In addition, always send out another e-mail two or three days before
your next get-together. This not only reminds people of the date but also
gives a final nudge to those who might not have done what they promised. It might read like this:

> *Hi Everyone,*
>
> *This is just a reminder that the homework committee will*
> *meet again this Monday at 7 P.M. at Judy's house (33 Main Street).*
> *Hope to see you there. If you can't make it, but have ideas or*
> *want to volunteer, please let me know.*
>
> *Cheers,*
Lindsay

JUST HOW POWERFUL ARE THE POWERS THAT BE?

Often, school administrators are not as powerful as you might think they are. While they certainly can make things better for your child alone, they might not be in a position to change policy overall. "As a principal, I don't have the autonomy that people think I do," admits one public elementary school principal from Westchester County, New York. "I don't believe in homework in the elementary years, but I have to follow my district's homework policy. The most I can do is take up homework with our school-based council, and then maybe the district will revisit the issue." So be prepared to go to the school board. Luckily, the members are elected officials who represent your community and are supposed to be responsive to residents' concerns. Even better, as a long-term project, try to get yourself, or someone who shares your views, elected to the school board.

Even at private schools, principals are not always all powerful. They and other school administrators are accountable to a board of directors and often conflicting parental demands.

If parents start demanding less homework, both public and private schools will have to respond. But even if public or private school officials agree that the homework policy needs to be modified, chances are they're not going to admit that to you. You can't really expect the administration to confess that the school is handing out too much homework, that the curriculum hasn't been reexamined in twenty-five years, and that the teachers are giving the same tired, ineffectual assignments year after year. Because of these constraints, they might even tell you that you have to live with the current homework load—or leave the school.

But don't despair. Although they might seem indifferent or unwilling to admit that there's a problem, virtually all school administrators do care about the quality of education. As Sara discovered, and as other parents we interviewed reported, a weird thing often happens: Just when you think you've reached an impasse, school administrators suddenly announce they are lightening the homework load. This is because, no matter how unresponsive they might seem, school administrators are often listening, reevaluating, and figuring out how to make changes without appearing to cave in to parent pressure.

Make the Most of a School or School Board Homework Meeting

After all this hard work, there's little doubt that you'll get homework onto the agenda of a schoolwide meeting. To make the most of this occasion, keep the following in mind:

WHAT TO BRING

- As many other parents as possible. (You really have to stack this meeting in order to make a big impression.)
- The results of your homework survey and/or logs.
- Excerpts from other schools' homework policies that you admire (see our selection in Tools for Homework Reform).
- A list of proposed changes to your own school's policy (even better: Write up the language you'd want).
- Your fact sheet on homework research.

ASSIGN ROLES

1. **Plan who's going to speak first.** Or else you might find that no one's willing to step forward when the time comes. If there's too long a pause, the chair might move on to the next agenda item. Your first speaker

should be prepared to touch on as many of the most important points as possible just in case time runs short. That said, the first speaker—and every speaker—should limit her remarks to no more than two minutes.

2. **Figure out who's going to say what.** While all of you will want to talk about the effect homework is having on your individual children, each person might want to cover a topic that she's particularly passionate about. Since every meeting has a limited amount of time, and since there will probably be lines at the microphone, be sure you have your strategy settled in advance. And if you notice that the committee member who was going to cover vacation homework is all the way at the back of the line, you might be sure to mention it, too.

Make Your Case

1. **Keep it short and simple.** People have limited attention spans, so you're better off making a few simple statements and sitting down. If you forget to say something important, don't worry. One of the following speakers will probably cover whatever you missed. But with a little planning you'd be surprised at how much you can cover. Remember to include the following:

- Who you are.
- The idea that everyone shares the same interests—to have bright, happy, successful, well-balanced kids.
- All of the various homework problems you've encountered—too much work, boring work, weekend and vacation work, etc.—and something personal about how homework affects your family or children.
- What you want—a task force, a policy change, a moratorium on homework until the problems can be looked at.

• What you're willing to do to help. Conclude by volunteering to examine the current policy, work on or with a school task force, be part of a focus group, or whatever else needs to be done.

Here's an example of a parent comment that clocks in at under two minutes:

Hi, I'm Sara and I have two children in this school, a son in the eighth grade and a daughter in the fifth. I'm speaking today on behalf of the Parents Coalition for Homework Reform, a group we started a few months ago to deal with the issue of homework at our school. I'm happy to be able to participate in this open forum.

Like everyone—other parents, teachers, and administrators—we care very much about the development of our children and we want them to grow up to be well-rounded adults, intellectually as well as artistically and emotionally. We think all of us in this room share the same goals—where we differ is in our beliefs in how to achieve them.

Personally, we see our own children losing interest in their schoolwork. At this point, the school is expecting them to do twice the amount of homework recommended by the National Education Association and the National PTA. The more that's expected of them, the more we see our children shut down. We don't mean to be unkind or rude, but much of the homework is fairly rote and uninspiring and it takes up most of the little bit of free time they have when they get home from school.

We'd like to see the school examine the type of homework it's giving, see whether it really is valuable, place time limitations on it, and have the teachers coordinate assignments so our children aren't bringing home vast amounts of work from each class. We'd like our children to have some time at the end of the day to sit

down with us as a family, have a leisurely conversation, read a
book of their own choosing, play their music, enjoy their friends,
and do many of the things that all this schoolwork is interfering
with. Paradoxically, we believe that less homework would actually
allow our children to learn much more, and be happier and more
balanced people. We'd also like to encourage the abolishment of
weekend, vacation, and summer homework, so that we can have
some real family time without any school tasks hanging over our
children's heads.

We'd like to suggest you form a task force to look into this issue
further, and that parents with different viewpoints be included.
I'd be happy to volunteer. Thank you.

2. **Practice, practice, practice.** It sounds silly, but the reason many
people feel awkward speaking in public is because they don't get much
chance to do it and they don't practice before they do. It doesn't hurt to
rehearse in front of a mirror at home—a tip many of us give our kids
before they have to give a speech.

3. **Speak from your heart, take a deep breath, and don't talk too
fast.**

One Parent's Story: Going the Distance

Robine Lewis, a mother of three girls in the tenth, seventh, and third
grades in Vista, California, was sick of how homework overload had
taken over her family's life and changed it for the worse. She reported, "I
saw my oldest daughter stop reading for pleasure when she got into high
school because of too much homework. My middle daughter stopped

taking dance classes because of too much homework. And I fight constantly with my youngest daughter to get her to do the homework." For years, Robine had met with her children's teachers countless times, pushing for less homework but never getting lasting results.

When her middle daughter started sixth grade, Robine encouraged several other parents to use their parent-teacher conferences to talk to their children's teachers about the homework problem. "Enough of us complained that the sixth-grade teachers got together, started talking about it, and cut back on the amount. There was a big disconnect on their part: They simply hadn't realized how long their assignments were taking the kids."

Robine knew, however, that homework was not just a teacher problem but "a systemic problem," especially in her school district where there was no written policy at all. So, encouraged, she decided to tackle the issue on a grander scale. She knew one of the school board members from her work on an earlier bond issue and they had discussed the homework issue at length. He agreed to try to get homework on the agenda as one of the school board's goals for the year, and called a special school board meeting in January 2005 to discuss it.

Robine was not afraid of speaking up. "You get three minutes, and often it only takes one loud voice. Luckily, I'm very loud. I'm the squeaky wheel," she says. But she wanted to make sure she made the most of every one of those minutes. So before the meeting, Robine gathered and prepared her thoughts, and scribbled a few notes on a piece of paper. "During the public speech part, I stood up and said that we had to discuss homework. I had done a lot of research and informed them about the ten-minutes-per-grade-level homework rule, as well as some of the other facts I'd discovered. I also told them that my high schooler had dropped her reading and social life, and I could see that resonated with everyone."

But Robine didn't stop there. For the next six months she went to every school board meeting and brought up the homework issue without fail. When other parents were too busy or too shy to attend the meetings with her, she asked them to send her e-mails about their concerns and, with their permission, she read them aloud to the school board as well. Often, Robine was the only parent who even attended. And she'd have to stay until midnight because homework was inevitably placed last on the agenda. "I even ended up missing Back to School Night. I stood up and told the board, 'It stinks that you put homework on the agenda on Back to School Night.' " But she stayed, and when it was finally her turn, she related still more research and stories about homework overload.

At least in part because of Robine's tenacity, in September 2005, more than six months after the initial discussion about homework, the school board took action. It made a commitment to review the district's current homework practices and develop and implement a sound district-wide homework policy during that school year.

At that point, the board created a committee of teachers, administrators, parents, and even students to examine homework and write a policy. Robine, of course, made sure she was one of the parents appointed. But had she not been, she says, she "would have yelled so loud that someone would have put me on the committee." And, if that hadn't worked, she would have attended anyway. "Anyone can go to any committee meeting," she explains. "The problem is knowing when they are and that they even exist."

While some of the teachers wanted to keep the status quo, those teachers who were also parents were more in touch with the homework-overload problem. They decided to look at homework policies from other districts and gather data by designing an Internet survey for parents, students, and teachers. As usual, Robine worked hard to make sure that people in the district knew about it by sending out mass e-mails. Robine also contacted the local newspaper, which had run an article about the homework committee when it was formed, and got the editors to run a follow-up story reminding community members to fill out their surveys.

In addition, after sending the committee chairs several homework policies she'd written herself, Robine was invited to help. "It was easier for them than dealing with me suggesting numerous edits and making constant queries about what was going on. We sat down with photocopies of many different policies and cut and pasted those that we agreed on." Robine even had to sign a confidentiality statement since she was working with the sensitive information contained in the district's survey. The draft they finally hammered out included a commitment to homework quality over quantity, an acknowledgment that family, weekend, and holiday time are important, and a requirement that teachers monitor the time assignments take by asking students and parents how long was spent on them.

In mid-June 2006, as we were going to press with the hardcover edition of this book, the draft policy was presented for the first time at a school board meeting. There, the board publicly stated that no student should be doing homework on holidays such as Thanksgiving. The board also requested that the schools in the district try out the new homework policy during the following school year and mandated that the policy be reviewed at the end of that trial year.

All in all, Robine was pleased with the outcome. "I'm pragmatic enough to recognize that not all battles can be won, so I try to pick the ones that are feasible. The honors students were excluded from some of the protections and the policy strongly discourages holiday homework, but doesn't prohibit it." Her next step will be to organize other parents and students to work on protesting the weaknesses in the draft policy. She also knows that she'll have to stay on top of the homework issue for a long time. As she says, "A policy is no good if the teachers don't follow it and the principals don't enforce it."

Don't Stop Now

As Robine and other parents have learned, keeping homework under control at your child's school doesn't end with one meeting. Even if the school decides to totally revamp its homework policy to your specifications, you will still have to stay on top of the issue to make sure that the policy is being enforced—so don't disband your coalition of parents yet. You'll still want to meet occasionally to monitor the situation and use all the strategies outlined in this chapter if the need arises. In fact, it wouldn't hurt to ask for a yearly meeting to keep the dialogue going so that if the school board, principal, or administration changes, you won't have to start from scratch.

If you get a new policy, but it's less than perfect, congratulate yourself on a partial victory and look at it as a starting point. Once you've opened the discussion and changed people's minds even a little, they are often more receptive to continuing the conversation. So keep lobbying, keep talking, keep at it.

Remember: Over and over again, parents found that even the smallest effort to relieve their children's homework burden paid off. They reduced overall loads, made schools accountable for the quality and coordination of assignments, put an end to punishments for incomplete work, and made sure their kids didn't have to miss recess to finish it. With a little more effort, parents discovered that they could make a real difference, not just for their own kids, but even at the school and district levels.

Let us leave you with one more idea: If every reader of this book pledges to write a note to their child's teacher or to a school administrator on the first Monday of every month, every school will have to admit that this problem is too big to ignore. The truth about homework will finally be out and we'll begin to see real change at schools across the country.

Our children deserve no less.

Tools for
Homework Reform

The Case Against Homework: A Fact Sheet

- According to a 2001 review of more than 120 studies of homework and its effects by Professor Harris Cooper of Duke University, the country's leading homework researcher, and his updated 2006 review of an additional sixty studies, there is very little correlation between the amount of homework and achievement in elementary school and only a moderate correlation in middle school. Even in high school, "too much homework may diminish its effectiveness or even become counterproductive," writes Cooper in his latest research review (Harris Cooper, *The Battle Over Homework,* second edition, page 26, and *Does Homework Improve Academic Achievement? A Synthesis of the Research 1987–2003, the Review of Educational Research* [Spring 2006]).

- Many countries with the highest scoring students on achievement tests, such as Japan, Denmark, and the Czech Republic, have teachers who assign little homework. Meanwhile, countries such as Greece, Thailand, and Iran, where students have some of the worst average scores, have teachers who assign a lot of homework. American students do as much homework as their peers in other countries—if not more—but still manage only to score around the international average (*National Differences, Global Similarities: World Culture and the Future of Schooling* by David P. Baker and Gerald K. LeTendre, Stanford University Press, 2005).

- Most teachers do not take courses specifically on homework during teacher training. In fact, research shows that the great majority are unaware of the research on the problems with homework (Stephen Aloia, "Teacher Assessment of Homework," *Academic Exchange Quarterly* [Fall 2003]). That's why, as Professor Cooper told the authors of *The Case Against Homework,* when it comes to homework, "Most teachers are winging it."

RECOMMENDED HOMEWORK GUIDELINES

- According to Professor Cooper, kids should be assigned no more than ten minutes per grade level per school night (Monday through Thursday only). In other words, this adds up to ten minutes in first grade, twenty minutes in second grade, and so on, up to a maximum of two hours per night in high school (Harris Cooper, *The Battle Over Homework,* second edition, page 26).

- The National Education Association and National Parent Teacher Association recommend no more than ten to twenty minutes of homework per night in grades K through 2, and thirty to sixty minutes per night in grades 3 through 6.

- And some education experts, such as Etta Kralovec, associate professor of teacher education University of Arizona South, and coauthor of *The End of Homework: How Homework Disrupts Families, Overburdens Children, and Limits Learning*, recommend none.

ADDITIONAL INFORMATION

- A 2006 national Scholastic/Yankelovich study found that reading for fun declined sharply after age eight. The number one reason: too much homework.
- Kids between the ages of five and twelve need ten to eleven hours of sleep each night; teens need 9.25 hours. According to the National Sleep Foundation's 2004 Sleep in America Poll, 54 percent of first through fifth graders sleep just 9 to 10 hours each night and 17 percent sleep less than 9 hours. According to the foundation's 2006 poll, 80 percent of teens don't get the recommended amount of sleep. At least 28 percent fall asleep in school and 22 percent fall asleep doing homework (all facts: National Sleep Foundation, *www.sleepfoundation.org*).
- According to a large study by the University of Michigan, family meals are the *single strongest predictor* of better achievement scores and fewer behavioral problems for children ages three to twelve (*Journal of Marriage and the Family*, May 2001).
- According to the American Psychological Association, typical schoolchildren today report more anxiety than did child psychiatric patients in the 1950s (*Journal of Personality and Social Psychology*, December 2000).
- Kids are more sedentary than ever before, and homework is a contributing factor. Since 1981, the amount of time kids spend playing sports has decreased by 58 percent for six- to eight-year-olds, 19 percent for nine- to eleven-year-olds, 43 percent for twelve- to fourteen-year-olds, and 28 percent for fifteen- to seventeen-year-olds (*Changing Times of American Youth: 1981–2003*, Institute for Social Research, University of Michigan, 2004). Since 1980, the number of overweight children in the United States has tripled, according to a 2004 report by the Centers for Disease Control (CDC). Even since 2000, there's been a significant increase: 17.1 percent of American kids under age nineteen are now considered overweight (*Journal of the American Medical Association*, June 2004), and the CDC predicts that one in three children born in 2000 will become diabetic (*Journal of the American Medical Association*, October 2003).

From *The Case Against Homework: How Homework Is Hurting Our Children and What We Can Do About It*, Sara Bennett and Nancy Kalish (New York: Crown Publishers, 2006).

Sample Homework Policies

Here are some excerpts from admirable homework policies that you might want to incorporate in your own school policy.

MASON-RICE ELEMENTARY SCHOOL
Newton, Massachusetts

- Limit the amount of homework given so children will have the energy and time to read every night. Develop and implement a system of communication for how much reading is taking place at home. Assign homework that is developmentally appropriate and matched to your curriculum. Do not assign busywork. Homework should be meaningful. Remember, it is not your job to "keep children busy" at home.
- Homework is kept within certain limits each night, as shown in this excerpt about third grade: "Children will be expected to complete 30–35 minutes of homework four nights each week. Included within this time is the expectation that children will read independently for fifteen minutes. In addition, parents are encouraged to read aloud to their children every night."
- Substantial research demonstrates that children learn to read by reading, and that reading success generally translates into success in school. Less important is what children read. Children should be encouraged to read outstanding fiction and nonfiction literature, but they will also benefit from reading age-appropriate magazines, newspapers, and so on.

PATRICK E. BOWE SCHOOL
Chicopee, Massachusetts

- *Kindergarten:* There is no formal Homework Policy at the Kindergarten Level. Occasionally, depending upon the individual needs of the child and/or the activities within the classroom, an assignment may be given.
- *Grade 1:* Homework will be assigned at the discretion of the teacher—no more than ten minutes per day—Monday–Thursday.

- *Grade 2:* Homework assigned regularly—no more than twenty minutes per day—Monday–Thursday.
- *Grade 3:* Homework assigned regularly—no more than twenty minutes per day—Monday–Thursday.
- *Grade 4:* Homework assigned regularly—no more than thirty minutes per day—Monday–Thursday.
- *Grade 5:* Homework assigned regularly—no more than forty minutes per day—Monday–Thursday.

PISCATAWAY TOWNSHIP SCHOOL DISTRICT
Piscataway, New Jersey
(no longer in effect)

Suggested total times for daily homework:

Kindergarten: . . . . Teacher discretion

Grades 1–3: . . . . 0–30 minutes

Grades 4–5: . . . . 0–50 minutes

Grades 6–8: . . . . 0–75 minutes

Grades 9–12: . . . . 0–120 minutes

Homework will not be graded.

RAYMOND PARK MIDDLE SCHOOL
Indianapolis

- Assign homework only when you feel the assignment is valuable. A night off is better than homework which serves no worthwhile purpose.
- Avoid assignments that require adult help.
- Perhaps the most important purpose homework can serve is to improve reading skills and develop an appreciation for reading. Much current and validated research shows that homework has little impact on improving achievement in the elementary grades. The one exception is reading.
- Design a form for students to log the time they spend each day on homework in each subject.

- Provide alternative ways for students with skill deficiencies to complete assignments. Make allowances for students who are unable to work at the pace of their peers.
- Give assignments only for instructional purposes, not as punishment.

THE BEACON DAY SCHOOL
Oakland, California

Beacon recognizes that families—however constituted—are partners in each child's education. It is important that children are able to participate in family activities and that parents and guardians determine how to spend time with their children instead of having to do schoolwork.

YESHIVAT NETIVOT MONTESSORI
Edison, New Jersey

All students at Yeshivat Netivot work very hard during their school day. It is therefore appropriate that upon arrival in their home environment they have time to unwind, reflect upon their day, and involve themselves in other areas of interest not offered at school; thus strengthening them for the next challenging day to come. At the elementary school level there may be reading assigned for homework. Research papers, book reports, etc. will be worked on during school hours.

THE CASTILLEJA SCHOOL
Palo Alto, California

- If you are designing a new assessment (homework assignment), do it yourself in advance to gauge how long it will take your students and make appropriate changes.
- If you give a month's notice on a major assignment or project, layering other homework assignments on top of it does not allow students the benefit of real time on task. Be sure to allow some dedicated time to work on the assignment.

- Regular use of the test calendar is required, and must include tests, "quests," quizzes, essays, projects, and field trips. Strive for balance.

ARLINGTON PUBLIC SCHOOL DISTRICT
Arlington, Virginia

- It is recognized that students vary significantly in the amount of time they spend on a given assignment. Therefore, these maximum amounts of time represent the teachers' estimate regarding times required by the average student for completion of the assignment.
- Assignments should be reviewed and/or evaluated to provide meaningful feedback to students in a timely manner.
- The length of time spent on homework assignments should avoid undue intrusion on the time students may spend in other activities outside the school day.
- Summer assignments . . . should . . . represent limited time commitments and minimal intrusion on the summer activities of the student and his or her family.

ST. BERNADETTE CATHOLIC SCHOOL
London, Ontario, Canada

Homework should not be assigned for Christmas vacation, March break, or the summer holidays.

OAK KNOLL ELEMENTARY SCHOOL
Menlo Park, California

- We will not provide weekly homework packets that have not been differentiated based on individual student needs. Weekly packets help parents and students manage time. However, packets of this nature almost always include homework of which the child has demonstrated in class that he has absolutely no need to complete.
- We will not assign homework for homework's sake.

SALEM ELEMENTARY SCHOOL
Sackville, New Brunswick, Canada

- Teachers will *not* assign homework:
  ○ during holiday breaks (Christmas, March break, Easter break).
  ○ on evenings of school functions (interviews, concerts, etc.).
- [There will be two] reading weeks where students will be *expected* to read anything they choose [and no other homework will be assigned].

Sample Parent Surveys

Here's a sample of the kind of introduction you might want to use:

> *We are a new committee at this school and we are interested in find-ing out the impact of homework on your family. Please take the time to fill out the enclosed survey. We're very much hoping to have every parent fill it in so that we can have a true sense of how this commu-nity is feeling about this issue. You can respond anonymously if you wish.*
>
> *Please don't feel boxed in by the questions below. If we've missed something that's important to you, feel free to add it. We're interested in everything you have to say. If you have more than one child, please fill out separate surveys—although you only have to fill out the com-ments sections once—and staple them together. Please return your survey to [X] by [X] date. If you would like to work with our commit-tee, please contact [X]. Thanks.*

SAMPLE SURVEY 1

(created by an Arlington, Virginia, homework committee set up by the local school board)

The committee would like to know your thoughts about homework:

1. Types of homework assignments your child receives (e.g., practice, preparation, and extension; also, summer assignments).

2. The quantity of homework (e.g., time per day; time per week; length of assignments).

3. Your role in your child's homework.

4. Relevance of homework to mastery of course content (helps them learn what they need to know).

SAMPLE SURVEY 2

(an excerpt from the survey we used to gather information for
The Case Against Homework)

Your name (optional): _____

Your child's age and grade: _____

1. How much time does your child spend on homework on an average school night? _____

2. How much time does your child spend on homework on an average weekend? _____

3. In general, do you think this amount is:
   ___ Too much?   ___ Not enough?   ___ Just right?
   Why do you feel this way? _____

4. Could you describe a typical evening in your family? What time do your kids get home from school, have a snack, do homework, eat dinner, watch TV, go to bed, etc.? _____

5. On average, how many nights each week do you eat dinner with your children? _____

6. Does homework ever involve you or your partner with your child in a positive way (increase closeness, give you insight into her or his school day, etc.)? _____
   If yes, please describe. _____

7. Does homework ever involve you or your partner with your child in a negative way (do you need to cajole, cheerlead, bribe, threaten, etc.)?
   _____
   If yes, please describe. _____

8. Do you or your partner ever help your child with assignments or projects? (Please check.)
   ___ Never   ___ Sometimes   ___ Often   ___ Always

9. If you help, have you or your partner done any of the following during this school year? (Check all that apply.)
   ___ Proofread
   ___ Edit
   ___ Type or handwrite
   ___ Read aloud required reading
   ___ Prepare for tests

___ Brainstorm on projects or papers
___ Help design projects
___ Explain math concepts
___ Help create sentences for spelling words
___ Stay up late after child has gone to bed to put finishing touches on work
___ Go over work and correct errors
___ Help decide what order to do homework in
___ Other (please specify) _____

10. Have you or your partner ever done part or all of an assignment for a child? _____
    If yes, please describe. _____

11. How much total time do you spend helping your child with homework each night? _____

12. Do you ever disagree with your spouse/partner/ex about how homework should be handled?_____
    If yes, please describe. _____

13. Does homework ever interfere with your child being physically active?
    If yes, please describe. _____

14. Does your child ever have to give up activities (play dates, music, scouts, religious activities, hanging out, etc.) in order to do homework? _____
    If yes, please describe what activities your child gives up: _____

15. Do you ever have to give up family activities in order for assignments to be completed?_____
    If yes, please describe: _____

16. How many nights each week does your child stay up past bedtime to complete homework? (Please circle.)
    0   1   2   3   4   5   6   7

17. Does your child ever show physical signs of stress from homework? ___
    If yes, please describe: _____

18. Does homework ever affect your child's attitude toward school? _____
    How? _____

19. Have you ever approached a teacher or the administration to complain/change things?_____
    If yes, please describe: _____

20. Any additional comments? _____

SAMPLE SURVEY 3

(created by the Vista Unified School District in Vista, California)

The Vista Unified School District Board of Trustees directed staff to investigate current homework practices in our schools in order to craft a district-wide homework policy. To help accomplish this goal, a district homework committee comprised of teachers, students, parents, and administrators formulated surveys for teachers, students, and parents.

Following is the parent survey, comprised of 19 questions. The questionnaire is anonymous; your identity cannot and will not be discovered through this survey. Please answer the questions as best you can; your sincere responses are essential to our fact-finding mission.

If several children in your household attend schools at Vista Unified, you may answer this survey up to three times to reflect each child's experience with homework. No more than three surveys are available for each family. Please keep in mind one child's experiences when answering each survey.

1. I help my child complete his/her homework.
   ___ never   ___ seldom   ___ often   ___ always

2. My child is assigned homework that requires family assistance.
   ___ never   ___ seldom   ___ often   ___ always

3. I am clearly informed by the teacher(s) about my child's homework assignments (homework packet, back-to-school night, monthly letter, Web site, homework hotline).
   ___ never   ___ seldom   ___ often   ___ always

4. My child's teacher(s) establishes and consistently follows a set format/routine for homework assignments.
   ___ never   ___ seldom   ___ often   ___ always   ___ I don't know

5. My child's homework assignments are graded and returned.
   ___ never   ___ seldom   ___ often   ___ always   ___ I don't know

6. My child is required to use a computer to do homework.
   ___ never   ___ seldom   ___ often   ___ always   ___ I don't know

7. My child has too much homework.
   ___ never   ___ seldom   ___ often   ___ always

8. My child does not have enough homework.
   ___ never   ___ seldom   ___ often   ___ always

9. On the average, my child spends the following length of time on daily homework:

___ 15–30 minutes	___ 2–2.5 hours
___ 30–45 minutes	___ 2.5–3 hours
___ 45 minutes–1 hour	___ 3–3.5 hours
___ 1–1.5 hours	___ 3.5–4 hours
___ 1.5–2 hours	___ More than 4 hours

I do not know how much time my child spends doing daily homework.

10. My child is assigned homework over the weekend.
___ never   ___ seldom   ___ often   ___ always

11. My child is assigned homework over vacations/holidays.
___ never   ___ seldom   ___ often   ___ always

12. Should homework be assigned over the weekend?
___ yes   ___ no   ___ sometimes

13. Should homework be assigned over vacation/during the holidays?
___ yes   ___ no   ___ sometimes

14. Comments: _____
_____

15. Please indicate your child's grade. (Please circle.)
K   1   2   3   4   5   6   7   8   9   10   11   12

16. Does your child attend an honors/Advanced Placement (AP)/International Baccalaureate (IB)/GATE class this school year?
___ yes   ___ no

17. Does your child belong to the English Language Development (ELD) program, created for students who learn English as a second language?
___ yes   ___ no

18. Does your child receive special education services this school year?
___ yes   ___ no

19. Did your child respond to a student survey about homework?
___ yes   ___ no   ___ I don't know

Resources

If you want to read more, the following books and Web sites can provide additional helpful information on homework and education in general.

Books

Allington, Richard L., and Patricia M.Cunningham, *Schools That Work: Where All Children Read and Write,* Needham Heights, Mass.: Allyn and Bacon, 2005.

Baker, David P., and Gerald K. LeTendre, *National Differences, Global Similarities: World Culture and the Future of Schooling,* Palo Alto, Calif.: Stanford University Press, 2005.

Beck, Isabel L., Margaret G. McKeown, and Linda Kucan, *Bringing Words to Life: Robust Vocabulary Instruction,* New York: Guilford Press, 2002.

Beers, Kylene, *When Kids Can't Read, What Teachers Can Do: A Guide for Teachers 6–12,* Portsmouth, N.H.: Heinemann, 2003.

Blessington, John P., *Let My Children Work,* New York, Anchor Press/Double-day, 1999.

Buell, John, *Closing the Book on Homework: Enhancing Public Education and Freeing Family Time,* Philadelphia: Temple University Press, 2004.

Cohen, Lawrence J., *Playful Parenting: A Bold New Way to Nurture Close Connections, Solve Behavior Problems, and Encourage Children's Confidence,* New York: Ballantine, 2002.

Cohen-Sandler, Roni, *Stressed-out Girls: Helping Them Thrive in the Age of Pressure,* New York: Viking, 2005.

Cooper, Harris, *The Battle Over Homework: Common Ground for Administrators, Teachers, and Parents,* Thousand Oaks, Calif.: Corwin Press, 2001.

Crain, William, *Reclaiming Childhood: Letting Children Be Children in Our Achievement-Oriented Society,* New York: Times Books, 2003.

De Carvalho, Maria Eulina P., *Rethinking Family-School Relations: A Critique of Parental Involvement in Schooling,* Mahwah, N.J.: Lawrence Erlbaum Associates, 2001.

Doherty, William J., Ph.D., and Barbara Z. Carlson, *Putting Family First: Successful Strategies for Reclaiming Family Life in a Hurry-Up World,* New York: Henry Holt and Company, 2001.

Elkind, David, *The Hurried Child: Growing Up Too Fast Too Soon,* Cambridge, Mass.: Da Capo Press, 2001.

Elkind, David, *The Power of Play: How Spontaneous, Imaginative Activities Lead to Happier, Healthier Children,* Cambridge, Mass.: Da Capo Press, 2007.

Fisher, Roger, and William Ury, *Getting to Yes: Negotiating Agreement Without Giving In,* New York: Penguin Books, 1991.

Gardner, Howard, *Changing Minds: The Art and Science of Changing Our Own and Other People's Minds,* Cambridge, Mass.: Harvard Business School Press, 2004.

Gardner, Howard, *The Disciplined Mind: Beyond Facts and Standardized Tests,* the K–12 Education That Every Child Deserves, New York: Penguin Books, 2000.

Goodnough, Abby, *Ms. Moffett's First Year: Becoming a Teacher in America,* Cambridge, Mass.: Perseus, 2004.

Kane, Pearl Rock, ed., *My First Year as a Teacher,* New York: Penguin Books, 1996.

Kennedy, Mary, *Inside Teaching: How Classroom Life Undermines Reform,* Cambridge, Mass.: Harvard University Press, 2005.

Kindlon, Daniel J., *Too Much of a Good Thing, Raising Children of Character in an Indulgent Age,* New York: Miramax, 2003.

Kohl, Herbert, *Stupidity and Tears: Teaching and Learning in Troubled Times,* New York: New Press, 2003.

Kohn, Alfie, *The Homework Myth: Why Our Kids Get Too Much of a Bad Thing,* New York: Da Capo Lifelong Books, 2006.

Kozol, Jonathan, *The Shame of the Nation: The Restoration of Apartheid Schooling in America,* New York: Crown, 2005.

Kralovec, Etta and John Buell, *The End of Homework: How Homework Disrupts Families, Overburdens Children, and Limits Learning,* Boston: Beacon Press, 2000.

Kralovec, Etta, *Schools That Do Too Much: Wasting Time and Money in Schools and What We Can All Do About It,* Boston: Beacon Press, 2003.

Krashen, Stephen D., *The Power of Reading: Insight from the Research,* Portsmouth, N.H.: Heinemann, 2004.

Leonhardt, Mary, *99 Ways to Get Kids to Do Their Homework (And Not Hate It),* New York: Three Rivers Press, 2000.

Leonhardt, Mary, *99 Ways to Get Kids to Love Reading and 100 Books They'll Love,* New York: Three Rivers Press, 1997.

Levine, Mel, *Ready or Not, Here Life Comes,* New York: Simon & Schuster, 2005.

Levine, Mel, *The Myth of Laziness,* New York: Simon & Schuster, 2003.

Levine, Mel, *A Mind at a Time,* New York: Simon & Schuster, 2002.

Llewellyn, Grace, and Amy Silver, *Guerrilla Learning: How to Give Your Kids a Real Education With or Without School,* New York: John Wiley and Sons, 2001.

Meier, Deborah, and George Wood, eds., *Many Children Left Behind: How the No Child Left Behind Act Is Damaging Our Children and Our Schools,* Boston: Beacon Press, 2004.

Mercogliano, Chris, *Teaching the Restless: One School's Remarkable No-Ritalin Approach to Helping Children Learn and Succeed,* Boston: Beacon Press, 2003.

Ohanian, Susan, *What Happened to Recess and Why Are Our Children Struggling in Kindergarten?,* New York: McGraw-Hill, 2002.

Pope, Denise Clark, *Doing School: How We Are Creating a Generation of Stressed-Out, Materialistic, and Miseducated Students,* New Haven, Conn.: Yale University Press, 2001.

Pope, Loren, *Colleges That Change Lives: 40 Schools That Will Change the Way You Think About Colleges,* New York: Penguin Books, 2006.

Sax, Leonard, *Why Gender Matters: What Parents and Teachers Need to Know About the Emerging Science of Sex Differences,* New York: Broadway Books, 2005.

Schenk, Jeb, *Learning, Teaching & The Brain: A Practical Guide for Educators,* Thermapolis, Wyo.: Knowa Inc., 2003.

Sothern, Melinda S., T. Kristian von Almen, and Heidi Schumacher, *Trim Kids: The Proven 12-Week Plan That Has Helped Thousands of Children Achieve a Healthier Weight,* New York: HarperCollins, 2001.

Steinberg, Jacques, *The Gatekeepers: Inside the Admissions Process of a Premier College,* New York: Penguin Books, 2003.

Thompson, Michael, and Teresa Baker, *The Pressured Child: Helping Your Child Find Success in School and Life,* New York: Ballantine, 2004.

Van de Walle, John A., *Elementary and Middle School Mathematics: Teaching Developmentally,* Boston, Mass.: Pearson, 2004.

Witkin, Georgia, *Kidstress: What It Is, How It Feels, How to Help*, New York: Penguin Books, 2000.

Magazines/Journals/Online Resources

Theory into Practice, The Homework Issue, 23, no. 3 (Summer 2004).

Encounter: Education for Meaning and Social Justice, www.great-ideas.org.

www.stophomework.com

This site, run by Sara Bennett, reports the latest homework news and provides forums for parents, students, educators, and mental health professionals.

www.susanohanian.org

This site, run by Susan Ohanian, a former teacher and author of several books on education, acts as a clearinghouse for the latest articles on homework, NCLB, testing, and other education issues and offers her outspoken—and interesting—opinions. Ohanian has won the National Council of Teachers of English's "NCTE Orwell Award" for her Web site's contribution to the critical analysis of education.

www.educatorroundtable.org

The Educator Roundtable convened with the goal of repealing NCLB. You'll find information about NCLB and can join efforts to dismantle the tests.

www.fairtest.org

This Web site of the National Center for Fair & Open Testing provides important information on all sorts of standardized tests, including K–12 testing and the SATs.

www.edweek.org

The online home of *Education Week and Teacher Magazine*, this site is geared toward teachers and other educators. But it covers all sorts of educational issues, and is definitely worth a visit from parents, too.

Acknowledgments

My first and biggest thanks goes to my husband, Joe Holmes, who has been with me through every step of this project, and every project that came before. For this book, he brainstormed the big ideas, read every single word, often two or three times, acted as first editor, took photographs for the Web site and jacket, and provided unwavering moral support and love. This book would not exist without him.

It was my children who inspired this project at the outset with their diverse passions and love of learning. For this book, my son, Julian, designed the homework survey Web site, gave incisive comments on the proposal, and inspired me with his courage and integrity in standing up—politely—to his teachers. My daughter, Sophia, offered invaluable comments on Chapter 1, was the model for the Web site photograph, and also inspired me with her strength in going to school with her homework assignments unfinished. I appreciate their insights, courage, patience, and understanding, and their ability to distract and relax me just when I needed it.

I wouldn't be where I am today if it weren't for my father, Avie, who pointed me in the right direction when I first told him of my book idea, gave me guidance and advice every step of the way, and was a great listener and reader. My mother, Bev, also gave much needed support. My brother David, a professional mediator, willingly spent many hours role-playing teacher-parent conversations, and then devoted even more hours to tweaking the wording of the conversations and letters in Chapter 9. (Of course, any mistakes are solely mine and Nancy's.) Over many years, I've had countless discussions about homework with my sister-in-law, Mary Bender, my sister Jane, and my cousin, Nancy Shapiro, conversations that helped me see the widespread nature of the problem and hone my response. I'm lucky that my brother Richard and sister-in-law, Paula, live nearby, because they provided endless support and welcome distraction. My sister Robin, a long-time educator, and my brother, Paul, also provided insightful comments on early drafts.

Several friends and educators also read drafts and I can't thank them enough for their speed and for their invaluable comments, as well as their moral support: Jo Andres, Alan Berger, Katherine Chew, David Easton, Sara Mandelbaum, Lily Mercogliano, Christine Poff, and Kristen Palmer. For moral support I also thank Steve Balser, Steve Buscemi, Shawn Dulaney, Suzanne Fiol, Apollonia Holzer, Cristiana Kahl Collins, Diane Roback, Ellen Schleifer, Karen Shapiro, Pam Shapiro, and Lynora Williams.

During the writing of this book, I spoke with many parents, educators, and psychologists, all of whom surprised and delighted me by giving generously of their time, their stories, their contacts, their areas of expertise. Without my asking, one teacher photocopied and passed out the survey address to six hundred at a teacher's conference. Others sent me research materials, their own books or books they thought I should read, and sample homework assignments. Some educators opened up their schools to me and allowed me to meet alone with their students. Untold parents passed the survey around to all of their friends and colleagues, posted the survey link on their Web sites, shared their stories, and sent sample homework assignments, letters to teachers, and homework policies. They often thought they were getting support from me without realizing what important support I was getting from them. They inspired me to work hard and fast, and it was truly fun to have long conversations with such a thoughtful group of people, including: Lois Allen, Jan Allison, Stephen Aloia, Gay Armsden, Valerie Barr, Wendy Barry-Owen, Kylene Beers, Peggy Bennett, Barbara Blinick, Ronald Bolandi, Daniel Collins, William Crain, Cymry DeBoucher, Terence Davidson, Daria Doering, Virginia Dorris, Deborah Duffy, June Edelstein, Thelma Farley, William Fogarty, Felicity Frisbie, Susan Gilbert, Kalman Heller, Marcy Holle, Tim Holmes, Mary Hynes, Jennifer Ingram, Etta Kralovec, Richard Krawiec, Robine Lewis, Paul Lockhart, Beverly Loos, Jon Mattleman, Kate McReynolds, Deborah Meier, Chris Mercogliano, Jenny Milan, Lori Myers, Steve Nelson, Susan Ohanian, Lynn Ostro, Denise Clark Pope, Jennifer Prost, David Puth, Leslie Puth, Pamela Potischman, John Prentice, Madeleine Ray, Paul Richards, Deanne Rohde, Angie Rome, Wendy Rosen, Todd Seal, Lisa Schreibersdorf, Jessica Sheppard, Amy Silver, Mark Springer, Mark Stephens, Karen Taylor, Lorraine Thompson, Todd Seal, Ayelet Waldman, Leslie Weber, Barb Wherry, and Susan Yohn.

At one of my children's schools, I was inspired by Jamie Kay, a parent who worked tirelessly to advocate for students with learning issues. And I am immensely grateful to the parents who stood up with me—Theresa Greenleaf, Karen Johnson, Kathy Libraty, Gilda Mooney-Dube, Donna Travers, Susan Valenti, and especially Cynthia Muldrow.

A very special thanks to a group of people from my lawyer side who are always there for me: Dorchen Leidholdt, Mary Lynch, and Charlotte Watson, the smartest, most dedicated, creative thinkers I ever had the honor to work with, and to my former clients Linda White and Patsy Kelly Jarrett, who wrongly spent years in prison but never lost their dignity, faith, or grace and help me keep a perspective on what's important in life.

I'm extremely grateful to Doug Pepper at McClelland and Stewart, who championed me when the book was just an idea and was there every step of the way, and to Rachel Kahan, who graciously helped me find an agent. At William Morris, I'd especially like to thank Georgia Cool and Erin Malone, who always went out of their way to help. Many people at Crown worked long hours to make this book happen and I truly appreciate their dedication and their willingness to work on a short schedule. Special thanks to assistant editor Lucinda Bartley, who made sure nothing fell between the cracks; Amy Boorstein, managing editor, who helped turn this into a book in an extraordinarily short amount of time; and Tina Constable and Jay Sones, who made sure the world knew about it. Thanks also to Leta Evanthes, Walter Friedman, Kristin Kiser, Dan Rembert, Steve Ross, and Barbara Sturman. I spent countless hours with my coauthor and neighbor Nancy Kalish whom I appreciate for her incredible talent at bringing words to life, her sense of humor, and her couscous salad. A huge thanks to our editor, Rachel Klayman, who gave me the gift of her trust and confidence, was amazingly astute, and helped me realize my vision. Most of all, I'd like to thank our agent, Suzanne Gluck, for taking me on as a first-time author and in whom I found a force of nature and a kindred spirit.

SB

First of all, I'd like to thank my coauthor, Sara Bennett, an amazing activist and advocate. My deep gratitude also goes to the hundreds of parents, teachers, and kids who shared their stories with us by survey, e-mail, and phone. Many experts broadened my understanding of the issues. I'd particularly like to thank Dan Kindlon, Kalman Heller, Larry Cohen, Harris Cooper, Catherine Davis, David Bennett, and the passionate Melinda Sothern of New Orleans, who agreed to be interviewed in the middle of rebuilding her house after the 2005 hurricane.

We were helped along the way by many people, including our extraordinary agent Suzanne Gluck of William Morris. There's no better person to have on your side. Thanks to her assistants Georgia Cool and Erin Malone. Thanks, too, to Avie Bennett and Doug Pepper for their astute advice throughout. Our talented editor, Rachel Klayman, helped hone our words and gave many insightful suggestions that enriched the book. The entire staff at Crown was terrific, including art director Dan Rembert, managing editor Amy Boorstein, Leta Evanthes and Walter Friedman in production; publisher Steve Ross; editorial director Kristin Kiser; and assistant editor Lucinda Bartley. My appreciation also goes to the tireless Tina Constable, director of publicity, along with publicist Jay Sones.

My cherished friends and fellow writers, Pamela Katz and Judith Newman, always knew exactly what to say when I was discouraged, and both gave excellent editorial advice. Gail Belsky was also an inspiration. I'm also grateful to Michael Rutter and Joan McCool, who were especially helpful when we were just getting started, as well as Frances Rutter. My parents, Lionel and Muriel Kalish, were wonderful first editors and endless sources of support. They read and read and read whatever I wrote, and invariably gave great suggestions. Linda and Steve Weiss were also always there when I needed them, ready with the perfect strategy.

My husband, Steve Rutter, put up with the grouchiest wife in Brooklyn during this process. Yet he was unfailingly supportive and a master at helping me figure out how to make the manuscript better. For this—and many other things—he'll always have my gratitude and love. My beloved daughter, Allison, who has suffered through endless hours of homework herself, helped by spreading the word about our homework survey to her wide circle of friends and beyond, and was always ready to offer her perspective and a hug. I am so lucky to have all these people in my life. I only wish I had been enlightened about homework while my child was still in elementary and middle school. If I knew then what I know now, I would certainly have taken more action, as I hope our readers will.

NK

Index

About the Authors

SARA BENNETT, host of www.stophomework.com, is a criminal defense appeals attorney and was the first director of the Wrongful Convictions Project of New York City's Legal Aid Society. She is an expert in the post-conviction representation of battered women and the wrongly convicted, and lectures widely on both homework and legal issues. Sara and her cases have been featured in the *New York Times* and on *60 Minutes II, Dateline NBC,* and the *Today* show. She successfully challenged and changed homework policies at her children's schools. She lives in Brooklyn, New York.

NANCY KALISH is a former senior editor at *Child* and columnist for *Redbook, Working Mother,* and *Selecciones.* She writes often for *Parenting, Parents, Real Simple, Reader's Digest, More, Ladies' Home Journal, Health, Prevention,* and other magazines. Nancy put several of the strategies in this book to work for her own daughter, always with positive results. She lives in Brooklyn, New York. Visit her website at www.nancykalish.com.

This book's website is www.thecaseagainsthomework.com.

Author photographs: Sara Bennett: Joseph O. Holmes/joesnyc.com, Nancy Kalish: Allison Rutter